THE POLITICAL ECONOMY OF CENTRAL BANKING

The Political Economy of Central Banking

Edited by

Philip Arestis

Professor of Economics, University of East London, UK

and

Malcolm C. Sawyer

Professor of Economics, University of Leeds, UK

Edward Elgar
Cheltenham, UK • Northampton, MA, USA

Published by
Edward Elgar Publishing Limited
8 Lansdown Place
Cheltenham
Glos GL50 2HU
UK

Edward Elgar Publishing, Inc.
6 Market Street
Northampton
Massachusetts 01060
USA

A catalogue record for this book
is available from the British Library

Library of Congress Cataloguing-in-Publication Data
The political economy of central banking / edited by Philip Arestis,
    Malcolm C. Sawyer.
    Papers from an international conference held at the University of
East London in 1997.
    Includes index.
    1. Banks and banking, Central—Congresses.   2. Banks and banking,
Central—New Zealand—Congresses.   I. Arestis, Philip, 1941–   .
II. Sawyer, Malcolm C.
HG1811.P65   1998
332.1'1—dc21   98–12817
                                                                CIP

ISBN 1 85898 742 3

Typeset by Manton Typesetters, 5–7 Eastfield Road, Louth, Lincolnshire LN11 7AJ, UK.
Printed and bound in Great Britain by Bookcraft (Bath) Ltd.

Contents

Figures

Tables

Contributors

Philip Arestis is Professor of Economics, and formerly Head of Department of Economics, University of East London. He has also taught at the Universities of Surrey and Cambridge (Department of Extra-Mural Studies) and Greenwich University (where he was Head of Economics Division). He was editor of the *British Review of Economic Issues* and joint editor of the *Thames Papers in Political Economy*, and is joint editor of the recently launched *International Papers in Political Economy*. He has been on the editorial board of a number of journals and an elected member of the Council of the Royal Economic Society. His publications include: his co-authored *Introducing Macroeconomic Modelling: An Econometric Study of the United Kingdom* (Macmillan, 1982); his edited *Post-Keynesian Monetary Economics: New Approaches to Financial Modelling* (Edward Elgar, 1988); his co-edited *Post-Keynesian Economic Theory: A Challenge to Neo-Classical Economics* (Wheatsheaf, 1984), *The Biographical Dictionary of Dissenting Economists* (Edward Elgar, 1992), *The Elgar Companion to Radical Political Economy* (Edward Elgar, 1994), *Keynes, Money and the Open Economy: Essays in Honour of Paul Davidson, Volume One* (Edward Elgar, 1996), *Employment, Economic Growth and the Tyranny of the Market: Essays in Honour of Paul Davidson, Volume Two* (Edward Elgar, 1996), *Capital Controversy, Post-Keynesian Economics and the History of Economics: Essays in Honour of Geoff Harcourt, Volume One* (Edward Elgar, 1997), *Markets, Unemployment and Economic Policy* (Edward Elgar, 1997); also his two books *The Post-Keynesian Approach to Economics: An Alternative Analysis of Economic Theory and Policy* (Edward Elgar, 1992), and *Money, Pricing, Distribution and Economic Integration* (Macmillan, 1997). He has published widely in journals and books in Post Keynesian economics, macro-economics, monetary economics and applied econometrics.

Sedat Aybar is a PhD student at the School of Oriental and African Studies (SOAS), University of London, carrying out research on 'Liberalisation and the Turkish Banking System'. He is a part time lecturer and tutor at SOAS and has worked on a project concerning institutional investors' decision-making process. He has previously researched at the Universities in Paris and Oxford and has published a number of papers. His research interests include financial economics and development, banking and international finance, economic theory and the economy of Turkey. He is a founder editor of SOAS *Economic Digest*, a research student quarterly.

Keith Bain is a Principal Lecturer in the Department of Economics at the University of East London, having taught previously in both Australia and Papua New Guinea. He studied at the University of Queensland in Australia. He has co-authored a number of books, the most recent being *Financial Markets and Institutions* (with Peter Howells, Longman, 1994), and has contributed chapters to books and articles to journals on international trade, international monetary systems and monetary economics.

Iain Begg is Professor of International Economics at South Bank University, London, and Programme Director of a major research programme on the Single European Market funded by the Economic and Social Research Council. He chairs a COST Action A7 (DG XII of the European Commission) on the evolution of rules for a single European market, has served as a specialist adviser to Sub-Committee A of the House of Lords' European Communities Committee for an enquiry into the Structural Funds and the Cohesion Fund, and is an expert adviser to the Economic and Social Committee. He has directed several studies for different directorates of the European Commission and for the European Parliament, and has published extensively on European policy issues. Recent publications include work on prudential supervision under EMU, on the EU budget, on the political economy of EMU and on regulation in the EU. He has recently been elected to serve as the joint editor of the *Journal of Common Market Studies*.

Jagjit Chadha is an Economist with the Monetary Assessment and Strategy Division of the Bank of England. He studied economics at University College, London and the London School of Economics. His research interests lie in mainstream monetary economics, in economic history and economic development. Prior to joining the Bank he collaborated with Morris Perlman on a project concerning the Bullionist Controversy and has several papers forthcoming in academic journals. His recent papers have included several analyses of the interaction among monetary policy, asset prices and real activity as well as a short history of monetary unions. He has presented papers at academic conferences throughout the sunnier parts of the world.

John Cornwall is McCulloch Emeritus Professor of Economics at Dalhousie University, Canada. He has also taught at Tufts and Southern Illinois Universities and the Copenhagen School of Economics. His publications include *Growth and Stability in a Mature Economy* (Martin Robertson, 1972), *Modern Capitalism: Its Growth and Transformation* (Martin Robertson, 1977), *The Conditions for Economic Recovery* (Martin Robertson, 1983), *Economic Recovery for Canada: A Policy Framework* (with Wendy Maclean, James Lorimer, 1984), *The Theory of Economic Breakdown* (Blackwell, 1990) and

Economic Breakdown and Recovery (M.E. Sharpe, 1994). His edited books include *After Stagflation: Alternatives to Economic Decline* (Blackwell and M.E. Sharpe, 1984) and *The Capitalist Economies: Prospects for the 1990s* (Edward Elgar, 1991). He is a Fellow of the Royal Society of Canada.

Wendy Cornwall is Professor of Economics at Mount Saint Vincent University, Halifax, Canada, and Adjunct Professor at Dalhousie University. Before this she held an appointment in the Economics Department at Dalhousie University. Her publications include *Economic Recovery for Canada: A Policy Framework* (with John Cornwall, James Lorimer, 1984) and *A Model of the Canadian Financial Flow Matrix* (with J.A. Brox, Statistics Canada, Ottawa, 1989). She has published articles on the flow of funds, applied econometrics and economic growth, both in journals and in books. She is currently writing a book with John Cornwall for Cambridge University Press, entitled *Modelling Capitalist Development*.

Paul Dalziel is Reader in Economics at Lincoln University in New Zealand. Since completing his PhD at the University of Otago in 1985, his research has focused on Post Keynesian macroeconomic theory and New Zealand economic policy. He has published extensively in this area in journals and edited books. He has also published three books on the New Zealand economy, most recently *The New Zealand Macroeconomy: A Briefing on the Reforms* (with Ralph Lattimore, Oxford University Press, 1996). His major current research project is a study of the role of bank credit in the creation of inflationary pressures.

Sheila Dow is Professor in Economics at the University of Stirling, where she has taught since 1979. She was educated at the Universities of St Andrews, Manitoba, McMaster and Glasgow. She worked for two years for the Bank of England and for four years in the Finance Department of the Government of Manitoba, latterly as Senior Economist. Her research interests include Post Keynesian economics, monetary theory, history of thought and methodology and regional finance. She has published and edited a range of books, the latest being *The Methodology of Macroeconomic Thought* (Edward Elgar, 1996). In addition she has published a wide range of articles and contributions to monographs.

Georg Erber is Research Officer, Department of Industry and Technology, German Institute for Economic Research. He is also Research Associate and Lecturer, Free University of Berlin. He was Assistant Professor in Statistics and Econometrics and Visiting Professor at Thammasat University of Bangkok, Thailand, Zhejiang University of Hangzhou, PRCh, Academy; and Counsellor at the National Planning Institute, Lima, Peru, and Lecturer at the Ecole National d'Administration et de Gestion, Vientiane, Lao PR. His principal fields of interest are industrial organization, macroeconomic theory and policy, technological change and unemployment, growth and structural change, and econometrics. He has published in these areas in journals and edited books. He has published a number of books and research reports including: *Catching-Up or Falling Behind, Relative Differences in Productivity and Price Competitiveness between U.S. and German Industries, 1960–1985*, Research Report (DIW, 1993); *Zukunftsperspektiven Deutschlands im Internationalen Wettbewerb: Industriepolitische Implikationen der Neuen Wachstumstheorie*, (with H. Hagemann and S. Seiter, Physica, Heidelberg 1998); *Sustainable Price Stability for Europe: Prospective Effects of a European Central Bank on Long-Term Growth and Employment* (with H. Hagemann, forthcoming).

Ilene Grabel is an Assistant Professor of International Economics at the Graduate School of International Studies at the University of Denver (USA). She has published articles in the journals *World Development, International Papers in Political Economy, Journal of Economic Issues, Journal of Development Studies, International Review of Applied Economics* and *Review of Radical and Political Economics*. She has contributed an entry to the *Encyclopedia of Political Economy* (Routledge Press, forthcoming) and has contributed chapters to the following books: J. Harvey and J. Deprez (eds), *Post-Keynesian Foundations in the Analysis of International Economics* (Routledge Press, forthcoming), R. Pollin (ed.), *The Macroeconomics of Finance, Saving, and Investment* (University of Michigan Press, 1997), S.D. Gupta and N.K. Choudhry (eds), *Liberalization and Structural Change* (1998), and G. Epstein, J. Graham and J. Nembhard (eds), *Creating a New World Economy: Forces of Change and Plans of Action* (Temple University Press, 1993).

Augusto Graziani is Professor of Economics at the University of Rome 'La Sapienza', Italy. At various dates he has been Visiting Professor in the Universities of Birmingham, Michigan (Ann Arbor), Collège de France (Paris), Paris III 'Sorbonne'. He is author of numerous books and articles on macroeconomics, money and distribution theories, and history of the Italian economy. He is a member of the Italian Lincei Academy, of the Orientation Committee of Ismea (Institute for the Study of Applied Mathematics and Economics) Paris, and of the editorial board of *Economie Appliquée*.

David Green is Dean of the Business School at Leeds Metropolitan University. Prior to his appointment at Leeds he was Head of School at South Bank

University. Before this, he spent a number of years working as a social policy and welfare rights adviser and researcher. His major research work at present is in the economics of international finance and banking supervision. He is currently directing an international research project funded by the European Commission on *The Future of Banking Supervision and Regulation in Selected Transitional Economies in Relation to European Monetary Union.* He has published in the areas of financial markets (domestic, European and international), social and economic policies and privatization. He broadcasts, publishes and lectures widely on contemporary economic questions.

Harald Hagemann is Professor of Economic Theory at the University of Hohenheim, Stuttgart. He has been Professor of Economic Theory and Political Economy at the Free University of Berlin (1980–81) and Assistant Professor at the University of Kiel (1977–80). He was a Fulbright Visiting Professor at the Graduate Faculty of the New School for Social Research in New York in 1986, Visiting Professor at the University of Cambridge in 1989–90 where he also became a Life Member of Clare Hall; he was also an Erasmus Visiting Professor at the University of Bologna in 1996. His main areas of research are macroeconomics theory and policy, technological change and employment, and the history of economic thought. He has published extensively in journals, and edited books. He is managing editor of *Structural Change and Economic Dynamics*, a member of the editorial board of the *European Journal of the History of Economic Thought* and of the advisory board of other international journals. He has recently been elected as a member of the Executive Committee and the Treasurer of the European Society for the History of Economic Thought, and became an honorary fellow of the Brazilian Association of Graduate Schools in Economics in 1996.

Laurence Harris is a Professor of Economics in the University of London and a Pro-Director at the School of Oriental and African Studies (SOAS). He has previously taught at the London School of Economics: Birkbeck College; the Open University; the University of California, Berkeley; UC Irvine; UC Riverside; and the University of Zimbabwe. Books he has written, co-authored or edited, include *Monetary Theory* (McGraw-Hill, 1981); *Rereading Capital* (Macmillan, 1981); *City of Capital* (Blackwells, 1983); *Dictionary of Marxist Thought* (Blackwells, 1983); *The Peculiarities of the British Economy* (Lawrence & Wishart, 1986); *New Perspectives on the Financial System* (Croom Helm, 1988) and his articles cover financial economics and macroeconomics as well as other subjects. He has contributed to economic policy analysis in several countries, especially South Africa, Mozambique and their neighbours. Currently his research is on international capital markets and public finance.

Dorene Isenberg is Associate Professor of Economics at Drew University, Madison, NJ, where she is also the director of the Semester on the European Union. She received her PhD from the University of California at Riverside in 1986 and began teaching at the University of Maine, Orono. In 1988, she spent the year at the Jerome A. Levy Economics Institute at Bard College as a Visiting Research Fellow. Her research interests have focused on the financial sector's relationship to and impact on the production sector in developed capitalist economies. Her research programme has ranged from investigating whether Minsky's financial fragility hypothesis helped to explain the Great Depression in the United States to her most recent work on the political economy of monetary policy in the European Union's integrating financial markets. She is also engaged in an ongoing international comparison of the impact of the process of financial integration and liberalization on housing markets and housing affordability. Results of these research projects have been published and presented in a variety of different venues. Research papers on the Great Depression have been published in the *Journal of Economic Issues*, *British Review of Economic Issues* and *New Perspectives in Monetary Macroeconomics* (edited by G. Dymski and R. Pollin). Research papers on financial liberalization and its effects on housing markets and affordability have been published in Japan and in a forthcoming collection, *Globalization and Progressive Economic Policy: Real Constraints and Real Possibilities* (edited by D. Baker, G. Epstein and R. Pollin).

Norbert Janssen is an Economist in the Bank of England's Monetary Assessment and Strategy Division. He studied economics at Tilburg University (the Netherlands). In 1995 he obtained his PhD degree, 'The definition and policy relevance of monetary aggregates in the Netherlands', at Maastricht University, the Netherlands. His publications include contributions to books, the *Bank of England Quarterly Bulletin* and academic journals. His main research interests are the demand for money and credit, reaction functions of monetary authorities and the transmission of monetary policy.

Carlos Rodríguez-Fuentes is Lecturer in the Department of Applied Economics at the University of La Laguna (Spain, Canary Islands) since 1991. From 1993 to 1994 he was granted financial assistance by the Stevenson Foundation (University of Glasgow) and the Spanish government (Ministerio de Asuntos Exteriores) to finish his PhD in the Department of Economics at the University of Stirling (Scotland), as a visiting postgraduate student. His PhD 'Monetary policy and regional economics' was awarded in 1996 and has been published by the Spanish Economic and Social Council (Consejo Económico y Social). His research interests are focused mainly on Post Keynesian economics, regional finance and methodology. Apart from having published several books and articles on the economy of the Canary Islands, he has also published some articles in several Spanish economic journals on Post Keynesian monetary theory and on the role of banks in regional development. Also, he is joint author with Sheila C. Dow of a survey on regional finance (*Regional Studies*, December 1997).

Malcolm Sawyer is Professor of Economics at the University of Leeds and formerly Head of Division of Economics at the same University, and Professor of Economics at the University of York. He is the author of several books including *Macroeconomics in Question* (Harvester-Wheatsheaf and M.E. Sharpe, 1982), *The Economics of Michal Kalecki* (Macmillan and M.E. Sharpe, 1982, 1985), *The Challenge of Radical Political Economy* (Harvester Wheatsheaf and Barnes & Noble, 1989) and *Unemployment, Imperfect Competition and Macroeconomics* (Edward Elgar, 1995). He is the managing editor of *International Review of Applied Economics*, joint editor of the recently launched *International Papers in Political Economy*, and editor of the series *New Directions in Modern Economics*, published by Edward Elgar. He has recently co-edited *The Biographical Dictionary of Dissenting Economists* and *The Elgar Companion to Radical Political Economy* (Edward Elgar). He has published widely in journals and books in the areas of industrial economics, macroeconomics and political economy. His current research interests include the theory of industrial policy and the conceptualization of competition and markets in economic theory, and the causes and cures for unemployment, as well as continuing to work on Post Keynesian macroeconomics.

Mario Seccareccia is Professor of Economics at the University of Ottawa, Canada. He is the author of numerous journal articles and chapters of books in the areas of monetary economics, history of economic thought and labour economics, and is co-editor, among others, of *Vers le plein emploi* (with P. Paquette, Presses de l'Université de Montréal, 1998), *Les pièges de l'austérité* (with P. Paquette, Presses Universitaires de Grenoble and Presses de l'Université de Montréal, 1993), and *Milton Friedman et son oeuvre* (with M. Lavoie, Presses de l'Université de Montréal, 1993).

H.-Peter Spahn is Professor of Economic Policy at the University of Hohenheim, Stuttgart. He studied Economics and Sociology at the Universities of Bochum and Freiburg where he was awarded his PhD in 1978 based on a study of the concept of stabilization policies of the German Council of Economic Advisers. He worked as Assistant Professor at the Free University of Berlin and finished his habilitation research project on stagnation problems in monetary economics in 1986. From 1985 to 1990 he was appointed research coordinator at the Science Centre, Berlin, supervising and pursuing studies in international financial markets and their impact on the scope of employment policy. From 1990 to 1992 he was Professor at the University of the Armed Forces in Munich. His main areas of teaching and research are monetary macroeconomics, stabilization strategies in open economies, history of monetary policy, problems of exchange rate systems and history of economic thought.

BK Title

Introduction

E58

Philip Arestis and Malcolm Sawyer

There have been rapid and substantial changes in the operation, significance and economic power of the financial markets over the past three decades or so. It is these markets that central banks have to influence in pursuit of their objectives. These developments have inevitably influenced the relationship between central banks and financial markets. Many students of financial and monetary affairs have suggested that central banks have lost much of their power over financial markets and that their abilities to regulate and influence are much diminished. On this argument, it is the financial markets which increasingly set the scene against which central banks have to operate, and also these markets limit the possibilities for effective regulation. This is especially so in the current environment of the globalization of financial markets, consciously helped by the policies of financial liberalization pursued by most, if not all, countries around the world. On the other hand, many other students of financial and monetary affairs have focused on the argument that central banks may have been given more power (at least relative to other arms of government) arising from a trend towards the granting of 'independence' to central banks (and often being given the objective of the single-minded pursuit of low inflation: and the recent 'operational independence' of the Bank of England in May 1997 is a case in point).

The importance of these developments cannot be exaggerated. In view also of the emphasis given to them by academics and practitioners alike, it was felt that the time for an international conference to address these issues was ripe. Jointly sponsored by the International Papers in Political Economy (IPPE) and the Post-Keynesian Study Group, a one-day international conference took place at the University of East London on Friday, 16 May 1997. The theme of the conference was appropriately 'The Political Economy of Central Banking'. Contributions focused on four areas: independence of central banks; enhanced power of financial markets; inflation targets and the associated cost in terms of growth and employment; and central banking in the context of financial liberalization in both developed and developing countries. The result is the present book, which contains the thirteen papers presented at the conference. The first six concentrate on theoretical issues and the rest are applications to a number of countries.

Sheila Dow and Carlos Rodríguez-Fuentes in Chapter 1, entitled 'The Political Economy of Monetary Policy', consider the meaning of, and possibilities for, monetary policy in an endogenous money framework. This contrasts with the neoclassical identification of monetary policy with money supply control. While the horizontalist endogenous money approach sees monetary policy in terms of interest rate setting, they consider a combination of endogenous money and liquidity preference theory which gives monetary policy a much more complex role. Further, it is argued that this role is contingent on context. First, interest rates themselves may be subject only to central bank influence rather than control. Second, central bank interventions may have their greatest influence on expectations about interest rates, or more generally about liquidity. Third, there is an interdependence between central bank intervention in markets to influence interest rates or liquidity, and prudential regulation of the banking system. In all of this, the possibilities open to the central bank depend on the state of expectations and liquidity preference. They also depend crucially on the stage of banking development.

Sedat Aybar and Laurence Harris in Chapter 2, under the title 'How credible are credibility models of central banking?', argue that the existing paradigm of monetary theory, while taking central bank credibility at its centre, omits some of the important features of the modern world. They focus in this chapter on two seemingly distant but interacting aspects. These are globalization of finance and money supply endogeneity. The dominant trend in the financial markets today is globalization, which implies a broader concept than open economies framework where financial flows are treated as flows between nations. Central banks seek to promote their policy credibility within global financial markets, characterized by new forms of devices. The models of monetary policy constructed in terms of national boundaries could be strengthened if the role of central banks in these markets is recognized and credibility is given high priority in relation to these markets. In addition to globalization of financial markets, endogenous growth of money supply put limits to central bank credibility in pursuance of monetary policy. The case study on Turkey, presented here, lends support to the structuralist view of money supply endogeneity where, in the presence of a liberalized financial system, the central bank is unable to accommodate fully demand for credit money by using open market operations and setting discount rates.

Keith Bain in Chapter 3, entitled 'Some problems with the use of "credibility" and "reputation" to support the independence of central banks', begins by considering the importance of the ideas of 'credibility' and 'reputation' to the theoretical argument for independent central banks. He does this by showing how these ideas can be used to provide an explanation for what has occurred in a particular case, such as the decision in May 1997 to grant the Bank of England the power to set interest rates for the UK economy. This is followed by a discussion of the arguments put forward to justify central bank independence, especially the time inconsistency argument. Time inconsistency arises in these models because of the conflict between market agents who are aware that there is no trade-off between inflation and unemployment and voters who act as if such a trade-off exists. The credibility literature makes no serious attempt to justify this difference in behaviour between market agents and voters. An alternative view is to be critical of the representation of the behaviour of market agents in the model. Even if one accepts that, from a macroeconomic perspective, there is no inflation–unemployment trade-off, it is very likely that for some subset of market agents, an expansionary macroeconomic policy will increase their chances of obtaining or retaining jobs and that this might have quite long-term consequences for them.

John Cornwall and Wendy Cornwall in Chapter 4, 'Unemployment costs of inflation targeting', examine the foundations for the growing claims that greater central bank independence will ensure, at no cost, that inflation is both lower and less variable. The three foundations for these claims are: a growing body of empirical evidence; recent developments in monetary theory; and the 'temper of the times'. These foundations are found to be extremely fragile. The empirical evidence rests upon simple correlations between an index of central bank independence and inflation rates, unemployment rates, productivity growth or output growth, or their variances. When such misspecification is rectified by including other relevant variables, the unemployment costs associated with central bank independence are shown to be significant. The purpose of greater central bank independence is to remove short-run monetary policy decisions from the political sphere, and put them in the hands of central bankers charged with pursuing longer-run price stability goals set by government. The theoretical arguments used to support the claim that this will reduce inflation without real costs are firmly based in neoclassical unemployment analysis, and are found to suffer from its unsupported and inconsistent assumptions. The 'temper of the times' is identified here as a belief system, and consequently cannot be refuted.

Peter Spahn in Chapter 5, 'Leadership and stability in key currency systems: a simple game-theoretic approach', considers some basic problems apparent in the working of a key currency system. A two-country model provides the general framework of the analysis where the active part is played by the interaction of central banks. The first question is how leadership by some country is established and why other countries accept their subordinate position. Two approaches which might cause such a systematic asymmetry are investigated: a model which highlights different market structures as to money demand; and another which shows that monetary policy preferences are the decisive factors. Whereas leadership in the gold standard depends on the priority attached to the preservation of external equilibrium at given exchange rates, the emphasis laid on price stability determines that currency which is chosen for intervention and reserve keeping purposes in paper standard systems like the European Monetary System (EMS). Welfare of member countries is affected by supply and demand shocks emanating from the leading country. Paper standard systems differ substantially from the classical gold standard as they exhibit a marked restrictive bias. This result offers some further reason for the evident instabilities of the EMS in the past years.

Ilene Grabel in Chapter 6, 'Coercing credibility: neoliberal policies and monetary institutions in developing and transitional economies', begins by reflecting on the reconstitution of developing countries along neoliberal lines over the last twenty years or so, and the more recent adoption of similar policies by the former socialist countries. Not surprisingly, under these conditions neoliberal economic policies and parallel institutional changes, such as independent central banks and currency boards, are recommended (and indeed have been implemented) by government and IMF/World Bank officials. It is argued that the criterion of 'credibility' is invoked today as a means of privileging neoliberal economic policies and independent monetary institutions, including autonomous central banks and currency boards. The chapter demonstrates that the credibility criterion is theoretically anti-pluralist and politically anti-democratic. In this connection, the chapter argues that credibility is always secured endogenously through political and economic power rather than exogenously through the inherent properties of economic theory. The chapter concludes by suggesting two alternative criteria by which policy regimes and the governance structure of monetary institutions could be adjudicated. These alternative criteria are termed the 'principle of democratic credibility' and the 'principle of fallibility'.

Georg Erber and Harald Hagemann in Chapter 7 under the title, 'Credibility: measurement and impacts. Central bank experience and Euro-perspectives', present a model of rational credibility and reputation formation under the assumption that credibility and reputation formation takes place in an economic environment of stochastic volatility which is assumed to be typical in international financial and money markets. This is considered to be an important topic ignored by many in the past, essentially because most economists use the terms without giving them an explicit formal meaning. To close this gap a simple model of credibility formation based on a cumulative stock approach and of reputation formation based on asymmetric adjustment processes including the possibility of hysteresis effects is formulated. The model assumes that stochastic volatility follows a Bayesian autoregressive stochastic process where the variance of the random variable follows a one-dimensional beta distribution. The chapter demonstrates that the process of forming a European Monetary Union has been, and still is, dominated by political decisions of national governments in the European

Union (EU) and the European Commission to reach a political consensus between the member countries of the EU. Other economically less-costly trajectories of monetary integration could have been chosen and these are discussed in the chapter.

Iain Begg and David Green in Chapter 8, 'The political economy of the European Central Bank', suggest that the proposed European Central Bank (ECB) is designed to enjoy financial and policy independence in determining and implementing monetary policy. However, the way in which the overall European economic policy mix will be decided under the envisaged regime of monetary union in Europe is unclear. The ECB will be unable to offset shocks with asymmetric regional implications by monetary measures. It is suggested that the European economy would benefit from a pan- European stabilization policy. If there is no mechanism for engaging in EU-wide fiscal stabilization there will be an *economic policy deficit*. This deficit may be further aggravated because it is not envisaged that the ECB or any other corresponding Europe-wide institution should have responsibility for banking supervision despite the ECB's duty to prevent systemic instability in the financial system. The ECB will be responsible for European exchange rate policy but there is no guidance as to the policies, aims or the instruments by which it will operate. The potent combination of *democratic and economic policy deficits* may lead to a 'responsibility vacuum' which could be a significant source of macroeconomic policy problems.

Dorene Isenberg in Chapter 9, 'The political economy of monetary policy: the effects of globalization and financial integration on the EU', argues that financial integration on a worldwide basis has been heralded as the culmination of the process of market globalization. This neoliberal vision of a dominant, solitary role for market decision making in the economy concomitantly promotes a diminished role for governmental action in economic matters. This chapter challenges not only the vision that markets should be the sole economic actors, but whether financial liberalization and integration within the borders of the European Union have eradicated the economic roles that government fills. The changes in monetary policies experienced in Belgium and France during the 'global age' of capitalism are investigated, to conclude that while international market forces have made an impact on domestic monetary policies, domestic actors, needs and structures still play a dominant role in the determination of national monetary policy. While national differences were apparent in the manifestion of these changes, both France and Belgium experienced domestic internalization. This process of domesticizing the international market forces evolved from the rearrangement in class forces that emerged during this period. There was a shift in power between financial capital and industrial capital which had a debilitating effect on labour.

xxiv   The political economy of central banking

Jagjit Chadha and Norbert Janssen in Chapter 10, 'Same tune, different words? The reaction function of G7 monetary authorities', examine monetary policy in the G7 countries. Following the end of the Bretton Woods system of fixed-but-adjustable exchange rates, national monetary authorities in the G7 adopted, with varying degrees of formality, forms of feedback rule for monetary policy. This chapter investigates the role of discretion in following stated rules. We adopt a simple description of each country's macroeconomy and motivate a reaction function for monetary authorities' official interest rates which may plausibly operate regardless of the stated policy. The reaction function is examined for the G7 countries with quarterly cyclical data since 1971. The authors find reasonable evidence to suggest that it is possible to characterize official rates as reacting to a similar set of cyclical variables, across countries and through time, irrespective of the declared policy rule, namely, that interest rate smoothing occurs, GDP and inflation expectations play a significant role and that the real exchange rate and broad money seem largely endogenous to the policy rate. The differences in relative weights attached to feedback variables in the G7 do not seem to be well explained by stated policy rules. It is not clear why there needs to be a difference between the rule which is stated and the rule which operates *de facto*. Inflation targets may be a recent way of writing down the sort of discretionary rule which seems to operate.

Augusto Graziani in Chapter 11, 'The independence of central banks: the case of Italy', argues that fundamental changes have taken place recently in terms of the relationship between governments and central banks. Complete institutional independence of central banks from the whims of governments is an accepted development throughout most, if not all, of the world. The motivation of such belief is that independent central banks can ensure price stability, an objective which cannot be achieved when central banks are under the control of governments. This is so since, it is alleged, the objective of central banks, monetary stability, is in conflict with governments' own objectives which are different from that of the central bank's. These aspects are dealt with in this chapter in the case of the Italian central bank. More specifically, the question of the autonomy of central banks is discussed in connection with the dual problem of monetary stability and control of the exchange rate. The problem acquires a considerable relevance in small open economies in a context in which the exchange rates among the main international currencies tend to fluctuate. In the Italian experience, the often contrasting requirements of the two different targets have been at the root of divergence between the central bank and the government authorities. In spite of its formal autonomy, the Bank of Italy has often been forced by circumstances to follow the policy line chosen by the government.

Mario Seccareccia in Chapter 12, 'Wicksellian norm, central bank real interest rate targeting and macroeconomic performance', begins by noting that while most central banks emerged as institutions responsible for handling government debt and as the fiscal agents of governments, along with note-issuing privileges, more recently they have been entrusted with the social responsibility of regulating the financial system and macroeconomic demand management. From this, the chapter moves on to discuss the proposition that, historically, while mainstream economists have given credence to the quantity theory of money, those who have dealt with the theory of central bank behaviour, both economists and policy makers, have subscribed widely to variants of what can be generally denoted as the Wicksellian norm of price-level stabilization. This thesis maintains that control of inflation requires an appropriate bank rate policy, which must necessarily assume that a certain degree of endogeneity of the money supply prevails. The basic Wicksellian norm is to raise the bank rate when prices are rising and to reduce it when prices are falling. Since the 1970s, both in Canada and internationally, monetary authorities have been following a hybrid version of this original Wicksellian policy, with the empirical consequences that both real interest rates and unemployment rates have been pegged at inordinately high levels during the last two decades.

Paul Dalziel in Chapter 13, 'New Zealand's experience with an independent central bank since 1989', begins by describing the Reserve Bank of New Zealand's autonomy in formulating and implementing monetary policy. This is a good example of how a central bank is given autonomy, which, however, is subjected to stringent accountability requirements based on a Policy Targets Agreement, which means that it still remains accountable to the country's elected representatives. It proceeds to explain how the failure to achieve the lower half of the Reserve Bank's target inflation band, together with the costs imposed on the tradables sector by tight monetary conditions in 1995 and 1996, created a political environment in which the inflation target was relaxed from 0–2 to 0–3 per cent. It is suggested that this step represents a cautious acceptance by New Zealand policy makers that a small amount of anticipated inflation may not cause as much harm to the economy as the costs of achieving strict price stability. The chapter also analyses the role played by exchange rate appreciations in achieving a predetermined CPI inflation target in a small open economy, and draws attention to the need for better understanding of the relationship between monetary policy and domestic non-tradables inflation, along the lines being developed in the Post Keynesian research programme in monetary economics.

Special thanks must go to the contributors for their willingness to respond to our comments and suggestions with forbearance and good humour. We are also grateful to the many participants to the conference, who created a truly academic atmosphere with their comments and questioning. Thanks are also extended to June Daniels and Christine Nisbet of the Department of Economics, University of East London, for their secretarial assistance and help in organizing the conference; and to Edward Elgar and his staff, especially Dymphna Evans, Francine O'Sullivan, Julie Leppard and Fiona Peacock, who as always have provided excellent support throughout the period it took to prepare this book. Financial support from the Royal Economic Society and the International Papers in Political Economy, is gratefully acknowledged.

1 The political economy of monetary policy

Sheila Dow and Carlos Rodríguez-Fuentes

1 Introduction

Most of macroeconomic theory presumes that central banks exert complete control over the money supply through monetary policy. In fact, most economic textbooks show the money supply curve as vertical and any change in the money stock is thus represented as a horizontal displacement of this line. This displacement is due to exogenous monetary management on the part of the central bank. The money supply is therefore considered to be exogenous in the sense that it is unilaterally determined by the monetary authorities.

However, some argue that, as financial systems develop, central banks lose their ability to control the money stock since the money supply becomes endogenous to the economic process. For some, the conclusion is that monetary authorities exert control by means of setting key interest rates, so that their control of monetary aggregates is indirect. For them, monetary policy of the form of controlling interest rates is substituted for monetary policy of the form of controlling the money supply. As long as the demand for money is stable, the outcome within a money market diagram, in terms of a determined money supply, is the same.

But for others, endogeneity has more profound consequences. Endogenous money for them means that any increase in liquidity depends more on banks' and borrowers' liquidity preference than on the central bank's direct interventions. An endogenous money supply in this more fundamental sense means that monetary policy, using whatever instrument, does not determine the money stock but is only one of its multiple determinants.

The aim of this chapter is to explore this last perspective on endogeneity with a view to specifying a much broader meaning for monetary policy than is conventionally employed.

2 A reconsideration of the meaning and role of monetary policy

The New Palgrave: A Dictionary of Economics defines monetary policy as follows: 'The term monetary policy refers to actions taken by central banks to affect monetary and other financial conditions in pursuit of the broader objectives of sustainable growth of real output, high employment, and price stability' (Lindsey and Wallich 1987, p. 508).

It would be difficult to argue with this very general definition of monetary policy. However, where differences among economists arise is when trying to expand on this definition. Orthodox monetary theory sees monetary policy as a simple combination of day-to-day interventions within financial markets. Hence, by monetary policy is usually understood injections (or withdrawals) of cash (outside money) in primary money markets, either through open market operations or through changes in the reserve requirement ratio. In its simplest form, monetary policy is then understood as shifts or displacements of the LM curve within the ISLM model, due to exogenous changes in the money supply which, in turn, are due to central bank interventions.

But discussions of the practicalities of monetary policy soon become heavily conditioned by the type of banking system under discussion. Chick (1986) has taken this furthest in specifying the different, distinct stages through which most banking systems proceed as they develop. She demonstrates that the form of monetary policy which is appropriate and feasible depends on the stage of development of the banking system. In particular, she demonstrates that the capacity for monetary authorities to exert direct control over monetary aggregates declines dramatically once a lender-of-last-resort facility is introduced. Then the central bank cannot determine the volume of reserves, and thus of credit and deposits.

If money is supplied by commercial banks which have a considerable degree of latitude in determining credit levels, how far is it possible to identify LM curve shifts due solely to the actions of the monetary authorities? Would there exist such a thing as a monetary policy if the money supply were endogenous? The argument we wish to develop here is that monetary policy cannot, in modern banking systems, be understood as the effecting of discrete changes in the money supply (either directly, or indirectly through interest rate control). Nevertheless this does not deny the possibility of effective monetary policy. But monetary policy needs to be understood as a much more complex intervention in a process within which money is endogenously generated. Further, the possibilities for monetary policy extend beyond manipulation of the traditional instruments (open market operations, and so on) to encompass such elements as bank regulation and supervision.

What we are suggesting here is that, as financial and banking systems develop and the money supply becomes endogenous, making it difficult for the monetary authorities to control liquidity, the very concept of monetary policy should also change in order to take account of such major changes. Of course central banks do still intervene in markets through open market operations despite money being endogenous, but we believe this is neither their only tool nor the most effective way to affect liquidity. As banking systems develop, monetary policies rely much more on indirect mechanisms than on direct ones; central bankers themselves are perfectly aware of their own limitations in affecting liquidity without risking financial instability. In other words, at higher stages of banking development, central banks are generally perfectly aware of the limits of the traditional textbook monetary policy rules, so that in practice they choose to affect liquidity through a variety of means, including influencing the mood of the market and bank supervision.

This view of the concept of monetary policy is to be distinguished from the more standard view which considers monetary policy always to work in the same way regardless of institutional factors, such as the degree of financial development. In fact, traditional monetary analysis has usually drawn a line between monetary and financial or regulation policy. Indeed this separation has now been enshrined in British institutional arrangements, and is implicit in the design of the European Monetary Union. Monetary policy is concerned with monetary control whereas financial regulation is concerned with financial stability. Furthermore, orthodox economists consider financial regulation as a *negative factor* that makes financial intermediation more expensive or less efficient. Sometimes it is argued that bank regulation (or overregulation) has been responsible for periods characterized by *missing money* or *credit crunch* which, in turn, has made monetary control more difficult to achieve.[1] Some others have claimed that central bank regulation may be seen as a *tax on transactions intermediated through banks*.[2] (Prudential) financial regulation is thus never seen as being either an integral part of the monetary policy itself or as a *positive factor* which may encourage lending by providing confidence into the workings of the financial system.

But the existence of a regulatory burden on banks' capital level, banks' portfolios, shares and so on, may give confidence to the consumers of financial services as they perceive that such a system is being backed by monetary authorities. Indeed, the development of banking can be seen in terms of the accretion of confidence in the banking system, which in turn allowed banks to grow while maintaining increasingly small reserve ratios. In other words, prudential regulation has made a positive contribution to the growth of banking, without which it is not clear that banks could now function effectively. Modern banking systems generate a money stock which is primarily inside money, that is, money which is the liability of the banking system, with only fractional backing by outside money. The confidence in inside money reflects a confidence not only in the outside money (bank reserves) but also in the panoply of regulation and supervision which facilitates a backing by only fractional reserves.

It is useful further to consider the balance between regulation for monetary control purposes and prudential regulation. The first form of regulation is likely to exert a larger effect the less developed the banking system is. The latter, however, will become more important the more developed the banking system is. This does not mean that central banks need refuse to use monetary control at higher stages of banking development but rather that they should use both kinds of policies to control liquidity since banks may bypass direct monetary controls. That is, as the financial system develops, monetary control relies more on the effects of central bank interventions on banks' and borrowers' behaviour than on simple monetary restraints.

Dow and Saville (1990) point out the relationship between monetary policy and regulation policy:

> Though the two kinds of official involvements (monetary policy and prudential supervision) have different aims, these are not completely distinct. Prudential supervision does not aim to affect the course of the monetary aggregates ... but it could do so [they are referring to the British monetary experience since 1971], and perhaps at times has done so. (p. 163)

Further: 'To some extent, then, the purposes of monetary policy and banking supervision run together; and it is worth considering whether the procedures of banking supervision could properly assist monetary policy more actively' (p. 168). By monetary policy, then, we would distinguish two different, but interrelated, ways through which central banks may affect the liquidity of the system (see Figure 1.1).

The first channel for monetary policy is a *direct channel* which would apply at lower stages of banking development and would fit well within the standard ISLM view. The direct effects work through the banking multiplier model which assumes exogenous and complete control of money by central banks. This concept would match with the most restrictive view of monetary policy and would only work in banking systems at low stages of development. However, as banking systems develop, this concept of monetary policy becomes less operative as central banks experience a reduced capacity to control liquidity.[3]

It is when central banks lose their power to exert a perfect control on liquidity that they try to exert their influence through alternative means. This is what we have labelled the *indirect channel* and this concept would apply mainly to a highly developed banking system. At this stage, it is through their influence on agents' (borrowers and lenders) financial behaviour that central banks affect liquidity rather than through the standard banking multiplier model. From this perspective, then, monetary policy would affect the liquidity of the system by means of changes in behavioural parameters that have always been considered as fixed. In fact, some have acknowledged this point. For example, Kaldor (1986) pointed out that 'the major effect of changes in interest rates is to be found "in their repercussions on the behaviour of financial institutions" rather than that of private individuals' (Kaldor 1986, p. 13).

Chick (1985, pp. 90–91) has also acknowledged that monetary authorities have relied, to some extent, on the *expectational effect* that an exogenous monetary intervention may have on agents' expectations and that a change in

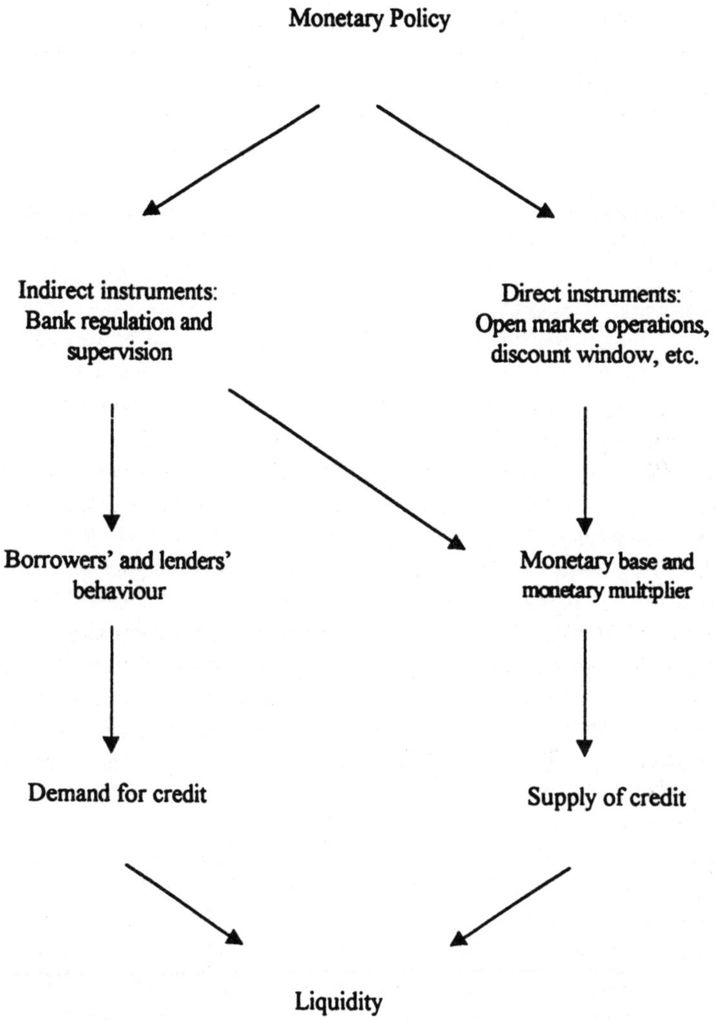

Monetary Policy

Indirect instruments:
Bank regulation and
supervision

Direct instruments:
Open market operations,
discount window, etc.

Borrowers' and lenders'
behaviour

Monetary base and
monetary multiplier

Demand for credit

Supply of credit

Liquidity

Figure 1.1   Influence of monetary policy on liquidity

interest rates is not essential to the transmission of monetary policy. There is in
any case an issue in terms of the capacity of the central bank to affect market
interest rates. Dow and Saville (1990, Chapter 4) point out that, when reserve
requirements are low, as in the UK, changes in the cost of borrowed reserves
have such a minor effect on bank costs that its influence on market rates is
necessarily diffuse. Changes in bank rate are taken by the market primarily as a
signal. But, depending on the current mood of the market, and the market's

perception of the behaviour of the central banks, the signal may or may not be taken seriously. Successful efforts to influence market rates must thus be endogenous to current behaviour and expectations in the market.

Because the *same monetary policy* may produce different effects as it might produce different expectational responses on behalf of economic agents, monetary policy influence on liquidity cannot be seen as being deterministic. This argument gathers force the more developed the banking system and the more the reliance on indirect channels of influence. Direct interventions would work mainly through changes in interest rates and reserves availability. However, the effectiveness of these two effects to slow down the demand for and supply of credit would depend both on the nature of borrowers and on the ability of the banking system to extend credit beyond their deposit base.

With regard to the effect of interest rates on the demand for credit its effectiveness will depend on how interest elastic the demand is: the more interest elastic, the stronger the effect. However, what is worth considering are the differences in terms of interest elasticity among personal, corporate and speculative demands. In this regard we would argue that as both speculative and personal demand for credit are less interest elastic than corporate demand,[4] it would be this latter which is most likely to be squeezed from credit markets when a rise in interest rates is being pursued.[5] This squeeze, however, is more likely to apply to small firms since these may be more dependent on bank finance.

Regarding the quantitative effect, that is, the change in credit availability, it is worth noting that the issue regarding whether tight monetary policies are able to reduce credit demand will depend on the stage of banking development. The lower the stage, the more central banks are able to constrain credit expansion by pursuing tight monetary policies. However, as long as bank credit no longer depends on bank reserves, since banks may have either ways to avoid monetary control by innovating or alternative sources of liquidity, the credit constraint is not likely to work unless it affects banks' expectations and thus banks' lending policy. However, the final effect will be mediated by the banks' behavioural response. It is on these variables that indirect monetary instruments, such as prudential regulation, exert their effects.

The issue of whether monetary policy so considered is able to affect the liquidity of the system will thus depend on variables such as:

1. the interest rate elasticity of demand for credit, since this will determine whether higher interest rates may reduce credit demand or not;
2. the stage of banking development, as this will determine whether monetary constraints may directly constrain bank-lending expansion;
3. banks' and borrowers' response to such monetary changes, since these will determine whether banks decide to meet all credit demand increases

or not. These responses will finally depend on how monetary policy affects banks' and borrowers' liquidity preference (willingness to assume risks) and agents' expectations.

From this perspective, monetary policy could be considered as an exogenous variable which is incorporated into the decision-making process of the private sector. It is exogenous in the sense that its changes are related to decisions taken by central banks. But at the same time, monetary policy may be considered as an endogenous variable because once its future lines are known these are incorporated into the decision-making process of private agents. Hence the announcement of future monetary policy intentions may affect current financial behaviour (the *announcement effect*) and so exert its effect on the economy through behavioural rather than structural parameters. Future monetary restraints may slow down current demand for credit because of a general increase in liquidity preference. It is this interrelationship, which has been labelled as the *identification problem* of money demand, that makes it difficult (if not useless) to draw the distinction between exogenous and endogenous variables which is usually made in economic analysis. It is to this issue, on whether money is exogenous to the economic system or not, that our analysis now turns.

Major outstanding issues in monetary policy
We turn now to analyse two main outstanding issues related to monetary policy. The first will deal with the issue regarding whether money is exogenously supplied by central banks, as orthodox theory sustains, or credit driven and demand determined, as Post Keynesians claim. In particular, we explore the Post Keynesian view further in order to assess how far it erodes the possibility of effective monetary policy. The second question relates to whether money is neutral or not. Thus, in the following subsection, we consider the implications of money, and monetary policy, for real economic conditions.

Money endogeneity We suggested earlier that, for orthodox economists, the money supply is exogenous to the system and so determined by central banks. Post Keynesians, on the contrary, consider the money supply to be credit driven and demand determined, that is, endogenous to the system. Some economists have therefore argued that, as long as the money supply is credit driven and demand determined, monetary policy becomes ineffective in terms of controlling the money stock. This argument is reinforced by the fact that the most extreme endogenous position, the horizontalist one,[6] considers banks as simple *price setters* and *quantity takers* in retail credit markets, that is, banks set prices and demand establishes the quantity to supply.

This horizontalist position argues that the money supply is demand determined and therefore all that monetary authorities can do is to set the general
level of interest rates at which banks would supply, at a marked-up interest
rate, as much credit as creditors demand.

This perfect endogeneity has sometimes been understood by orthodox
economists as meaning that money does not matter. For orthodox theorists,
any exogenous variable is automatically significant as a cause of disturbance
from equilibrium; once a variable is endogenous it loses causal force. However, this extreme horizontalist position is not widely shared by all Post
Keynesians economists,[7] since for some it is not enough to say that *demand
creates its own supply*, but it must be explained *how the private sector
commands the money supply it wants* (Chick 1973, p. 88). While we share the
endogenous money approach, we shall argue that some factors put limits on
the endogeneity of the money supply and, furthermore, that some of these
limits will come both from the activities of a monetary authority which tries
to control the liquidity of the system, as well as from the banks themselves,
which may also put limits on their credit extension. Our argument will be that
monetary policy does matter even if money is endogenous. As Wray (1992)
puts it[8]

> banks do not fully accommodate the demand for flows of credit even if their
> expectations move in the same direction as those of borrowers. ... This does not
> mean that we must accept the textbook 'deposit multiplier' or the orthodox posi-
> tion that the central bank controls the quantity of money. However, the central
> bank can make it very difficult for banks to extend their balance sheets if it so
> chooses. (pp. 1163–4)

In principle we shall assume the money supply to be horizontal at some
level of interest rates. In so doing, it must be emphasized that the money
supply schedule employed here is itself the outcome of a process *over time*,
unlike the orthodox money supply schedule which represents a range of
simultaneous possibilities. This distinction is central to the analysis of Arestis
and Howells (1996) which unpacks the money supply curve into a shifting
series of credit demand and supply curves.

It has been argued by several authors that the horizontal cannot be extended
indefinitely. Instead, there must be some point (M1 in Figure 1.2 below),
beyond which 'banks might require higher interest rates to compensate for
greater perceived risk as balance sheets expand' (Wray 1992, p. 1160). This
point would be where, following Minsky's analysis, 'the internal workings of
the banking mechanism or Central Bank action to constraint inflation will
result in the supply of finance becoming less than infinitely elastic – perhaps
even approach to zero elasticity' (Minsky 1982, p. 107). The point where the
money supply approaches zero elasticity is labelled M2 in Figure 1.2.

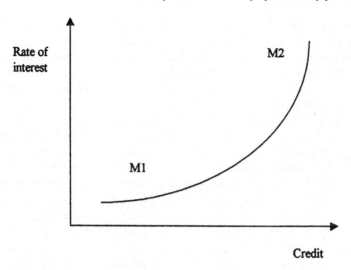

Figure 1.2 Lending expansion

But what are the factors that determine changes in money supply? We follow Minsky's work on financial instability[9] in order to explain why the two turning points (M1 and M2) are likely to exist and why they are also likely to move (backward and forward) along with business cycles. Let us start first by analysing the factors determining these *turning points* in the money supply curve. Bank lending expansion is likely to arise during economic upturns since it is then that economic optimism fuels both demand for and supply of credit as new business opportunities arise. It is during economic upturns that the number of people willing to incur debt grows and this in turn may make credit demand more interest inelastic. Hence, banks not only face a growing demand for credit but also a less elastic one. Banks can thus charge higher interest rates without any fear of loss of market share. It could be argued that growing competition both between banks and between banks and non-bank financial intermediaries would drive prices (interest rates) down. However, and despite competitive pressures that may put bounds to interest rates rising, it is likely that, sooner or later, interest rates will rise and that this policy will be followed by all institutions simultaneously.[10]

As bank lending increases, banks become less liquid and borrowers become less creditworthy than before (personal indebtedness has already increased and this might affect personal creditworthiness). On the other hand, as demand for bank lending increases it is likely that riskier and more speculative projects come into banks' portfolios. Furthermore, lending expansion may also drive banks to accept new customers whose risk is difficult and costly to assess. This factor would in turn explain why banks may begin to ration credit not only by raising interest rates but also by asking for higher collateral requirements from their new customers.

The effect of these higher interest rates may well displace some projects (investments) which cannot sustain higher interest rates within the very short term; for example, long-term projects which demand low interest rates until they begin to produce cash flow to pay off debts. Only those projects with higher profit expectations within the very short term will be able to afford this higher financial cost. Some of these projects are likely to be speculative, so that speculative activities will displace productive activity from financial markets.

One important byproduct of these displacements is that the demand for credit will become more interest inelastic, so that higher interest rates will have a weaker effect on the demand for credit. At this point banks may decide to ration credit themselves despite the fact that the demand is still going up. In addition, as banks' lending portfolios increase, banks' fears about their own financial stability may arise, driving banks into more prudent and conservative behaviour as regards their lending policies.

Another factor which may halt the lending-expansion process is the running of both a tight monetary and banking-supervision policies. These factors may affect lending expansion since it would make it more expensive and difficult for banks to extend lending further and, what is more important, may affect banks' attitude towards lending (banks' liquidity preference). We are not arguing here that central banks can control liquidity by means of quantitative ratios which make more difficult the provision of credit by commercial banks. Instead we believe, as Dow and Saville (1990) clearly state, that central banks' power is more a *qualitative* than a *quantitative* matter. They put the argument in the following way:

> Banks are older than central banks, and if central banks were abolished, banks would undoubtedly survive. ... One or more large banks could indeed in principle provide the services now provided by the central bank, so that the extreme position in which the banking system became completely independent in this respect is not inconceivable. ... That situation is not, in practice, likely to arise. For the game is essentially a political one: the central bank could always control the banks in other ways, as all parties are aware. (pp. 148–9)

It is the combination of all these factors, both quantitative and qualitative, that explains the increasing slope of the money supply as bank lending expands. The extension of lending may finally stop when both central and commercial banks begin to implement restrictive policies to slow down credit expansion at any cost.

So far we have concentrated our analysis on studying how a bank-lending expansion may entail an upward-sloping money supply function, even when money is endogenous. However, there is another feature of the process that we would like to stress here: the different path that this process may take along economic business cycles. Neither M1 nor M2 can be considered as fixed points but are likely to move, either forward or backward, along with economic upturns and downturns.

We now consider the argument that the whole money supply curve may change slope with the phase of the business cycle. We explicitly suggest that money supply is likely to be more elastic in upturns than in downturns and that this differential behaviour is explained by changes in the overall liquidity preference of the economy (see Figure 1.3). It is worth noting that these changes are mainly due to changes in financial behaviour which have the capacity to change the functioning of the whole financial system:

> individual actions which are rational in themselves generate outcomes which act against the collective interest. ... In an expansion, the supply of money may increase to such an extent that ... fuels the speculative expansion. ... An extreme euphoria followed by collapse may even irrevocably destroy the confidence in the outside money ... which had allowed the financial system to function as it did. In the aftermath of the bursting of the speculative bubble, the supply of credit is inelastic relative to demand ... [and this] inelasticity of supply with respect to demand is so great as to force bankruptcies and impede investment plans, thus contributing to the contraction of output and employment. (Dow, 1993, pp. 39–40)

In terms of Figures 1.2 and 1.3, point M1 moves because of the higher (lower) banks' liquidity preference during downturns (upturns). The more

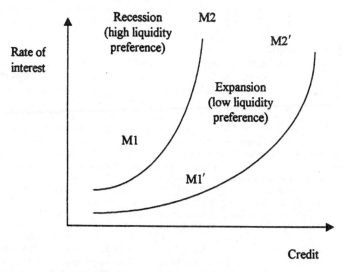

Figure 1.3   Lending expansion; recession and expansion

confident banks are (the lower their liquidity preference is), the later they will begin to charge higher interest rates on new loans. Point M2 in turn is also able to move because of the central banks' interventions. The tighter the monetary conditions the central banks establish, the more likely it is that commercial banks will begin to cut back on their lending expansion.

This overall argument suggests that the money supply is *sometimes horizontal* and, depending on some factors, *sometimes vertical* (Wray 1990, pp. 91–3). Table 1.1 summarizes the relationship between the endogenous/ exogenous character of money and the elasticity/inelasticity of the money supply, as well as the effect that monetary policy, banking development and liquidity preference may have on such variables. This table shows that at lower stages of banking development, an elastic supply of liquidity can only exist when central banks are implementing a loose monetary policy and, at the same time, both banks and borrowers are willing to lend and borrow, respectively. In all other cases, either because central banks are pursuing tight

Table 1.1   Endogeneity of money and liquidity expansion

Degree of endogeneity	Monetary policy	Stage bank development	Liquidity preference		Liquidity expansion
			Banks	Borrower	
Exogenous	tight	low	regardless	regardless	inelastic
Exogenous	loose	low	low	low	elastic
Exogenous	loose	low	high	low	inelastic[a]
Exogenous	loose	low	low	high	inelastic[b]
Exogenous	loose	low	high	high	inelastic[c]
Endogenous	regardless[d]	high	low	low	elastic
Endogenous	regardless[d]	high	high	low	inelastic[a]
Endogenous	regardless[d]	high	low	high	inelastic[b]
Endogenous	regardless[d]	high	high	high	inelastic[c]

Notes:
a. Banks may decide not to lend despite having funds available because of their high liquidity preference. Instead they would prefer risk-free investments such as public bonds, large companies rather than small ones, and so on. Some credit rationing may exist.
b. Although banks are willing to lend, borrowers may decide not to borrow because of their unwillingness to invest. High economic instability, low profitability, higher risks and so on may explain this kind of conservative behaviour.
c. In this case, both borrowers and lenders are unwilling to run into debt and to lend, respectively. Banks decide not to lend or borrowers to borrow. This situation is labelled as *defensive financial behaviour*;[11] a situation where the low availability of credit will be explained by both a weak supply and demand for credit.
d. Once the banking system reaches some level of development, monetary authorities lose their power to perfectly control liquidity. However, monetary authorities may still exert some effect on the liquidity of the system by affecting banks' and borrowers' financial behaviour. Hence, monetary and financial policy may play this role at this stage and these influences should be considered.

monetary policies which make banks' reserves scarce, or because banks or borrowers are unwilling to lend and borrow, respectively, an inelastic supply of liquidity is likely to exist. However, a high stage of bank development does not necessarily mean that an elastic supply of liquidity exists, but it rather reinforces the fact that liquidity expansion relies much more on banks' and borrowers' liquidity preference than for lower stages of banking development.

Monetary policy non-neutrality   We have suggested that monetary theory has traditionally drawn a sharp distinction between *real* and *monetary* variables. This distinction has led most economists to study how these two relate to each other, in the form of the monetary transmission mechanism. Real economic variables are usually assumed to depend only on real factors such as physical capital and labour, whereas money is seen just as a device to ease the exchange of goods and services already produced. Therefore the only role which has been left to money is to determine the general level of prices. Providing the system is working properly, monetary flows should thus mirror real flows. From this point of view, money (and by implication monetary policy) is considered to be neutral because a change in its quantity leads to 'a change in the absolute level of prices, but leaves relative prices, the rate of interest, real income, real wealth (including real money balances), and hence real output, unaffected' (Patinkin 1987, p. 640). Furthermore, 'money is said to be superneutral – or long-run neutral – if changes in the steady-rate of growth of the money supply do not affect the growth path of real economic variables' (Danthine 1987, p. 608). The neutrality of money simply means that economic agents are free from *money illusion* or, more formally, that demand functions are *homogeneous of degree zero* in the money prices and in the initial quantity of financial assets, including money.[12]

However, some chances for money not being neutral have been recognized, at least within the very short term. For example, some have pointed out that an increase in the price level, which is always seen as a monetary phenomenon, may have a stimulating effect on production since this 'keeps alive a spirit of industry in the nation' (Hume 1752, pp. 39–40, as quoted in Patinkin 1987, p. 18). Others have relied on the redistributive effects that such a monetary change could produce, for example, the redistributive effects that inflation may cause between lenders and borrowers, and the redistributive effects that high interest rates may have on profits, wages and personal indebtedness.[13]

Monetarists, in turn, have recognized that money may not be neutral in the short run although they claim its neutrality in the very long run. But rational expectations theorists have pointed out that this effect of money on output and employment within the short run only happens when the monetary change is unforeseen by economic agents. Otherwise, the effect will be totally on prices. That is, only a non-systematic (unanticipated) monetary policy is able to affect output within the short run. However, in the long run, money is neutral.

Price stickiness, either in nominal interest rates or wages, is often noted as another source of monetary non-neutrality. Indeed, much of the standard Keynesian view on monetary effects has relied on such price stickiness. This approach underpins New Keynesian theories of non-neutrality, which have explored the role of asymmetric, or otherwise imperfect, information in generating market failure. In particular, asymmetric information is seen as causing credit rationing, where capital markets are not sufficiently perfect to provide substitutes for bank credit. However, if information were full, costless, complete and available to all agents, money would be neutral.

The implication of this literature is that, as long as there are market imperfections, money is non-neutral, and monetary policy is important (Laidler 1990, p. 21). It is because of this that most of the empirical literature dealing with the issue of whether money is neutral has looked at one or more of the following questions:

1.   how different economic sectors respond to exogenous monetary shocks;
2.   the degree to which anticipations of monetary changes matters;
3.   whether credit markets are rationed.

However, this approach is rather misleading because it applies only to a theoretical framework which splits economic activity into the real and the monetary. The starting point is a world of exogenous money where real variables are determined only by real factors and money determines prices. The question then is, under what conditions would an exogenous change in the money supply have real effects? Within this model, money would be neutral if it were unable to affect real variables.[14] It is only from this very particular perspective that the issue regarding monetary neutrality (non-neutrality) makes some sense.

However, if money were not exogenously introduced into the system but endogenously created by the banking system to finance economic activity, how could we address the issue of whether money is neutral? In particular, how could we discuss the effects of a money supply increase without first discussing the expenditure plans which generated the demand for credit, and the bank behaviour which led to the demand being net? If we introduce these factors,[15] then the issue is no longer restricted to whether money is neutral or not but when and why it has been so. The issue is not then to determine whether the banknotes dropped from the helicopter affect output and employment. *It matters who receives the money* (Dow and Earl 1982, p. 254). Only by assuming that what is going on in the *real economy* is strictly independent of what is going on in the *helicopter* could we safely analyse the theoretical matter of whether money is neutral or not. Otherwise the relevant question to be addressed would be a more specific one: why the money dropped in this place has not produced the same effect as that dropped a little further away.

What we are suggesting here is that the issue of the neutrality of money is related to the issue of how money comes into the economy. If we assume that money is endogenous to the system, then the issue of its neutrality does not make any sense any more since the question regarding whether money helps to increase production or employment will depend on factors such as (i) what money is used for, and (ii) the response of investors, banks, savers and so on to monetary changes. Hence, the pure analysis of the neutrality of money which ignores these considerations can only make sense in a theoretical framework which assumes the banking system to play a passive (neutral) role in the economic process. It cannot make sense in a framework which assumes money to be endogenously supplied by the system:

> There always has been a conflict between those who see banks as the operators of a safe and secure payments mechanism and those who see banks as an essential institution for the capital development of the economy. The first group views banking and financial intermediation as essentially passive processes by which a predetermined amount of savings is allocated among alternative uses. The second group views banking and financial intermediation as active agents in the economy that, by financing investment, force resources to be used to put investment in place, thereby fostering the development of the economy. (Minsky 1993, p. 82)

Within the neutrality/non-neutrality debate we can identify two different dimensions: quantitative and qualitative. The quantitative dimension, which we shall call the *structural effect*, would apply mainly to an economy where money is exogenously determined and would be concerned with the effect that exogenous monetary changes may have on different sectors, level of employment, output and so on. We have named this quantitative effect because it is able to be quantified through the calculus of simple elasticities. This, in turn, helps to explain why most research has paid so much attention to this dimension. Focus on this dimension, however, can explain at best only one half of the process. The other half, we suggest, would be explained by what we have labelled the qualitative dimension of the process.

The qualitative dimension, which highlights what we call the *behavioural effect*, would instead fit in a world of endogenous money. Here, the question to be addressed is how economic and current monetary conditions[16] may affect agents' financial behaviour and how those, in turn, may affect economic activity (employment and output). In other words, the question to be addressed here is how financial behaviour affects the real economy, bearing in mind that financial behaviour is determined both by financial variables (monetary policy and financial regulation) and by real variables (economic expectations and so on) and neither a clear-cut nor a one-way causal relationship between the two can be established. It is clear that the behavioural effect is not open to being fully quantified

Conclusions

Our aim has been to clarify the meaning of the concept of monetary policy when money is endogenous to the economic process. It has been argued that, as the financial system develops and therefore money creation becomes endogenous, the concept of monetary policy has to be widened in order to include the factors which may affect banks' and borrowers' behaviour, since these will determine credit expansion/destruction. Accordingly it is not possible to draw a clear distinction between monetary policy and financial regulation since this latter is probably the most important determinant of credit expansion in financially developed economies.

Regarding the endogenous character of money, we suggested that an endogenous money supply does not necessarily mean that the demand for money is passively accommodated, or that money loses its causal power. But by the same token, if money is generated endogenously, its causal role is suffused within the overall economic process.

It has been argued here that, under certain conditions, the money supply may become inelastic in spite of money being endogenous: for example, when there exists high liquidity preference among borrowers and lenders. Furthermore, it was suggested that the money supply is likely to be more elastic during expansions rather than during downturns. That is to say, the pattern of credit expansion follows a cyclical pattern, as do changes in liquidity preference.

As far as the analysis of the effects of monetary policy on economic activity is concerned, we pointed out that the debate over whether *money matters versus does not matter* makes sense only if (i) there is a sharp distinction between the real and monetary sides of the economy and (ii) money is perfectly exogenous to the system. Only this would allow us to analyse what happens to the real side when we introduce an exogenous change in the money supply. Only by assuming that economic activity depends on real factors such as labour, physical capital and so on, and monetary flows simply mirror real ones, can it be ensured that money and monetary policy are neutral with respect to output and employment. Otherwise, the issue regarding whether money is neutral would not make any sense, just as it would not make sense to consider whether labour or physical capital, for example, were neutral.

If such a clear distinction between real and monetary sides of the economy are not drawn, then efforts should be put into studying *when and how* rather than *whether* monetary policy is neutral or not. Whether monetary policy is neutral or not could only be addressed from a theoretical standpoint which, by assuming money to be exogenous to the economic process, tries to determine the long-run effect of an exogenous increase in the money supply. However, if money were not exogenous then this matter would be of no relevance. Then the issue to analyse would rather be how exogenous monetary interventions in financial markets affect the liquidity of the system and thereby economic activity.

We also argued that two dimensions have to be distinguished when analysing the effects of monetary policy on economic activity: a structural dimension and a behavioural dimension. The first is concerned with the effects of exogenous monetary changes on different economic variables. The second dimension is related to the effect that such changes may have on agents' behaviour. The more developed the financial system is, the more relevant this second factor will be.

Bearing this in mind, it is clear that the issue to study is no longer whether exogenous monetary changes affect output or not but when and how they do, especially in financially developed economies. This is so because the final effect of any monetary change will depend on the final use given to the new money which is supplied. This is what Chick (1973, p. 132) has labelled the second half of the monetary transaction. In this sense, an endogenous money supply perspective would mean that the place in which, and time at which, the helicopter throws the money is of crucial importance when analysing its effects.

The view that monetary policy enters into an endogenous process, where its effects are context dependent, therefore clears the way for analysis of what that monetary policy should consist of in particular contexts. This in turn requires understanding, not only of the structure of the banking system and of the economy as a whole, but also of the determinants of behaviour. In particular, this approach draws attention to the fact that behaviour is conditional on an institutional structure which emerged as a result of past behaviour. In other words, modern banking systems function on the foundation of confidence which is the product of institutional arrangements, and experience of central bank behaviour, built up over many years. Minsky's work highlights the interdependence between financial behaviour, the state of confidence, and output and employment. What we have argued here is that this interdependence should be borne in mind when designing monetary policy. Specifically this requires attention to bank regulation and supervision, with a view to maintaining financial stability, as a central plank of monetary policy.

Notes

1. See Duca (1993) and Clair and Tucker (1993) for an account of these arguments.
2. Wills (1982, p. 249).
3. Interbank lending, discount window and lender-of-last-resort facilities, access to external financial markets, increased banking competition, financial innovation and so on, would be among the factors which would explain this process.
4. Speculative demand is likely to be less sensitive to changes in interest rates because speculative activities will probably mean higher, and riskier, returns within the very short term. As regards personal demand, especially households' borrowing, this will probably show a low interest rate elasticity since households' borrowing depends much more on income expectations (wages, employment and so on) rather than on the cost of borrowing itself (this later is specially true in the case of borrowing for the acquisition of durable goods).
5. Credit demand for speculative activities (speculative demand) is likely to be less interest elastic as these activities may have attached higher returns, because of their risky nature, within shorter periods of time. As regards personal demand this could also show low interest elasticity since personal borrowing decisions are likely to be determined by personal income expectations (wages, employment and so on) rather than by its cost (interest rates). The former is reinforced by the fact that personal borrowing is sometimes aimed to provide households with goods of first need (low price elasticity, such as housing and so on).
6. Being Moore (1988) the leading author.
7. See Cottrell (1994) for a survey.
8. Dow and Saville (1990) have also made a similar point to this. They have distinguished two points in bank intermediation. The first one is a *potential equilibrium point* whereas the second one would be the *operative equilibrium point*, both of which would move forward in a growing economy. The *potential equilibrium point* is defined as the *desired lending* by final lenders and borrowers, and the *operative equilibrium point* that one which banks *themselves find* profitable. See Dow and Saville (1990, pp. 23–7).
9. See Minsky (1982), especially Chapters 5 to 7.
10. Dow and Saville argue that 'although banks are many and separate, collectively the banking system behaves in some respects as a bloc. ... The conformity in behaviour probably reflects not oligopoly but other reasons ... Banks are in the business of maturity transformation ... Short-term funding will become harder to obtain if doubt develops about the quality of bank loans ... Thus, it is essential to each bank to maintain market confidence in its management, and this in general will require following lending policies similar to those other banks' (1990, p. 55).
11. Dow (1992) offers a full account of such a concept as well as an application to the Scottish case.
12. For a more detailed account on these two concepts, see Patinkin (1987).
13. The papers by Moore (1989), Niggle (1989), Ash and Bell (1991) and Arestis and Howells (1994) have dealt with some of the redistributional effects of high levels of interest rates.
14. However, one wonders how money could possibly matter within a model which explicitly assumes real variables (real income) to depend only on real factors (physical capital and labour). If by definition we take money away from the real sector, how could it matter for real purposes? How could the labour force matter if we consider that output does not depend on labour?
15. This is what Chick has labelled as the other half of the monetary change (see Arestis and Dow (eds) 1992, pp. 159–60).
16. By monetary conditions we do not only mean interest rates, but also expectations on future interest rates, economic growth, and any other variable (information) which may affect borrowers' and lenders' behaviour.

Bibliography
Arestis, P. and S.C. Dow (eds) (1992), *On Money, Method and Keynes*, London: Macmillan.
Arestis, P. and P. Howells (1994), 'Monetary policy and income distribution in the UK', *Review of Radical Political Economics*, **26** (3), 56–65.
Arestis, P. and P. Howells (1996), 'Theoretical reflections on endogenous money: the problem with convenience lending', *Cambridge Journal of Economics*, **20** (5), 539–51.
Ash, C. and D.N.F. Bell (1991), 'The regional impact of changes in interest rates', University of Stirling, Mimeo.
Chick, V. (1973), *The Theory of Monetary Policy*, Oxford: Basil Blackwell.
Chick, V. (1985), 'Keynesians, Monetarists and Keynes: the end of the debate or a beginning?', in P. Arestis and T. Skouran (eds), *Post Keynesian Economic Theory. A Challenge to Neo Classical Economics*, Brighton: Wheatsheaf, Armonk, NY: M.E. Sharpe, pp. 79–98.
Chick, V. (1986), 'The evolution of the banking system and the theory of saving, investment and interest', *Economies et Sociétés 20, Monnaie et Production*, **3**, 111–26.
Chick, V. (1993), 'The evolution of the banking system and the theory of monetary policy', in S.F. Frowen (ed.), *Monetary Theory and Monetary Policy: New Tracks for the 1990s*, London: Macmillan, pp. 79–92.
Clair, R.T. and P. Tucker (1993), 'Six causes of the credit crunch', *Federal Reserve Bank of Dallas, Economic Review*, 3rd Quarter, 1–20.
Cottrell, A. (1994), 'Post-Keynesian monetary economics', *Cambridge Journal of Economics*, **18** (6), 587–605.
Danthine, J.P. (1987), 'Superneutrality', in J. Eatwell, M. Milgate and P. Newman (eds), *The New Palgrave. A Dictionary of Economics*, Vol. 3, London: Macmillan, pp. 608–9.
Dow, S.C. (1992), 'The regional financial sector: a Scottish case study', *Regional Studies*, **26** (7), 619–31.
Dow, S.C. (1993), *Money and the Economic Process*, Aldershot: Edward Elgar.
Dow, S.C. (1994), 'Endogenous money', in G.C. Harcourt and P. Riach (eds), *The Second Edition of Keynes's General Theory*, Vol. 2, London: Routledge, pp. 61–78.
Dow, S.C. and P.E. Earl (1982), *Money Matters: A Keynesian Approach to Monetary Economics*, Oxford: Martin Robertson.
Dow, J.C.R. and I.D. Saville, (1990), *A Critique of Monetary Policy. Theory and British Experience*, Paperback edn, Oxford: Clarendon Press.
Duca, J.V. (1993), 'Regulation, bank competitiveness and episodes of missing money', *Federal Reserve Bank of Dallas Economic Review*, 2nd Quarter, 1–23.
Kaldor, N. (1986), *The Scourge of Monetarism*, 2nd edn, Oxford: Oxford University Press.
Laidler, D. (1990), *Taking Money Seriously*, New York: Philip Allan.
Lindsey, D.E and H.C. Wallich (1987), 'Monetary policy', in J. Eatwell, M. Milgate and P. Newman (eds), *The New Palgrave. A Dictionary of Economics*, Vol. 3, London: Macmillan, pp. 508–15.
Minsky, H.P. (1982), *Inflation, Recession and Economic Policy*, Brighton: Wheatsheaf.
Minsky, H.P. (1993), 'On the non-neutrality of money', *Federal Reserve Bank of New York, Quarterly Review*, **18** (1), 77–82.
Moore, B.J. (1988), *Horizontalists and Verticalists: The Macroeconomics of Credit Money*, Cambridge: Cambridge University Press.
Moore, B.J. (1989), 'The effects of monetary policy on income distribution', in P. Davidson and I. Kregel (eds), *Macroeconomic Problems and Policies of Income Distribution. Functional, Personal, International*, Aldershot: Edward Elgar, pp. 18–41.
Niggle, C.J. (1989), 'Monetary policy and changes in income distribution', *Journal of Economic Issues*, **23** (3), 809–22.
Patinkin, D. (1987), 'Neutrality of money', in J. Eatwell, M. Milgate and P. Newman (eds), *The New Palgrave. A Dictionary of Economics*, Vol. 3, London: Macmillan, pp. 639–45.
Wills, H.R. (1982), 'The simple economics of bank regulations', *Economica*, **49**, 249–59.
Wray, L.R. (1990), *Money and Credit in Capitalist Economies. The Endogenous Money Approach*, Aldershot: Edward Elgar.
Wray, L.R. (1992), 'Alternative approaches to money and interest rates', *Journal of Economic Issues*, **26** (4), 1145–78.

20 - 37

ES1 ES2 ES8 oll (Turkey)

2 How credible are credibility models of central banking?

Sedat Aybar and Laurence Harris

1 Introduction

The theory of monetary policy has, since the 1980s, developed within a thoroughly modern paradigm but in historical perspective it is the latest stage of an old debate. There are a number of candidates for its starting point. For some, today's literature may be seen as the full maturity of the Chicago case for a monetary rule, whose terms were set out in 1936 by Henry Simons (Simons 1936). In longer perspective it may be seen as another staging post on the long road monetary theory has travelled since the birth of economics, the road defined originally by the early nineteenth-century debates between the currency and banking schools (Viner 1937; Rist 1940; Hicks 1967; Arnon 1991). Today, the case for rules or discretion ('authority') employs the modern concepts of rational expectations, credibility, commitment and dynamic (in)consistency. But is it an appropriate framework; has the modernity of theory been gained at the expense of losing touch with the actually existing modern world?

In this chapter we argue that the standard models of central banking, which lie at the heart of the theory of monetary policy, do, indeed, omit important features of the modern world. We focus upon two absences: an international dimension that properly reflects 'globalization' of finance; and endogeneity of the money supply. Although the simplicity of central banking models is a virtue, enabling them to generate powerful results, their framework of purely national (rather than global) markets and a vertical supply curve of money severely limits their applicability.

The models' standard concept of credibility illustrates those points. The models assume that credence refers to the perceptions of employers and workers and their impact on the labour market: but central bankers actually pay attention, arguably much greater attention, to their credibility in the eyes of international financial markets. Moreover, although the models define credibility in terms of the central bank's actions on policy instruments, assuming that policy is immediately translated into changes in money supply, in actual economies the credibility of those instruments themselves is equally relevant: do rational agents believe the money supply is wholly determined by central bank policy instruments?

In the following section we summarize the existing paradigm. In Section 3 we discuss its limitations in a world marked by global financial markets, and in Section 4 we consider the relevance of theories of endogenous money supply. In Section 5 we consider a case study of the empirical significance of endogenous money supply, using data from Turkey. Section 6 concludes.

2 Credibility and the central bank's objective function

The existing paradigm of the theory of monetary policy has the central bank's credibility at its centre. The central result, in a world of rational expectations and no information asymmetries, is that discretionary monetary policy has an inflationary bias. That bias can only be eliminated, with a consequent gain in social welfare, if the central bank is pre-committed by strictly tying monetary expansion to a rule. The inflationary bias of discretionary policy exists because central bank announcements are not credible. Here lack of credibility is identical with dynamic inconsistency. If the central bank announces a zero-inflation policy, the public, with perfect information including information about the bank's objective function, rationally expects the bank to adopt a different, surprise, policy to expand employment once inflation expectations have been formed, and therefore determines its actions on those fully informed expectations. Dynamic inconsistency means that the bank's announced policy is not credible (Kydland and Prescott 1977; Barro and Gordon 1983b; Cukierman 1995).

Extensions to the model, permitting asymmetric information, uncertainty in the minds of the public, and sophisticated strategies in the central bank/public game lead to related results, but rather than credibility being simply present or absent, it is a function of reputation, influenced by central bank actions and a variety of institutional arrangements (Barro and Gordon 1983a). The world has been experiencing a wave of institutional reforms in central banking. They include moves towards central bank independence, the appointment of central bank governors with 'conservative' reputations (in terms of the weight given to unemployment and price stability in their objective function), and contractual or constitutional rules regulating relations between government and the central bank. The theoretical rationale for each is located in such models of credibility-increasing institutional arrangements. Therefore the underlying concept of credibility deserves scrutiny, starting with the question 'who has to have confidence in the credibility of monetary policy?'.

The agents around which the model revolves are workers and employers and their critical actions occur in negotiating wages in the labour market. Specifically, they negotiate the nominal wages that will obtain over a period in an attempt to attain an optimum real wage over that period; thus, their negotiations reflect expected inflation over the period and, hence, the credibility of central bank policy announcements. Central bank credibility, therefore, is credibility in the eyes of labour market actors. If the bank lacks credibility, nominal wage settlements will rise faster than otherwise and, given technology and the degree of monopoly, that rate of wage inflation will be reflected in a higher rate of price inflation.

The models' focus on credibility in the labour market can also be seen in their assumption about the central bank's objective function, or loss function. Its two variables are inflation and unemployment, the determination of which is located in the labour market. With given inflation expectations in the labour market, a short-run Phillips curve would exist, apparently offering a trade-off between inflation and unemployment. If the central bank announces a policy ('zero inflation') it would not be credible to workers and employers because they know that dynamic inconsistency exists. That is, if the expectation of zero inflation were held, after announcing its zero-inflation policy the bank would then seek to maximize its objective function (minimize loss) by reneging on its announcement. It would try to reduce unemployment below its 'natural rate', and raise inflation, moving along that short-run Phillips curve to the point where it is tangential to an indifference curve of the objective function. Knowing that the bank has that incentive for dynamic inconsistency, nominal wage negotiators in fact generate a higher inflation rate. Thus, the driving force for the inflationary bias of discretionary monetary policy is lack of central bank credibility in the eyes of labour market actors.

Since that basic model became established, the theory of central banking has developed within a political economy framework. In it, a key additional player is the elected political authority ('government'), for, as Waller and Walsh (1996, p. 1139) put it, such models address 'the continual tensions between the Federal Reserve and the US Congress as well as the ... worldwide moves toward redesigning central banking institutions'. Fratianni et al. (1997), for example, examine a variety of institutional arrangements as outcomes of the desire to solve a political principal–agent problem. The public (principal) finds that the central bank (agent) operates suboptimally because its ties to the government, whose objectives are reelection, affect its credibility. The effects of a variety of institutional arrangements are examined, with independence or performance contracts having the best effect. Similarly, Waller and Walsh (1996) examine optimal institutional arrangements in the form of the length of term of the central banker's appointment and the principle of appointing a conservative central banker, showing that long terms of appointment may be too costly if society's preferences shift permanently. However, the political economy models of optimal institutional design, with inflation and unemployment in the objective or social welfare function, are also driven by labour market reactions and credibility perceived in the labour market.

Cukierman (1995) develops a political economy framework as a positive theory orientated towards explaining the existence of inflationary monetary policy, and goes beyond a simple inflation–unemployment objective function. Recognizing that actual central banks both historically and today have a number of roles, his model includes revenue raising for the state (seigniorage), stabilization of the banking system and financial markets, and balance-of-payments objectives, as well as domestic macroeconomic responsibilities (inflation–unemployment) among them. Thus, monetary expansion and inflation might arise either from the standard inflationary bias and credibility problems, or from attempts to optimize the state's revenue from seigniorage, or from short-term interest rate smoothing in pursuit of financial stabilization, or for balance-of-payments reasons. As we suggest in the following section, that perspective increases the model's applicability to existing central banks, but misses important aspects.

A more thoroughgoing attempt to go beyond the labour market orientation of central bank models, is Epstein's construction of a model (Epstein 1994) in which the structural characteristics of the labour market are integrated with other structural features of the economy to explain the determinants of monetary policy. In that case the underlying research programme is, unusually, a puzzle over the absence of expansionary monetary policy (Epstein 1993). In his 1994 model, which is seminal within the structural economics paradigm, Epstein demonstrates how the interaction between four structural features can determine monetary policy: in addition to the structure of the labour market they are the relation between the central bank and the state, the connection between the industrial and financial sectors, and the economy's position in the world economy.

3 Credibility in globalized markets

The basic model of central banking, which revolves around monetary policy's credibility in the labour market has an unduly restrictive focus. In reality, whatever the relevance of monetary policy for labour market outcomes, monetary policy is conditioned by central bank credibility in other markets. In particular, money market rates, bond yields, equity returns and foreign exchange rates are highly sensitive to the credibility of the central bank.

Consequently, the design of central banking arrangements, such as independence, or the installation of a 'conservative' central banker, is driven to a large extent by the need to win credibility in financial and foreign exchange markets. Similarly, the actions of central banks are frequently designed to strengthen the bank's reputation in those markets. Arguably, credibility and reputation in those markets has been the dominant force in modern central banking. But the basic model, with its restricted concept of credibility, is unable to engage with that reality, and the political economy models such as Cukierman's and Epstein's which do introduce the central bank's concern for financial markets do not include a developed concept of central bank credibility in those markets.

Any attempt to introduce into our models the central bank's relationship to financial and foreign exchange markets immediately exposes another limitation of the existing models, for they define central banks in terms of their national boundaries while in reality financial markets are increasingly global. That discrepancy is a serious problem for the applicability of central banking models, and requires some consideration at this stage.

The difference between a model defined in terms of national boundaries and a globalized world is not the same as the distinction between a closed and an open economy. Models such as Cukierman's, which includes a 'balance-of-payments motive' for monetary policy, and Epstein's are both open economy models, but they remain 'national economy' models. Open economy models treat international finance as flows between nation states; residents of the country or another country move their own or their principals' funds between financial markets located in the country and financial markets elsewhere. And those choices of residents are reflected in balance-of-payments accounts.

The notion that financial markets are globalized is rather different. It implies that financial markets have no national identity, and the flows between them are similarly without citizenship.[1] The interest rates on a particular country's paper, or the country's exchange rate, may be determined in offshore markets located anywhere in the world and, according to the concept of globalization, the physical location of those markets in a particular country does not detract from their global character; the Eurodollar markets in London in the 1970s, for example, were quite independent from conditions in the UK economy, having a global role that was an early form of today's globalization (Harris and Coakley 1983). Similarly, in a globalized economy, important financial flows as well as financial markets lack national identities. They consist of global funds, such as hedge funds, rather than portfolios easily identified with residents of particular countries.

It would be wrong to claim that the world economy is fully characterized by globalization (Harris 1995) and the concept itself is open to criticism, but it describes a rising trend along which financial markets and flows are arguably more advanced than others. To that extent models of central banking would be strengthened if, instead of being constructed in terms of national boundaries, they were able to recognize central banks' roles in those markets.

Having had a key role in the creation of more global markets – especially through liberalization of foreign exchange and financial markets and the shift from extensive control over bank assets to capital adequacy controls – a driving force behind central bank design and monetary policy is the high priority to be given to credibility in respect of those markets.

Placing matters in that context highlights a further weakness in the existing models of central bank design. All consider purely domestic devices for increasing the credibility of monetary policy, but in reality the world of global markets both requires and delivers new forms of international devices to bolster credibility. Weak central banks have their policy's credibility in global markets strengthened by publicly subordinating it to a programme agreed with the International Monetary Fund, or by linking their currency to a strong central bank's through a variety of currency board type arrangements. And even well-established central banks may seek to strengthen their policy's credibility in global markets by adhering to an exchange rate bloc or currency union.

4   Credibility of policy implementation: endogenous money supply

In addition to the weaknesses already identified in central banking models' concept of credibility, a rather different problem exists. Instead of problems concerning the markets affected by the credibility of the bank's intentions (whether they are labour markets, other 'national' markets, or global markets) we now draw attention to credibility concerning the central bank's ability to implement its policy. The central problem here is that in standard models the central bank is assumed to be able to control the money supply and, thereby, to control inflation. But in modern economies the rate of growth of the money supply is not directly under the control of central banks, being determined, instead, by the interaction of central banks, commercial banks, and the non-bank private sector, interactions mediated by financial markets. The complexity of those interactions accounts for the failure of experiments by central banks such as the Bank of England in aiming for monetary growth targets, and makes policy targets incredible.

Within monetary economics one theory of an endogenous money supply attempts to capture the extreme, but apparently plausible, consequence of such complex determinants of the money supply, the idea that the central bank has no control over it, but there are alternative models of money supply endogeneity. In this section, we review the arguments and advance a structuralist version. In the following section, we outline empirical evidence relating to endogeneity in one case study, the Turkish economy.

A basic notion underlying money supply endogeneity is that the demand for money creates its own supply. Banks create credit money whenever they extend loans or, more generally, fiat and credit money is created whenever the central bank or commercial banks purchase assets and issue their own monetary liabilities. Banks hold cash reserves to maintain the convertibility of credit money into liquid form which enables credit money to retain its moneyness and general acceptability as a means of payment.

The supply of credit money responds to changes in the demand for bank credit. Since modern commercial banks are price setters (setting their margins over the central bank rate of interest) and quantity takers in both their retail deposit and loan markets, the total quantity of money is both credit driven and demand determined.

In a reversal of the standard textbook bank money multiplier model, decisions about lending are made prior to acquisition of reserves; endogenous money supply models assume that banks create loans and seek reserves to support the outcome of lending decisions. Alternative views on exactly how commercial banks obtain those reserves divide endogenous money supply models into two schools.

The 'accommodative' or 'horizontalist' school argues that banks are always able to obtain reserves at a given interest rate by borrowing from the central bank. Central banks target and administer the short-term interest rate and therefore, instead of having a money supply target, lend reserves to banks, in response to demand, at the targeted interest rate. Thus, the money supply curve is horizontal at the pegged interest rate so that whenever economic units desire to increase their money balances they will always be able to do so without a change in bank interest rates, which are set with a mark-up over the central bank's administered interest rate. Some proponents of this view of endogenous money supply would argue that providing reserves at a given interest rate is not simply a policy choice which some central banks make at certain times[2] but, instead, a logical necessity arising from the nature of money and finance in all modern credit money economies. The argument rests on the proposition that, to be accepted, credit money requires a central guarantee of the stability of the system. Since Walter Bagehot, that guarantee has been the central bank's commitment to act as 'lender of last resort', but to carry out that role the central bank has to lend whatever reserves the commercial banks demand at the existing discount rate.

Furthermore, the central bank's inescapable responsibility for the financial system's stability leads it to stabilize market interest rates at target levels, correspondingly relinquishing control over the money supply. In its role as ultimate liquidity provider, the central bank plays a crucial role of controlling the quantity and price of the net inflow of funds into the wholesale markets. Depending on the extent to which it supplies funds to the wholesale markets relative to the wholesale markets' net demand for funds, the central bank is able to raise or lower general short-term wholesale interest rates. By far the bulk of the central bank's open market operations involve continuously injecting into or withdrawing funds from the wholesale markets defensively in response to changes in net inflow and outflows of funds so as to maintain the depth and liquidity of the financial markets. Central banks do not have it in their power not to accommodate; that is, they are powerless to constrain the supply of credit money quantitatively. All central banks can do is to set the price and terms at which they supply fiat money on demand to the financial system.

The accommodative or horizontalist school comprises Basil Moore, who in his book *Horizontalists and Verticalists* (1988b) uses the horizontal money supply curve to distinguish between the endogenous and exogenous concepts of money supply determination, Kaldor (1982, 1985), Kaldor and Trevithick (1981), and Weintraub (1978a, 1978b).

The alternative, 'structuralist', view of endogenous money supply is that banks are altogether more active in seeking reserves to legitimate their credit expansion, and central banks are less passive. Pollin (1991) following Holmes's dictum 'banks extend credit, creating deposits in the process, and look for reserves later' (1969, p. 73) argues that the process of 'looking for reserves later' is problematical in the horizontalist. According to Pollin, Rousseas, and others, central bank efforts to control the growth of non-borrowed reserves through open market sales do introduce quantity constraints on reserve availability, for discount window borrowing is not a close substitute for reserves created through open market operations. Following from the observation that risk-averse, profit-maximizing banks do not treat borrowed reserves as perfect substitutes for non-borrowed reserves, central banks do have an impact on banks' reserves instead of simply supplying reserves which validate banks' credit expansion. However, that does not mean that central banks can control the money supply directly even if they choose to, for in modern banking systems, banks operate by obtaining reserves on a range of sophisticated money markets. When central banks choose to restrict the growth of non-borrowed reserves through open market sales, commercial banks generate reserves by borrowing in interbank (federal funds), Eurodollar and Certificate of Deposit (CD) markets, and a range of innovatory liability management techniques. Rousseas (1986), Pollin (1991), Palley (1991), and Arestis and Howells (1996), advance a number of theoretical and empirical arguments for the view that the money supply is endogenous because of banks' active innovatory liability management techniques rather than central bank accommodation.

Although similar identification of a bank balance sheet is recognized by the 'horizontalists', the foundations for the structuralist approach are located in a non-simplified bank balance sheet. Assets and liabilities fall into two categories; retail and wholesale. In their retail deposit and loan markets banks are price setters and quantity takers; and they are price takers and quantity setters in the wholesale markets. We can also distinguish commercial bank assets as marketable and non-marketable assets. The latter are mainly bank loans and advances. The principal difference between the non-marketable and marketable assets is that non-marketable assets are created on the initiative of bank borrowers. The former are bills, notes and standardized short-term paper of various kinds which could be transformed into liquid form more quickly and are traded on the wholesale markets; they comprise banks' defensive assets and these exceed required reserves with a margin. This defensive margin enables banks to meet reserve or cash requirements should they be confronted with unanticipated withdrawals of deposits. In this situation, banks can borrow from interbank markets, stop rolling over overnight loans to other banks, sell CDs, present maturing Treasury Bills instead of cash, or issue securities, bills or other term deposits, either outright or under a repurchase agreement. In that context, structuralists, in contrast to accommodationists, argue that there could be no proportionality in the relative movements of loans and reserves because of modern banks' liability management. Active liability management enabled banks to shift their liabilities from demand deposit accounts to CDs and Federal Funds where reserve requirements are lower. As a result, even when the central bank is controlling the absolute level of reserves, a given level of reserves will support a non-unique level of deposits, and demand deposits will support a non-unique volume of loans and advances. Moreover, while active liability management thwarts the possibility of direct central bank control over the quantity of money, it does mean that interest rates fluctuate, and such pressures on interest rates, in times when the authorities attempt a restrictive monetary policy, stimulate further financial innovation so that active liability management is practised in an increasingly facilitating environment. What are the implications of endogenous money supply for the concept of credibility in models of central banking? The structuralist approach to money supply endogeneity implies that central banks' announced policies for money supply growth cannot be credible since the bank does not have direct control over the money which is, instead, determined endogenously. Since the active liability management that underlies that endogeneity occurs in markets which are prone to rapid change through innovation, the transmission mechanism from central bank actions to endogenous variables (monetary aggregates and rates) is not predictable. Thus, even if the central bank's policy is announced in terms of inflation targets rather than targets for monetary aggregates, they lack credibility. These considerations, moreover, are closely linked to the criticism of credibility-based models, in the light of globalization, outlined in Section 3. In addition to raising questions about the appropriateness of national-economy-based models, globalization of financial markets has been the basis on which broad, deep and liquid money markets have developed and, therefore, has facilitated the growth of active liability management.

5   Empirical evidence on endogenous money supply: a case study

In this section we report some empirical results concerning the relationships involved in endogenous determination of the money supply, using Turkey as a case study.

We report on three sets of statistical relationships. In all three we use monthly data from International Financial Statistics (IFS) statistical publications of the central bank of the Republic of Turkey from 4 January 1987 to 1 February 1997. Yearly averages are calculated from monthly data. Subperiods coincide with events that changed the financial environment in the process of Turkey's liberalization programme. We examine three propositions of the theories of endogenous money supply, propositions on which the 'accommodationist' and 'structuralist' approaches take different views:

- the proposition that bank loans are proportional to reserves is one form of the proportionality hypothesis underlying the 'accommodationist' view and is rejected by structuralists; first, we test for proportionality in the time series;
- the proposition that banks treat borrowed reserves and unborrowed reserves as close or perfect substitutes underlies the accommodationist view and is rejected by structuralists, for the latter believe that central banks' open market operations can affect restriction by changing unborrowed reserves and banks then seek to overcome it by active liability management instead of automatically obtaining borrowed reserves: second, we test for the substitutability between borrowed and unborrowed reserves;
- the accommodationist proposition that the central bank targets interest rates contrasts with the structuralist proposition that interest rates are determined by the interaction of central banks' open market operations and banks' liability management: third, we examine causality relations between different interest rates and suggest interpretations in accordance with theory.

Proportionality in the time series
Proportionality of relative movements of loans and reserves was examined after establishing a control for changes in required reserves and the lag structure for loans and reserves. The null hypothesis is stationarity over time. If the central bank could fully accommodate loan demand, the L/R ratio should be relatively stable where L is the total loans of the commercial banks and R is the total reserves. If the central bank could not accommodate and the L/R ratio rose this would imply some restrictiveness and importance of financial innovations which increases lending capacity. In order to examine changes in the mean of L/R further test is conducted following the identity:

$$\log (L/R) = \log (L/D) + \log (D/ML) + \log (ML/R) \qquad (2.1)$$

where D is total deposits (sight and time deposits) of the commercial banks, ML is managed liabilities. Following Ersel (1990) and Iskenderoglu (1991), ML is derived from a simplified version of the Central Bank of Republic of Turkey balance sheet and is the sum of (CDs, Treasury Bills held, claims on other institutions by the private banks).

The rate of change on a monthly basis is defined as:

$$\frac{\Delta \text{Log } X / Y}{\Delta t} = \text{Rate of change.} \qquad (2.2)$$

Table 2.1 presents evidence on the test for L/R in Turkey between 1987 and 1997. The full period is divided into three subperiods to observe differences. The findings indicate that the mean of L/R ratio increases throughout three subperiods.

Table 2.1   Mean, standard deviation and covariance of L/R *ratios in Turkish commercial banking system*

	Full period	1st period 4.1.87–4.1.91	2nd period 5.1.91–3.1.94	3rd period 4.1.94–2.1.97
L/R				
Mean	7.90	6.00	7.87	10.67
Standard deviation	2.67	1.22	0.74	3.05
Covariance	0.34	0.20	0.09	0.29
L_{t-1}/R_t				
Mean	8.33	6.24	8.25	11.43
Standard deviation	2.94	1.28	0.76	3.34
Covariance	0.35	0.20	0.09	0.29

Source: Calculated from Datastream (1997).

Table 2.2   Selected ratios from Turkish commercial banking sector (annual % rates of growth)

	Full period 1987–2.1.1997	1st period 4.1.87–4.1.91	2nd period 5.1.91–3.1.94	3rd period 4.1.94–2.1.97
Loans/reserves (*L/R*)	7.73	4.67	8.46	10.67
Loans/deposits (*L/D*)	0.48	0.26	0.54	0.03
Deposits/ managed liabilities (*D/ML*)	0.75	0.67	5.49	–4.01
Managed liabilities/reserves (*ML/R*)	6.50	3.74	2.43	14.68

Source: Calculated from Datastream (1997).

From Table 2.2 we can specify the varying proportions of different types of deposits created with lending activity. *D/ML* indicates proportionality of traditional deposits to managed liabilities. We can also observe that, from period 1 to period 2 the ratio of *D/ML* grew dramatically together with *L/R* and decreased between 1994 and 1997. The largest change during the 3rd subperiod is in the increase of *ML/R*. This could be explained in terms of central bank intervention when a run on the Turkish lira (TL) resulted in a financial crisis in 1994. The central bank exerted its control of the system by extending reserve and liquidity requirements to asset-backed securities as well as deposits and non-deposit liabilities in foreign currency.

Substitutability between borrowed and unborrowed reserves
In order to restore market stability, the authorities introduced 100 per cent guarantees for individual bank deposits. The stabilization programme of 1994 included measures to strengthen central bank autonomy in implementing monetary policy. The system of short-term advances to the Treasury by the central bank was tightened. The programme also accentuated the lender-of-last-resort function of the central bank, enabling it to extend credits for up to one year to insolvent banks; previously this was for four months. The second set of tests we have carried out is to examine whether borrowed reserves, *B*, are close substitutes for non-borrowed reserves, *NB*. Table 2.3 presents the size of borrowed reserves relative to total reserves, *TR*. *B* represents the sum of free reserves and central bank claims on private banks and *NB* is the difference between total reserves and *B*.

Table 2.3   Borrowed reserves as a share of total reserves (average % change)

	Full period	1st period	2nd period	3rd period
B/R				
Mean	18	23	17	11
Variance	0.8	0.7	0.5	0.8

Source: Calculated from Datastream (1997).

If borrowed reserves were viable substitutes for non-borrowed reserves we would expect to see an increasing trend in the mean. Table 2.3 shows that in Turkey, *B* constitutes a significant proportion of total reserves. But the *B/R* ratio follows a declining path. This would indicate that the central bank's ability to determine the quantity on non-borrowed reserves through discount window lending is diminishing although still significant. From the 1st period to the 3rd, the *B/R* ratio decreases below the full period's average. This may result from two causes: The first relates to liquidity requirements. Banks were required to keep 5 per cent of their liabilities in the form of highly liquid assets comprising interest free deposits with the central bank and vault cash, and to keep 12 per cent in government paper. By gradual increase in 1991–92, banks were required to keep 30 per cent of their liabilities in the form of government bonds. The second reason is the tight monetary policy pursued in 1995 when no credit could be extended to the banking sector through the discount window (OECD 1993, 1995, 1996). Since banks are profit maximizers they attempt through arbitrage to equate their marginal cost of funds across sources. As the differential of the central bank fund rate over discount rate increases banks are induced to borrow from the central bank. Thus, if *TR* were constant, changes in *NB* will be negatively correlated with the changes in *B*. Then the total of

$$\Delta NB + \Delta B = 0. \tag{2.3}$$

In order to evaluate this formally we have conducted a bivariate regression on the following equation (all variables in logarithms):

$$B = \alpha + \beta \, (NB). \tag{2.4}$$

Table 2.4   Borrowed and non-borrowed reserve substitutability

	α	β	*DW*	$\bar{R}^2$	*F*-statistic
Full period					
(4.1.87–2.7.97)	0.14	–2.23*	2.24	0.52	128.00
	(6.5)	(–11.33)			
1st period					
(4.1.87–4.1.91)	0.80	–1.22*	2.40	0.29	19.77
	(2.9)	(–4.44)			
2nd period					
(5.1.91–3.1.94)	0.22	–4.32*	2.67	0.92	450.42
	(11.79)	(–21.22)			
3rd period					
(4.1.94–2.1.97)	0.16	–2.17*	2.19	0.54	42.14
	(4.26)	(–6.49)			

Notes:
t-ratios in parentheses.
*   significant at 1% level.

An intercept term is used at the degree of unity. B is taken as dependent variable and NB as independent. Monthly data is used for the full term and for the subperiods. Ordinary least square results are as given in Table 2.4. Borrowed reserves/total reserves are determined by calculating from the simplified central bank of Turkey balance sheet.

Regression tests were performed for the full period and three subperiods. From the table we can observe that there is a stronger relationship between variables during the 2nd period as opposed to the 1st and 3rd periods. F-statistics indicate that during the 2nd period negative correlation between two variables is much stronger. The adjusted R^2 shows that variation in the independent variable explains 92 per cent of variation in the dependent variable (B) during the second period.

Causality relations between different interest rates
The third test is carried out to determine the direction of interest rate causality by using monthly data. Four types of interest rates are taken as variables: (i) 3-month commercial banks' time deposit rates (deposit); (ii) money market rate (MMar.); (iii) 3-month Treasury Bill rate (TB3); (iv) 6-month Treasury Bill rate (TB6). The rates, calculated by the central bank, are 3-month Treasury Bills and 6-month Treasury auction rates. A geometric lag/lead structure was used in specifying the independent variables. Lags were carried back and leads forward four months. The Granger–Sims causality test is structured by formulating the regression as:

$$i_t^m = \sum_i \beta_i i_{t-n}^{cb} + \sum_i \alpha_i i_{t+n}^{cb} + \varepsilon_t \qquad (2.5)$$

for market rates and for the central bank controlled rates:

$$i_t^{cb} = \sum_i \beta_i i_{t-n}^m + \sum_i \alpha_i i_{t+n}^m + \varepsilon_t \qquad (2.6)$$

where i_t^m represents market rates and i_t^{cb} central bank controlled rates. As usual with these kinds of tests, we reversed the dependent and independent variables for each regression. We would then expect to see a reversal of the results. The results are presented in Table 2.5.

The regression data is downloaded from Datastream. Regressions are calculated by using Microfit package. The null hypothesis is that there is no Granger and Sims causation between variables for the number of observations. Regression results indicate that causality runs from market rates to deposit rates for the full period between 4 January 1986 and 5 January 1997. When we look at the relationship between MMar. and TB6, they interact. Nevertheless, detailed analysis indicates that there is a stronger causality running from TB6 to MMar.

Table 2.5   Causality tests for various interest rates

Variables					Causality	
Dependent	Independent	α	$\bar{R}^2$	DW	Σ lags	Σ lags
1. Deposit	MMar.	0.17 (0.19)	0.95	2.17	B⇒A	B⇒A
MMar.	Deposit	0.27 (1.04)	0.74	2.01	B⇒A	A⇔B
2. TB(6)	MMar.	21.90 (2.47)	0.83	1.81	B⇒A	A⇒B
MMar.	TB(6)	1.86 (0.99)	0.10	2.32	No causality	No causality
3. TB(3)	MMar.	−0.99 (−0.80)	0.91	1.70	A⇔B	B⇒A
MMar.	TB(3)	1.02 (2.61)	0.58	1.98	A⇔B	B⇒A
4. TB(3)	TB(6)	−10.74 (−0.41)	0.20	2.46	B⇔A	B⇔A
TB(6)	TB(3)	−4.73 (−2.45)	0.18	2.49	B⇔A	B⇒A
5. Deposits	TB(6)	1.66 (2.21)	0.89	1.73	B⇒A	B⇒A
TB(6)	Deposits	−17.66 (−1.34)	0.93	2.43	B⇒A	B⇒A
6. Deposits	TB(3)	1.66 (2.20)	0.89	1.73	B⇒A	A⇔B
TB(3)	Deposits	−17.66 (−1.34)	0.92	2.43	B⇒A	B⇒A

Data used for this regression covers the 1991–94 period. Towards the end of this period the central bank used its Open Market Operations (OMOs) to prevent a run on the Turkish lira. When we consider short-term Treasury Bills and market rates they strongly interact, especially for the period between 4 January 1986 and 11 January 1993. Causality tests between the short-term Treasury Bill rate and the 6-month Treasury Bill rate also indicate strong interaction except when calculated with leads. Thus causality runs from short-term rates to 6-month Treasury rates in leads for the period between 6 January 1992 and 11 January 1993. One reason for this could be that short-term claims on the central bank increased as the Public Sector Borrowing Requirement (PSBR) increased during this period, as is the case. When we look at the causality between 3-month Treasury Bills and short-term bank deposit rates it is evident that lead structure of the regression specifies a strong causality from bank deposits to short-term Treasury Bills during 6 January 1991 to 11 January 1993. Possible interpretation of this is that banks as profit maximizers raised reserves from markets by using their liability management instruments. During this period, the central bank set ceilings on certain types of interest rates so that interest rate ceiling aversion played a role. This could explain why causality runs from 6-month interest rates to deposit rates. The central bank was able to influence interest rate levels in the longer run as is evident from the causality tests for the period 4 January 1986 to 11 January 1993.

6 Conclusion

Institutional reform of central banking structures, which currently dominates the restructuring of states and economies around the globe, has a foundation in economic models of monetary policy. Although most such models are well established within a paradigm where central bank credibility is the focus, their concept of credibility and associated assumptions regarding central bank objective functions is limited. Derived from the inflation–unemployment tradition which Bill Phillips's eponymous curve originally put on the macroeconomic agenda, credibility in modern models of monetary policy has an almost exclusively labour market focus.

In this chapter, it has been suggested that credibility is extremely important in two other dimensions of central bank activity. One is credibility in the context of external capital markets and foreign exchange markets, and, in order to encompass that dimension fully, consideration has to be given to the character of such markets in a period of globalization. The other is credibility in respect of the instruments of monetary policy. If money supply is endogenous, monetary policy in the form of money supply targets is not credible since the central bank does not have control over the money supply aggregate. That problem exists whatever the nature of endogeneity, and the chapter outlines two alternative models of endogenous money supply. Monetary statistics from Turkey illustrate aspects of money supply endogeneity and focus our discussion on structuralist versus accommodationist models of endogeneity.

Notes
1. Citizenship here is a broad term. Applied to people, its broad meaning includes forms of quasi- or near-citizenship such as 'residency'.
2. Outstanding examples of central bank targeting of interest rates are the US and British policies in the second half of the 1940s of trying to achieve and maintain low interest rates, which required them to engineer a horizontal supply curve of money at those rates. Those particular attempts were adopted as discretionary policies in line with governments' desire to avoid a predicted postwar slump, and also to reduce the costs of government debt incurred to finance reconstruction programmes.

Bibliography

Akkurt, E. (1995), 'Developments in the Turkish banking sector: 1980–1990', in K. Aydogan and H. Ersel (eds), *Issues on Banking Structure and Competition in a Changing World*, Ankara: Central Bank of Turkey.

Akyuz, Y. (1990), 'Financial system and policies in Turkey in the 1980s', in Tosun Aricanli and Dani Rodrik (eds), *The Political Economy of Turkey: Debt, Adjustment and Sustainability*, London: Macmillan, pp. 98–131.

Arestis, P. and P. Howells (1996), 'Theoretical reflections on endogenous money: the problem with convenience lending', *Cambridge Journal of Economics*, **20**, 539–51.

Arnon, A. (1991), *Thomas Tooke, Pioneer of Monetary Theory*, Ann Arbor: University of Michigan Press.

Barro, R. and D. Gordon (1983a), 'Rules, discretion and reputation in a model of monetary policy', *Journal of Monetary Economics*, **12**, 101–22.

Barro, R. and D. Gordon (1983b), 'A positive theory of monetary policy in a natural rate economy', *Journal of Political Economy*, **91**, 589–610.

Cukierman, A. (1995), *Central Bank Strategy, Credibility, and Independence: Theory and Evidence*, Cambridge, MA: MIT Press.

Epstein, G.A. (1993), 'Monetary policy in the 1990s: overcoming the barriers to equity and growth', in G.A. Dymski, G. Epstein and R. Pollin (eds), *Transforming the US Financial System: Equity and Efficiency for the 21st Century*, Armonk, NY: ME Sharpe, pp. 65–98.

Epstein, G.A. (1994), 'A political economy model of comparative central banking', in G.A. Dymski and R. Pollin (eds), *New Perspectives in Monetary Macroeconomics*, Ann Arbor: University of Michigan Press, pp. 231–77.

Ersel, H. (1990), *Monetary Policy in a Changing Financial Environment*, Central Bank of Turkey Discussion Papers, No. 9004.

Fratianni, M., J. von Hagen and C. Waller (1997), 'Central banking as a political principal–agent problem', *Economic Enquiry*, **25**, 378–93.

Goodhart, C.A.E. (1984), *Monetary Theory and Practice*, London: Macmillan.

Harris, L. (1995), 'International financial markets and national transmission mechanisms', in J. Michie and J. Grieve Smith (eds), *Managing the Global Economy*, Oxford: Oxford University Press, pp. 199–212.

Harris, L. and J. Coakley (1983), *City of Capital*, Oxford: Basil Blackwell.

Holmes, A. (1969), 'Operational constraints on the stabilization of money supply growth', Federal Reserve of Boston, *Controlling Money Aggregates*, June, 65–77.

Hicks, J.R. (1967), *Critical Essays in Monetary Theory*, Oxford: Clarendon Press.

Iskenderoglu, O. (1991), *The Turkish Banking Sector: Income Statement (1983–1989) and Balance Sheet (1981–1989)*, Central Bank of Turkey Discussion Papers, No. 9101.

Kaldor, N. (1982), *The Scourge of Monetarism*, Oxford: Oxford University Press.

Kaldor, N. (1985), 'How monetarism failed', *Challenge*, **28** (2), 4–13.

Kaldor, N. and Trevithick, J.A. (1981), 'A Keynesian perspective on money', *Lloyds Bank Review*, **139**, 1–19.

Kydland, F.E. and E.C. Prescott (1977), 'Rules rather than discretion: the inconsistency of optimal plans', *Journal of Political Economy*, **85**, 473–92.

Moore, B. (1983), 'Unpacking the Post-Keynesian black box: bank lending and the money supply', *Journal of Post Keynesian Economics*, **5** (4), 537–55.

Moore, B. (1988a), 'The endogenous money supply', *Journal of Post Keynesian Economics*, **10** (3), 372–85.

Moore, B. (1988b), *Horizontalists and Verticalists: The Macroeconomics of Credit Money*, New York: Cambridge University Press.

Moore, B. (1991), 'Money supply endogeneity: "reserve price setting" or "reserve quantity setting"?', *Journal of Post Keynesian Economics*, **13** (3), 404–13.

Onder, I., O. Turel, N. Ekinci and C. Somel (1993), *Turkiye'de kamu maliyesi, Finansal Yapive Politikalar [Public Finance in Turkey, Financial Structure and Policies]*, Istanbul: Tarih Vakfi Yurt Yayinlari.

Organization for Economic Cooperation and Development (OECD) (1993, 1995, 1996), *OECD Economic Surveys – Turkey*, Annual Reports.

Palley, T.I. (1991), 'The endogenous money supply: consensus and disagreement', *Journal of Post Keynesian Economics*, **13** (3), 397–403.

Pollin, R. (1991), 'Two theories of money supply endogeneity', *Journal of Post Keynesian Economics*, **13** (3), 366–96.

Rist, C. (1940), *History of Monetary and Credit Theory from John Law to the Present Day*, London: Allen & Unwin.

Rousseas, S. (1986), *Post Keynesian Monetary Economics*, Armonk; New York: M.E. Sharp.

Simons, H.C. (1936), 'Rules versus authorities in monetary policy', *Journal of Political Economy*, **44**, 1–30.

Uygur, E. (1993), *Liberalization and Economic Performance in Turkey*, UNCTAD Discussion Paper, No. 65, The United Nations Conference on Trade and Development, Switzerland.

Viner, J. (1937), *Studies in the Theory of International Trade*, New York: Harper.

Waller, C.J. and C.E. Walsh (1996), 'Central bank independence, economic behaviour, and optimal term lengths', *American Economic Review*, **86**, 1139–51.

Weintraub, S. (1978a), *Keynes, Keynesians and Monetarism*, Philadelphia: University of Pennsylvania Press.

Weintraub, S. (1978b), *Capitalism's Inflation and Unemployment Crisis*, Reading, MA: Addison-Wesley.

3   Some problems with the use of 'credibility' and 'reputation' to support the independence of central banks

Keith Bain

1   Introduction

It has long been clear that a major requirement for an idea to achieve long-run (equilibrium) popularity in economics is that it permits and indeed encourages the telling of superficially appealing stories. Parables and allegories play an important role in converting complex reality into a form which can be modelled and then analysed using apparently objective and scientific methods. The ideas at the base of the stories being told may depend on a very specific interpretation of the world which can, and frequently has, been challenged, but as long as the idea is flexible in terms of the number and variety of stories it can generate, it will survive; indeed, economists will happily make policy recommendations on the basis of it.

One of the most successful ideas in story-telling within economics over the past twenty years has been that of credibility and reputation. As we have seen in the UK in 1997, stories about credibility and reputation have been at the heart of the debate over the independence of central banks. 'Credibility' and 'reputation' could be put to use in the simplification of reality to explain not just why the Chancellor of the Exchequer, Gordon Brown, and his advisers came to accept the view that the Bank of England should be made independent but also why the previous Conservative government did not move significantly in that direction.

2   The credibility model and Bank of England independence

The Conservative government's failure to act is well described in Milesi-Ferretti (1995) where it is proposed that in order to increase their electoral chances, incumbents may forgo policy measures that improve the relative standing of their opponents in the eyes of the voters. The paper deals specifically with the choice between fixed and flexible exchange rate systems: an inflation-averse government may refrain from choosing fixed exchange rates in order to capitalize on the inflationary reputation of its opponent. However, as the author points out, the idea can easily be applied to the question of the independence of central banks.

Thus, the refusal of the previous Chancellor, Kenneth Clark, to do more than stage regular consultations with the Governor of the Bank of England could be interpreted as an attempt to keep inflation, on which the Labour Party was thought to be politically vulnerable, as a political issue. Equally, the pre-election indications from the Labour Party of a movement towards the acceptance of an independent Bank of England could be interpreted as a way of overcoming an inflationary reputation which might otherwise have lost it vital votes. In Milesi-Ferretti's words, 'the choice of an independent central banker that cannot be fired, or delegation of monetary policy to a "foreign" country through exchange-rate pegging, removes monetary policy skills as an issue in the electoral process' (p. 1381).

This explanation of the development of Labour Party policy in this area can be strengthened by the argument that the party knew well that the election appeared to hang on the votes of a relatively small number of middle-income earners in relatively affluent constituencies, who were more likely than the majority of voters to be worried by inflation and could be assumed to be likely to vote against Labour, despite their dislike of the Conservative Party on many issues, if they thought that a Labour government would be soft on inflation.

This, of course, does not explain why, having been elected, Gordon Brown chose to put control over interest rates into the hands of the Bank of England. The academic credibility/reputation literature can produce at least two types of explanation for this. First, it could be argued that Brown and his advisers believed the whole credibility/reputation explanation of sacrifice ratios, the self-fulfilling nature of inflation expectations and the natural rate of unemployment. Then, if we continue to assume that Labour governments had a worse reputation than their Conservative opponents regarding the control of inflation, Brown would have been aware that the equilibrium, time-consistent rate of inflation would rise with no gain in terms of lower unemployment unless he acted to precommit the government to a tighter monetary policy than the market expected. In these terms, it is more important for a left-leaning government to accept an independent central bank than for a right-leaning government which is automatically more trusted by the markets over inflation.

The alternative view allows us to think of the Labour government as one which continued to be more concerned about unemployment than inflation and thus as one which would be tempted to create inflationary surprises. Being aware, however, of the importance of reputation, the government had an incentive to pretend to be tough on inflation for some time. It would thus seek to establish a reputation for low inflation and to maintain it until it was no longer profitable to do so. Thus, Gordon Brown's action on 6 May 1997, could be interpreted as part of a pretence to be a low-inflation-at-all-costs government. According to this view, we should expect the government over time to show its true colours and eventually to inflate the economy. A successful masquerade would require the inflation-prone government to appear to give away the ability to inflate the economy while not in reality doing so. But forward-looking market agents should have been aware of this possibility and should have studied carefully the precise form in which power appeared to have been given away.

We had therefore a neat set of stories we could use to explain real-world events which were flexible enough for us to be able also to explain what happened next, whatever happened next. We have some confirmation of the explanatory power of these stories because they seem to have been accepted by both the Governor of the Bank of England and by the financial markets. Thus, Eddie George, in expressing his pleasure with the Chancellor's decision, commented that the decision would allow long-run interest rates to fall. And, indeed, in the days immediately after the announcement the yield spread on the benchmark ten-year gilt over ten-year German government bonds fell from 1.7 per cent to below 1.4 per cent while the price of the 20-year bond rose sharply. Further, the series of increases in short-run interest rates made in the following months by the newly created monetary committee of the Bank of England did not cause the usual sharp falls in equity prices on the stock exchange. The message seemed clear – the risk premium attached to sterling was coming down. At a stroke, the Chancellor had lowered the time-consistent equilibrium inflation rate and could look forward to lower government borrowing costs in the long term.

But let us consider some implications of this application of the credibility model to Bank of England independence. A standard problem of the model is that there is no clear answer to the question of what determines the reputation of governments in the minds of voters/market agents; or of how existing reputations are changed. The obvious elements to include for an incumbent government or an independent central bank are the past inflation performance of the country and the institutional arrangements governing monetary policy decisions.

Thus, the long-term strength of the Deutschmark is usually attributed to Germany's past low rates of inflation and the political independence of the Bundesbank. Arguments that the independence of the Bundesbank and the low rate of inflation are joint products of a disinflationary culture in Germany raise the possibility that central bank independence may merely be an indicator of an anti-inflationary attitude of a population and leave us with the question of what causes these attitudes. The favourite candidate is the German inflations following both world wars. This suggests that attitudes towards inflation are extremely tenacious and that reputation derives not from a repeated set of games as in the general run of credibility models but from some disastrous 'metagame'. In such a case, the anti-inflation attitude should apply to all potential governments and the control of inflation should not be a political issue.

This does not appear to help in the analysis of a case in which different political parties seemingly do have different reputations with regard to the control of inflation. The starting point here should again presumably be past performance in government. But what if the non-incumbent party has been out of power for a considerable period? Recent performance of the economy is no guide. One obvious possibility is that reputation in the British case comes from some general idea that Labour governments are more interested in the welfare of workers who, on average, have only small amounts saved in financial assets while Conservative governments look after the interests of those with (relatively) substantial savings. If it were true that such attitudes led a significant number of voters/market agents to believe that Labour was less able to be trusted on inflation, we need to know what was needed for Labour to change its reputation. The more tenacious the attitudes, the less likely it should be that a soft-on-inflation reputation could be changed by a statement that power was being conceded to an independent central bank without a very careful examination of the terms on which independence was being granted.

Here we run into some difficulties in regard to 6 May. As is well known, all attempts to assess degrees of independence of central banks are subjective and open to much criticism. A normal requirement for a central bank to be classed as highly independent, however, is that operational independence for the bank should be accompanied by some anti-inflation objective which is embedded in the country's constitution. Even where this is done, there is much discussion over the relationship between the inflation objective and other objectives which may be included and how clearly control of inflation is given priority. The absence of a written constitution denies the UK the possibility of embedding a commitment to control inflation in this way. In any case, the Chancellor of the Exchequer has specifically retained the right to set the inflation target.

Second, the independent central bank literature usually implies that a high level of independence is associated with a long term of office for members of the executive board of the bank and preferably no possibility of reappointment at the end of that term. Six of the nine members of the new monetary policy committee of the Bank of England will have three-year terms and will be able to be reappointed.

A third problem everywhere relates to the need for governments to preserve the ability to override the decisions of the central bank in times of crisis, a power which the Labour government is going to retain. This, entirely desirable though it may be, normally leaves open interpretations of 'crisis' and can influence the behaviour of the central bank in response to output shocks. Lohman (1992) considers the case of a policy maker who cedes partial independence to a conservative central banker who places a higher weight on inflation stabilization than the policy maker. The central banker implements a lower average time-consistent inflation rate at the cost of a distorted response to output shocks, inducing a deadweight loss which is larger for extreme shocks. If the policy maker retains the option to override the central banker at some positive but finite cost, the central banker is induced to implement a non-linear policy rule: in normal times setting the inflation rate independently but in extreme situations accommodating the policy maker's *ex-post* demands in order to avoid being overridden. Differences in interpretation of what constitutes a severe output shock were seen in negotiations leading up to the signing of the stability pact for membership of the European Monetary Union (EMU).

Other issues may be mentioned in passing. A commonly expressed view among supporters of central bank independence (for instance, Issing 1993) is that it is desirable to separate the central bank role from that of responsibility for bank supervision if moral hazard is to be avoided for central bankers. That is, combining the monetary policy and supervisory roles may lead to the central bank being less firm in its attitude towards inflation than it might otherwise be. To this extent, the new British monetary policy regime conforms to the strict requirements for central bank independence since the Bank of England is also to lose its powers of supervision of the banking system.

Again, there is much discussion in the central bank independence literature (for example, in Walsh 1995) regarding the incentive structure needed to ensure that the central bank acts to achieve the objectives which are set for it. The three-year term plus possible reappointment for six of the members of the monetary policy committee of the Bank of England does allow reappointment to be tied to the Bank's success in achieving the targets set for it, but this cannot be guaranteed.

Thus, by the rigorous standards of supporters of independent central banks, the newly independent Bank of England may not score very highly at all. Any index would, of course, place it significantly above its position prior to 6 May, but almost certainly would put it comfortably below the Bundesbank. If a soft-on-inflation reputation is indeed difficult to lose, would one normally expect the 1997 monetary policy changes to be sufficient to cause the observed responses on the part of the Governor and the financial markets and, indeed, the dismay among the many Labour supporters opposed to central bank independence (see, for instance, Keegan 1997)?

There seem to be two possible explanations for this. First, the move could be interpreted as a prelude to EMU membership, if not in the 'first wave' then as soon as the economy was judged to be ready. This might help to explain the market reaction (if not that of the Bank of England Governor) if it were not for the fact that the concurrent strength of sterling was being interpreted as being based in part on the perceived status of sterling as a safe-haven currency for investors who feared that other EU nations would join a weak EMU. The markets had been signalling for some time an increased belief that Spain and even possibly Italy might be allowed into EMU and thus an increased willingness on the part of the UK to join also was hardly likely to be taken as a firm commitment to low inflation.

The second possible explanation is that the markets (and the Governor) had come to believe that the Chancellor was fully committed to low inflation even at high real 'short-term' costs and that the announcement of Bank of England independence merely confirmed that view. Thus, the Chancellor could be trusted to set tight inflation targets – New Labour was being interpreted by the markets as being totally different from its predecessor and as having succeeded in wiping away the Labour Party's previous soft-on-inflation reputation. The dismay on the part of many Labour Party supporters could derive from the confirmation of a fear that they had already had regarding the likely economic policy of the new government. This type of interpretation fits comfortably with the idea that central bank independence is principally a signal of policy intentions. As Issing (1993) put it:

> every society ultimately gets the rate of inflation it deserves and basically wants ... [but] resistance to making the central bank independent always reflects the intention of reserving access to money creation to policy-makers. ... In view of the temptations inherent in the political process, a society can signal its determination to safe-guard the stability of its money only by choosing the appropriate institutional arrangement. In this context the independence of the central bank comes top of the list. (p. 36)

None the less, telling the story of the events surrounding Bank of England independence entirely in credibility/reputation terms becomes rather strained and requires a good deal of *ad hoc* interpretation of motives and of market behaviour. This, then, raises the question of whether people do genuinely believe the underlying ideas. Or is it rather just another (seemingly successful) attempt to conceal reality – an attempt to dress market-clearing equilibrium in modern garb? Let us look at just a few of the problems associated with the approach.

3 Theoretical problems of the credibility model
In a very general sense, reputation is clearly important for governments wishing to influence markets since markets do provide classic examples of self-fulfilling prophecy. Thus, it is reasonable to propose a model in which wage negotiators take the expected inflation rate into account in bargaining

for money wage increases and in which anticipated government economic policy is one factor taken into account by negotiators in determining their goals. But the goals of wage negotiators are, in turn, only one factor influencing the rate of growth of money wages. Such an approach plainly leads us to only a very weak role for credibility.

The strong credibility/reputation model requires in contrast not only that market agents correctly assess the policy rules being followed by government and do not make systematic mistakes in inflation expectations but also that the rate of inflation is a purely monetary variable and that governments have full control over the rate of growth of the money supply. The strong version of the credibility model is, in other words, dependent on a modern version of money acting as a veil over the real economy (another powerful metaphorical expression of the neoclassical story). The unemployment–inflation rate trade-off (renamed the sacrifice ratio) then turns out to be a product of the extent of the anti-inflation credibility of governments. Rejection of any part of the story presents problems regarding the application of the model. Our interest here, however, is not with the vertical Phillips curve, the natural rate of unemployment, and the neutrality of money but, rather, with the incentive structure which governments are assumed to face in the standard time-inconsistency model (Kydland and Prescott 1977; Barro and Gordon 1983).

This includes a set of community indifference curves indicating preferences regarding combinations of inflation and unemployment. These may be interpreted as the expression of the social welfare function transmitted by the electoral system. According to the standard analysis, once governments have convinced voters/market agents of the credibility of their monetary policy, they are bound to reoptimize by expanding the economy along the now relevant short-run Phillips curve to an indifference curve representing higher welfare. This is so, even though this welfare gain is only temporary. The net result is (at the time-consistent equilibrium inflation rate and the natural rate of unemployment) a much lower level of welfare. Market agents soon realize this and thus the economy remains stuck at the lower welfare level determined by the government's reputation regarding inflation and the natural rate of unemployment. All governments are bound to behave in this way; the only difference among political parties is the level of the time-consistent equilibrium inflation rate.

There is, however, a basic problem here since if all market agents know that no long-run trade-off is possible between inflation and unemployment, the social welfare function should not reflect the belief that such a trade-off is possible. And yet it is only the apparent existence of this belief in a trade-off which provides the incentive for governments to behave in a time-inconsistent manner. The problem seems to be that there is an assumption that the economy's objective function is formed entirely separately from the voters' understanding of how the economy works. But rational behaviour among voters as well as among market agents requires the maximization of utility within constraints and the economic model which accompanies the social welfare function informs voters that inflation–unemployment trade-offs are not possible even in the short run. Yet many of the public choice criticisms of government intervention in the macroeconomy are based on the idea that voters do not understand the constraints imposed upon them by the economic system. Brittan (1987) expresses this view in its most general form, arguing that, at a macroeconomic level, people expect too much from government action at too little cost.

There are a variety of ways of attempting to explain this apparent conflict. For example, it is possible to postulate that rational forward-looking market agents are only a subset of voters – by definition a minority, since otherwise the political system would not be dominated by myopic behaviour; or that the same group of people behave rationally within markets but irrationally at the ballot box – that the nature of the democratic process causes people to continue to be wrong about what is possible even while they are aware as market agents what is possible. That is, the nature of the voting process forces them to be irrational in the sense that they go on making mistakes even in the long run.

It might be possible to argue, for instance, that voting is a social act and that social pressures lead people to vote for outcomes which they know to be impossible. But it is equally arguable that the reverse is true. After all, much market activity is strongly influenced by social and institutional factors, while in the world of politics there is a fairly commonly expressed view that a significant number of voters may tell polling organizations that they intend to vote in one way because they feel under some social pressure in that direction but that in the privacy of the voting booth, they behave differently. Another possibility is that the excitement of an election temporarily clouds people's judgement as to what can be achieved and at the moment of voting people expect governments to be able to create an unemployment–inflation trade-off at the same time as they know as market agents that such a trade-off is not possible. This hardly fits with the large number of people who choose not to vote because they feel that government cannot or will not do anything to help them.

A quite different possibility is that people are not mistaken at a political level – rather, that the apparent conflict between political and market decisions is rational. This might arise if people behaved in the way that they did at the market level (as if there were no trade-off) because the nature of the market constrained them to do this even though they were *correctly* aware that a trade-off might exist. Such a model could easily be developed within a prisoner's dilemma framework under conditions of uncertainty about the future inflation rate. Thus, at a macroeconomic level (as expressed in social judgements made through the voting system), people might be willing to accept a fall in real wages (as a result of an expansionary policy which generates both more employment and higher inflation). But at a microeconomic level, to fail to build into next period's wages and prices a possible higher level of inflation would leave the market agent open to the possibility of a fall in relative income if all other market agents did build the higher rate of inflation into their calculations. Such a model would seem to provide a case for a prices and incomes policy.

A basic problem of theorizing in this way is that no serious attempt is made by new classical writers to consider the microeconomic impacts of macroeconomic policies. Thus, it appears to be assumed that if market agents are aware that an expansionary policy will lead to higher inflation with no long-run increase in employment, then this will be the experience of each individual within the system. Yet even if there were no overall gain in output and employment, there would very likely be some gainers from the expansionary policy through redistributions of income. Most obviously, there would be gains or losses resulting from differential abilities within the population to protect themselves from inflation and resulting from differential holdings of financial assets.

But it is very probable that there would also be employment effects. Any given average rate of inflation is associated with a variety of inflation rates across industries. Further, industries have different degrees of sensitivity to given rates of inflation. Thus a particular average rate of inflation may involve a redistribution of employment within an unchanging total and the pattern of redistribution might be different at different rates of inflation. Hence, if we assume voters to be behaving like rational market agents and voting entirely out of self-interest, some groups of voters would appreciate that an expansion in demand might create job opportunities for them and would, in casting their vote, weigh up the benefits from an increased probability of their finding employment against the costs to them of inflation. This would remain true even if they were aware that there would be no increase in the total number of jobs in the economy, especially since, from the point of view of the individual, obtaining a job in the present might well increase the probability of being employed in the future. They would vote as if there were a trade-off between inflation and unemployment because, for them as individuals, there would indeed be a trade-off.

Of course, voters who lived on unearned income or whose employment was quite secure at any imaginable rate of unemployment and who had something to lose from increased inflation, would not face a trade-off and would vote for the lowest available rate of inflation. This would also be true for workers who correctly understood that increased inflation might put their jobs at increased risk. Many voters who did not fear unemployment as a result of increased inflation and thought that they could adequately protect their real incomes during periods of inflation would remain neutral. In a model of this type, the kind of social welfare function which causes so many problems within the Barro–Gordon framework could only be generated if those people who correctly understood that they personally might gain from increased inflation outnumbered those who appreciated that they would lose. In any more realistic model where there are net employment and output effects, at least in the short run, judgement about the desirability of the policy depends on comparisons between considerable numbers of winners and losers. In this case, the refusal to accept the political outcome represents simply a judgement regarding the distribution of income.

One way or another either the nature of the utility function in the model is difficult to justify, *given the assumption that the economic system is best represented by a vertical Phillips curve* or the notion that the vertical Phillips curve is an absolute constraint at a macroeconomic level is a narrow and mistaken one.

4 Conclusion

This chapter questions the importance of the notions of credibility and reputation in the debate over the independence of central banks in two quite distinct ways. First, it argues that the credibility/reputation notion is so flexible that it can be used to explain at a shallow level almost any development which occurs in relation to the movement towards independence of a central bank such as in the case of the Bank of England in May 1997. However, closer examination shows that these stories leave important questions unanswered. With regard to Bank of England independence, it is far from clear why the statements by the UK Chancellor on 6 May and in the following weeks should have been sufficient to change significantly the reputation of Labour governments with respect to inflation. Credibility/reputation stories are probably better seen as providing a justification for conservative monetary policies than a convincing explanation of differential rates of inflation among countries.

Second, the chapter raises severe doubts about the nature of the standard time-inconsistency model which is used to provide a theoretical justification for removing the control of monetary policy from elected politicians. In particular, it considers the possibility that many people in an economy may face an unemployment–inflation trade-off, *even if there is no apparent trade-off at a macroeconomic level.* The refusal to accept the outcome of a voting process which reflects the distinction between microeconomic and macroeconomic experience may be seen as a rejection of democratically validated changes in income distribution.

References

Barro, R.J. and D. Gordon (1983), 'Rules, discretion and reputation in a model of monetary policy', *Journal of Monetary Economics*, **12**, 101–21.
Brittan, S. (1987), *The Role and Limits of Government*, rev. edn, London: Wildwood House.
Issing, Otmar (1993), *Central Bank Independence and Monetary Stability*, Occasional Paper 89, London: Institute of Economic Affairs.
Keegan, W. (1997), 'Help! Labour's lost its monetary marbles', *The Observer*, 11 May, Business section, p. 2.
Kydland, F. and E. Prescott (1977), 'Rules rather then discretion: the inconsistency of optimal plans', *Journal of Political Economy*, **85** (3), 473–92.
Lohman, S. (1992), 'Optimal commitment in monetary policy: credibility vs flexibility', *American Economic Review*, **82** (1), March, 273–86.
Milesi-Ferretti, G. (1995), 'The disadvantage of tying their hands: on the political economy of policy commitments', *Economic Journal*, **105** (433), 1381–402.
Walsh, C.E. (1995), 'Optimal contracts for central bankers', *American Economic Review*, **85** (1), 150–67.

4   Unemployment costs of inflation targeting
John Cornwall and Wendy Cornwall

1   Introduction*

In the view of a prominent monetary theorist and policy maker, there is a
rising acceptance within the economics profession and in central bank and
government circles of the need for an 'independent' central bank. This view
is founded upon a growing body of empirical evidence, recent theoretical
developments in monetary theory and what the author designates as the
'temper of the times' (Fischer 1995). In this chapter we examine these three
foundations. We argue that while each helps to explain the desire for central
bank independence (CBI), none provides support for the benefits independence is claimed to bring. The primary claim is that CBI lowers both the rate
of inflation and its variance, yielding greater price stability. In many studies
there is no mention of any long-run impact on real economic variables; others
make a second claim, that CBI has no effect on such real variables as output
growth and unemployment, in short, that inflation targeting is a 'free lunch'.
We intend not only to document the unemployment cost of inflation targeting, but to examine each of the three alleged foundation stones to discover
why mainstream economists and others have either ignored or denied the real
costs of central bank reform.

Critical appraisal of each foundation requires a different method. Refuting
the statistical studies is the most straightforward, since there are widely
accepted criteria for evaluating econometric work. To challenge the theoretical foundation requires a less direct approach. Here it is necessary to examine
the broader context and assess the usefulness of neoclassical unemployment
theory, which is the theoretical framework of the models devised to bolster
the case for greater CBI. Among other things, this reveals damaging inconsistencies in the assumptions of the theoretical models.

We find it appropriate to define the temper of the times as a body of
economic beliefs that are not refutable because there is no accepted test of
their truth or validity, such as statistical criteria for acceptance or rejection or
standards of logic that must be maintained. Rather they are akin to meta-
physical beliefs considered by their protagonists as almost irrefutable.[1] In
this chapter we treat certain tenets of the neoclassical 'counterrevolution' in

*   We wish to thank the Dalhousie Faculty of Science and the Mount Saint Vincent University
Research and Development Fund for financial support for this work.

macroeconomics as part of the relevant belief system. This system is identifiable as the present mainstream view in macroeconomics that replaced the Keynesian perspective, and has dominated macroeconomic thought since the late 1960s to early 1970s. In particular, the neoclassical counterrevolution includes the views of mainstream economists, central bankers and government officials, among others, with respect to the workings of capitalism and the policies required to ensure its proper functioning. This includes a reevaluation of the role of the state and of the economic and political forces thought to be endangering the economy. Defined in this way, we argue that this belief system plays a critical and independent role in the growing acceptance of greater CBI, but we also find that this counterrevolution has led to a serious misunderstanding of the current problems facing the developed capitalist economies.

By examining the issue in this way, we hope to do more than evaluate the arguments for greater CBI and its unemployment costs. By offering an illustration of how incorrect policy recommendations emerge from inappropriate assumptions, we hope to shed light on the inadequacies of current macroeconomic thought and policy in other areas.

The next section contains a brief general discussion of the main issues, followed in Section 3 by an evaluation of the empirical studies. Section 4 summarizes the theoretical arguments used to support the alleged main benefit of greater independence, the reduction of the endemic inflationary bias of democratic capitalism. Sections 5, 6 and 7 broaden the discussion, taking up and evaluating the theoretical foundations of the CBI models. The implications for CBI analysis are then taken up in Section 8, while Section 9 considers the degree to which the main tenets of the prevailing 'temper of the times' are supported by the historical record of three capitalist economies. This study of the political economy of CBI concludes that its foundations are weak, and cannot support the claims made for it.

2   Why independence is considered important

Underlying the argument for an independent central bank is the belief that democracy, unless suitably constrained, suffers from an inherent economic weakness, an inflationary bias. This arises out of the desire of elected representatives (hereafter the government), motivated by self-serving 'opportunistic' reasons, to pressure the central bank into initiating inappropriate and harmful changes in previously announced policies, the so-called 'time-inconsistency' problem. It may even generate a political business cycle (Nordhaus 1975). These harmful changes take the form of discretionary stimulative aggregate demand policies which lead to unanticipated increases in prices, output and employment. While perhaps prolonging the career of some elected officials, such actions destabilize an otherwise self-regulating system. This follows from the more basic assumption that in the absence of such interventions the economy always tends in some long run to its (variously defined) equilibrium rate of unemployment and level of output.[2] At this equilibrium, involuntary unemployment is either zero or, if positive, it is classical; it cannot be decreased permanently by expansionary policies. As a result, the impact of such policies on the real sector is only temporary, as there is no long-run trade-off between inflation and either unemployment or output. Further, since politicians' demands for stimulative policies are ever present as well as successful, in the absence of the appropriate financial institutions continuous upward pressures on prices result. In this world of real-wage bargaining, long-run vertical Phillips curves and political business cycles, without institutional safeguards an unfortunate economic consequence of democracy is an inflationary bias.[3]

The remedy has already been suggested. Under democratic capitalism, strong inflationary tendencies can be contained only if monetary policy is made 'independent' of short-run political pressures; it must be constrained by formal or informal rules prescribing welfare goals for the central bank. However, it is recognized by some of its advocates that in a democracy this independence must be limited (Cooper 1994). The long-run goals of monetary policy must be firmly established by government, perhaps by statute, subject to periodic review and revision. In this way the central bank can be relieved of short-run political pressures from the government currently in power without sacrificing any of the basic tenets of democracy. Throughout this chapter, greater CBI will be defined as the establishment of regulations that give the central bank the means and the responsibility to pursue these long-run targets unhampered by politically motivated interventions.

3 The empirical evidence
Recent claims that greater central bank independence can deliver lower inflation at no real economic cost rest upon several bases. Here we consider two dimensions of the empirical base. Consider the much cited Alesina and Summers (1993) claims, which rest upon scatter diagrams depicting simple correlations between an index of central bank independence and the rates of inflation, unemployment, real GDP growth and real per capita GDP growth, and their variances. These measures suggest that while independence of the central bank has a salubrious effect on inflation rates, it has no 'downside', that is, it does not have any effect on the real variables. The index they use is based partially on Grilli et al. (1991), who reach the same conclusions. Cukierman et al. (1993), whose index covers several dimensions of the legal relationship between central banks and their governments, also find a negative relation between independence and inflation for the industrialized economies; they do not test the real variables.

These conclusions are severely weakened in two ways. First, even if it can be assumed that the indices of central bank independence are without flaws, the conclusions rest on simple correlations, or on simple regressions with CBI as the sole regressor. The implicit assumption in this work is either that inflation depends only on the level of independence of the central bank, or that central bank independence is uncorrelated with any other causal variables. The credence given the low or zero correlation between CBI and the real variables similarly depends on the assumption that CBI is uncorrelated with whatever else determines their values. If neither of these assumptions is correct, the models are misspecified. If other variables contribute to explaining inflation, unemployment and growth, their omission results in biased sample statistics, whether these are estimated coefficients and their standard errors, or simple correlation coefficients.

Because of the wide acceptance of the statistical conclusions, a reminder in the simplest terms serves to stress the problems. The purpose of multiple regression analysis is to account for the influence of each regressor on the dependent variable, while holding the remaining ones constant. The estimated coefficients are partial coefficients, and it is the partial correlations that provide the information. Only if the regressors are independent of each other are the simple and partial correlations the same. Since data series used in the social sciences rarely display such independence, simple and partial correlation coefficients differ, both in their sign and, often substantially, in their magnitudes, so that simple correlations are usually misleading.[4]

Particularly misleading is the zero simple correlation between central bank independence and unemployment. When there are several explanatory variables, the influence of any one of them cannot be individually measured when any of the rest is changing. Multiple regression analysis provides a method that approaches the *ceteris paribus* condition that is needed. In Table 4.1, we present regression results for a reduced-form unemployment equation, derived from a model in which governments attempt to optimize a preference function subject to the prevailing Phillips curve.[5] The model was originally specified to trace unemployment outcomes to some key characteristics of the institutional and political substructures that influence economic behaviour and economic mechanisms. In this work, central bank independence was interpreted as a measure of aversion to inflation, which would influence effective political preferences regarding policy targets. These preferences may reflect 'grassroots' anti-inflation sentiment, or they may result from the influence of powerful business or financial sector interest groups. The original specification, reported in equation (1) in Table 4.1, using the Cukierman et al. index (CWN),[6] shows quite clearly that central bank independence is positively related to unemployment rates. To verify that this result is not dependent on the particular index used, the equation was reestimated using the Alesina and Summers (ALE) and

Table 4.1   Regression results for the reduced-form unemployment equation

	Equation (1)	Equation (2)	Equation (3)	Equation (4)
Proportion of left-of-centre votes	−4.877 (4.02)	−5.055 (3.58)	−3.387 (1.99)	−3.304 (1.94)
Central bank CWN index	3.046 (2.64)	3.332 (2.38)		
Central bank ALE index			0.823 (2.51)	
Central bank GMT index				0.258 (3.31)
Dummy variable for EMS membership	3.016 (4.60)	2.651 (3.56)	2.504 (3.33)	2.551 (3.60)
Log of strike volume lagged one period[a]	1.005 (8.05)	1.125 (8.34)	1.335 (7.85)	1.238 (9.16)
'World' unemployment[b]	0.944 (4.04)	1.091 (4.12)	1.154 (4.30)	1.033 (4.17)
Average inflation lagged one period	0.195 (3.43)	0.208 (3.36)	0.199 (3.23)	0.230 (3.85)
Constant	4.210 (5.65)	4.398 (5.05)	3.286 (2.76)	2.806 (2.57)
Adjusted R^2	0.8222	0.8218	0.8239	0.8386
No. of observations	72	52	52	52

Notes:
a. Days lost per thousand workers.
b. For each country this is the average unemployment rate for the other countries in the sample, weighted by its own exports to GDP ratio, used as a measure of external demand conditions.
The absolute values of the t-statistics are in parentheses.
There are four observations for each country, for the periods 1960–67, 1968–73, 1974–79 and 1980–89; more recent data do not cover a full business cycle, and are complicated by German unification.
Equation (1) uses the full sample of 18 countries, that is, US, Japan, Germany, France, Italy, UK, Canada, Australia, Austria, Belgium, Denmark, Finland, Ireland, Netherlands, New Zealand, Norway, Sweden and Switzerland. Equations (2), (3) and (4) omit Austria, Finland, Ireland, Norway and Sweden, since these are excluded from at least one of the ALE or GMT indices.
The dependent variable is the average unemployment rate for each period.

Sources: Voting data, T. Mackie and R. Rose (1991), *The International Almanac of Electoral History*, London: Macmillan; strike data, *International Labour Organization Yearbook of Labour Statistics*, various issues; OECD data are used for the remaining variables. Further details are available from the authors on request.

Grilli et al. (GMT) indices. These indices cover a smaller group of countries, so the Cukierman index was also used with the smaller sample for comparison purposes. The results are reported in equations (2), (3) and (4) in Table 4.1, and suggest that the choice of index is of no significant consequence. The coefficients of the remaining variables demonstrate considerable robustness, both to the changes in the sample size and to the alternative specification, the adjusted R-squares are virtually the same, and the indices all have coefficients that are significantly different from zero. These results strongly suggest that there is no free lunch.

The second empirical problem concerns what exactly these CBI indices are measuring. As suggested above, to interpret them as measures of aversion to inflation is one possibility. We are of the same view as Debelle and Fischer (1994), who show that countries with a greater aversion to inflation will tend to have more independent central banks. Posen (1996) attributes central bank independence to the level of effective opposition to inflation by financial interest groups. He shows an index of this opposition to be strongly corre-lated directly with the degree of central bank independence and negatively correlated with inflation. Hall (1994) stresses the joint action of CBI and the extent of coordination of both wage bargaining and fiscal and monetary policy if low inflation is to be achieved without high unemployment costs. These points are important. The first suggests that lower inflation is not achieved by changing the nature of the central bank, rather that the degree of CBI is endogenous, depending upon a preexisting aversion to inflation. The second implies that the unemployment costs of low inflation depend on factors other than CBI. In summary, the statistical foundation of the argu-ments that greater CBI reduces inflation and does so without real costs cannot withstand close scrutiny.

4   Modelling costs and benefits of central bank independence
Theoretical arguments supporting greater independence as a means of reducing the inflationary bias begin with a Lucas supply function or the expectation-augmented Phillips curve with real-wage bargaining (solved for the rate of unemployment). Write

$$Q_t = \overline{Q}_t + \beta(\dot{\mathbf{p}}_t - \dot{\mathbf{p}}_t^e) + \varepsilon_t \qquad (4.1)$$

and

$$U_t = \overline{U}_t + \alpha(\dot{\mathbf{p}}_t - \dot{\mathbf{p}}_t^e) + \mu_t \qquad (4.2)$$

where $Q_t, \overline{Q}_t, U_t$ and $\overline{U}_t$ are actual output, equilibrium output, the actual un-employment rate and the equilibrium unemployment rate, respectively, $\dot{\mathbf{p}}_t$ and

$\dot{p}_t^e$ are the actual and expected rate of inflation, respectively and ε_t and μ_t are random error terms.[7] Each relation implies a vertical long-run Phillips curve and a short-run trade-off between inflation and either output or unemployment.

The alleged shortcoming of democracy, a strong potential inflationary bias, is easily restated in terms of either equation. We shall do so using equation (4.2). As is clear, unemployment may deviate from its equilibrium level only because of a divergence between the expected and actual rates of inflation (ignoring shocks). Therefore the monetary authorities can temporarily reduce unemployment below its equilibrium by exploiting the short-run trade-off between unemployment and inflation through 'price surprises'. Unless central bankers are allowed freedom to carry out anti-inflation policies unencumbered by the desires of elected officials, the imposed preferences of the latter will generate a costly inflationary bias. The earlier mentioned political business cycle is one variant of this bias. Greater independence for the central bank is designed to give it this freedom to reduce or eliminate inflation. Moreover, since output and unemployment in the long run need only differ from their equilibrium value by a random error, the central bank can successfully concentrate on the inflation goal since the real sector is assumed to take care of itself. Everybody gains.

In the recent literature there are two classes of theoretical models that incorporate the potential inflationary bias of democratic capitalism and the alleged improvement of performance made possible by greater CBI. They are designated the conservative-central-banker policy model and the principal–agent policy model.[8] They differ primarily in the design of the inflation target assigned the central bank. In the conservative-central-banker policy model, the proper setting of the instrument variable involves minimizing a quadratic loss function in which both inflation and the variability of output or unemployment are the arguments. For example, in the oft-cited Rogoff model (1985), greater central bank independence is achieved by replacing the loss function of the general public with that of the central banker. Increased independence for the central bank is measured by the greater weight given to inflation in its loss function. In principal–agent models the central bank (the agent) is held accountable for achieving an inflation goal set by some elected body (the principal). In order to deter any temptation to 'cheat', penalties are imposed on the central bank for non-compliance with the target.

In general terms, there are two kinds of benefits allegedly yielded by these policies of greater CBI. First, they will give greater credibility to announced restrictive policies and thereby reduce their real costs, including the costs of eliminating past mistakes in policy. Second, policy mistakes that induce higher rates of inflation will be avoided in the future, because central bankers will not alter their behaviour in response to political pressures, that is, the problem of time inconsistency is avoided. Overall, proponents of greater CBI envisage improved macroeconomic performance and even in some cases Pareto-improved macroeconomic performance. There now exists a vast literature illustrating variations of these policy models. For reasons developed in the next four sections, it is not necessary to consider these embellishments.

5 Neoclassical equilibrium analysis

We would like to argue that the theoretical models employed in support of the welfare-improving impact of increased CBI are themselves flawed and therefore no more supportive than the statistical evidence. This is done by analysing the CBI issue within a broader theoretical context which provides the underlying rationale for greater CBI. This rationale formalizes a basic tenet of the counterrevolution cited earlier. We first discuss and evaluate certain key assumptions that are only implicit but absolutely essential in the CBI theoretical models. They must be considered along with the explicit assumptions of these models in order to evaluate properly the theoretical arguments advanced in support of greater CBI.

A key assumption of the neoclassical counterrevolution is that the private sector of a capitalist economy is basically self-regulating in some unspecified long run. Deviations of the economy from steady growth, low unemployment and politically acceptable rates of inflation are due to exogenous disturbances, including policy error, or 'market imperfections' which can be corrected if there is the 'political will'. This fundamental assumption is formalized in a very particular macroeconomic framework, characterized by its exogenously determined equilibrium. This equilibrium is unique, given the values of a set of exogenous variables, the 'supply side' in common usage. The absence of any independent long-run role for endogenous demand variables and the uniqueness of the equilibrium are defining features of neoclassical macroeconomic equilibrium analysis. A third defining feature, essential to the stability of the equilibrium, is a mechanism to ensure the passive adjustment of aggregate demand to the exogenously determined aggregate supply in the long run (Cornwall and Cornwall 1997).

What is properly designated the neoclassical equilibrium theory of unemployment exemplifies this approach, and is the basis for the claimed beneficial effects and lack of unemployment costs of greater CBI. All versions of this theory have as a common feature an expectation-augmented Phillips curve with real-wage bargaining, as in equation (4.2) above. In a 'well-behaved' system, for any given values of the exogenous supply-side variables, the long-run equilibrium unemployment rate is unique; at any other unemployment rate, inflation rates accelerate or decelerate without limit. The stability of the unemployment equilibrium follows from the additional necessary (but weakly supported) assumption that there exists a mechanism to bring aggregate demand into line with aggregate supply in the long run.

6 Evolving neoclassical equilibrium unemployment theory

The natural rate version
It is important to understand the strengths and weaknesses of neoclassical unemployment theory because the conclusions of the CBI argument depend absolutely on these macroeconomic underpinnings. In the earliest exposition of equilibrium unemployment theory and the vertical long-run Phillips curve, Friedman (1968) designated the equilibrium unemployment rate the 'natural rate'. Although his description of the properties of the natural rate allows for market imperfections, following a shock equilibrium is nevertheless regained by competitive haggling between buyers and sellers of labour until the market clears. In the Friedman model, the natural rate of unemployment is the full employment rate. Subsequent vertical Phillips curve models in the full employment tradition were less prone to simply assume competitive 'flexprice' markets and invisible hands. Instead they allowed price and wage rigidities in the short run, but assumed that Keynes and Pigou effects functioned as long-run mechanisms adjusting aggregate demand to aggregate supply at the full employment level. This ensured stability of the equilibrium rate. It is clear that in these models, an independent central bank can target inflation with no long-run unemployment cost.

The non-accelerating inflation rate of unemployment (NAIRU) version
However, an inherent difficulty with the natural rate version of neoclassical unemployment analysis is its inability to explain high rates of involuntary unemployment. Involuntarily unemployed workers are by definition willing to take work at the going real wage or less. Ironically, despite the growing evidence that the larger share of the rise in unemployment over the past 25 years has been caused by rising involuntary unemployment, the popularity of neoclassical unemployment theory has grown, although with some modification of the natural rate version.[9] Rather than the natural rate, these models refer to the equilibrium unemployment rate as the NAIRU. Moreover the distinction between involuntary and voluntary unemployment lost favour in this literature, to be replaced by a distinction between classical and Keynesian unemployment.[10]

NAIRU analysis developed to explain the persistent high unemployment since the mid-1970s. According to its advocates, it is only natural rate theory, not equilibrium unemployment theory in general, that cannot explain high unemployment. NAIRU analysis is distinguished from natural rate theory by allowing involuntary unemployment to exist in the long-run equilibrium.[11]

Even though mass unemployment may exist at the NAIRU, it is classical, and must be accepted unless policy changes on the supply side can reduce the exogenously determined NAIRU. As in the natural rate version, restrictive aggregate demand policies have no adverse real effects in the long run, only beneficial effects on inflation. Greater CBI allows consistent inflation targeting, ensuring that these benefits will be realized.

7   An appraisal of NAIRU analysis

The relevance of the NAIRU version of equilibrium unemployment theory as an explanation of unemployment tendencies is highly questionable. It is implausible because its assumptions are both implausible and inconsistent. The strength and effectiveness of the mechanisms that must bring aggregate demand into line with aggregate supply in NAIRU models (as well as in natural rate versions) have been largely ignored in the literature, even though the supply-determined equilibrium framework requires a convincing adjustment mechanism if it is to have any explanatory power. In particular the assumed mechanism adjusting aggregate demand to the exogenously determined supply side must act with sufficient speed and strength to always offset both the impact of shocks and any shock-induced cumulative movements of aggregate demand, output and employment.

There is little empirical or theoretical support for the view that Keynes and Pigou effects work quickly and forcefully enough to dominate movements on the demand side of the market either in the short or in the long run.[12] Without an effective adjustment mechanism, the equilibrium is unstable, a situation reminiscent of the Harrod–Domar knife edge in growth theory.[13] And without stability, any variant of neoclassical unemployment theory is reduced to nothing more than the concept of a unique equilibrium rate of unemployment. NAIRU analysis suffers from a second handicap in its reliance on contradictory assumptions. To justify retaining the unique equilibrium and vertical Phillips curves in periods of high unemployment, NAIRU advocates chose one of two routes. The first was to ignore the distinction between the full employment rate of unemployment and a NAIRU with positive rates of involuntary unemployment. The second was to assume that whatever involuntary unemployment exists at the NAIRU, it is classical, that is, unresponsive to aggregate demand increases. Neither route can salvage neoclassical unemployment theory.

The first simultaneously assumes wage bargaining to be in real terms and allows involuntary unemployment at the NAIRU, contrary to the definition of involuntary unemployment. This internal contradiction seriously impairs the validity of the NAIRU version of vertical Phillips curve analysis.[14] The second route is an attempt to reconcile high levels of involuntary unemployment with the assumption of real-wage bargaining. It assumes that stimulative macroeconomic policies cannot permanently reduce involuntary unemployment, because real wages are too high; unemployment is involuntary but classical. However, this argument cannot hold, because money wages, not real wages, are set in the labour market. Real wages are set in the product market when business decides how much to mark up over costs.[15] Labour cannot set the real wage too high because it is determined by employers, a point stressed in Keynes's *General Theory*. As long as labour does not set the real wage, unemployment is not classical.

8   Implication for CBI analysis

What then remains of neoclassical equilibrium unemployment theory, and what are the implications for CBI? The natural rate version, defining equilibrium unemployment as the full employment rate of unemployment, while free from contradictory assumptions is not relevant in today's world. The only resolution of the internal contradiction in the NAIRU model is to drop the assumption of real-wage bargaining over the range of unemployment rates at which involuntary unemployment exists. This modification has radical implications. Over this range there will exist a long-run trade-off between unemployment and inflation rates; multiple equilibria exist with each corresponding to a different level of aggregate demand and a different constant rate of inflation. Moreover, as the rate of unemployment in equilibrium is demand determined, discretionary aggregate demand policy has a role to play.[16] Neither the natural rate nor the NAIRU forms of neoclassical unemployment theory are adequate to the task of modelling unemployment tendencies. Neither can explain movements in the unemployment rate nor provide a plausible formal model of a self-regulating system.[17]

This has obvious and serious implications when evaluating the theoretical case for greater CBI. Most of the force of the CBI arguments stems from the assumption that capitalism can be modelled as a system with stable, unique (and sometimes even full employment) equilibrium tendencies and a vertical long-run Phillips curve.[18] Indeed, the conclusions that there are no real costs to reducing inflation rates, that capitalism suffers from an inflation bias which is due to 'opportunistic' behaviour by the central bank, that 'time inconsistency' illustrates a failure of democracy and that setting either a fixed or flexible inflationary target is always welfare improving either follow from or fit conveniently with the implicit assumptions of neoclassical unemployment analysis. If, as we have argued, there are in fact no strong supply-determined equilibrium tendencies, but instead the authorities are faced with a long-run trade-off between inflation and unemployment, restrictive aggregate demand policies have real costs, and it is incorrect to speak of measures designed to increase CBI as *a priori* welfare improving, let alone Pareto improving. Such measures are political choices in the sense that some groups will benefit and others will be hurt.[19]

60   *The political economy of central banking*

9   The temper of the times and the historical record

This brings the discussion to the 'temper of the times' and in what sense it supports institutional monetary reform. Earlier we stated that the temper of the times could be appropriately defined as the neoclassical counterrevolution in macroeconomic thinking with respect to the proper role of the state and the economic and political forces thought to be endangering the economy. While this change in views has many aspects, it is sufficient here to consider two of them: a shift (i) from a Keynesian perspective of capitalism as a system in need of periodic intervention to prevent serious unemployment to what we defined as a neoclassical view of an economy that is self-regulating in some long run; and (ii) from the position that periodic shortfalls of aggregate demand are the main macroeconomic concern to one in which excessive aggregate demand is the danger. Certainly these altered beliefs are part of the support system for greater CBI as they are widely supported by influential groups. But the important issue is whether these sentiments can be said to have a factual basis. If they do, then there is the possibility that proponents of CBI are right, but for the wrong reasons; capitalism is self-regulating, in the absence of misbehaviour on the part of central bankers and politicians, even though the neoclassical theory of unemployment is an unacceptable formalization of the invisible hand metaphor. This suggests looking at the historical record.

Table 4.2 gives unemployment rates covering three-quarters of a century for Canada, the United Kingdom and the United States. The average unem-

Table 4.2   Average annual unemployment rates and the number of years unemployment equalled or exceeded 3 per cent and 6 per cent

	Average annual rate	Unemployment 3 per cent or more		Unemployment 6 per cent or more	
	1920–95[a]	1920–38	1950–95	1920–38	1950–95
Canada[b]	7.1	14 of 19	43 of 46	9 of 19	26 of 46
United Kingdom	6.6	18 of 19	27 of 46	19 of 19	16 of 46
United States	6.8	17 of 19	42 of 46	11 of 19	18 of 46

Notes:
a.   Excludes 1939–46.
b.   Excludes 1920.

Sources: A. Maddison, *Phases of Capitalist Development*, Oxford: Oxford University Press, 1982; R. Layard et al., *Unemployment, Macroeconomic Performance and the Labour Market*, Oxford: Oxford University Press, 1991, Table A3; and *Economic Outlook*, Paris: OECD, December 1996, Table A22.

ployment rate for the 1920–95 period (excluding the war years and the early years of conversion) varied between 6.6 and 7.1 per cent. As well, in all three economies unemployment rates were equal to or exceeded 3 per cent in most years, for example, in 59 out of 65 years in the US, and were equal to or exceeded 6 per cent approximately one-half of the time in the same economies. While it is common practice in evaluating the unemployment record today to compare actual unemployment rates with estimates of the NAIRU, the relevant welfare baseline statistic is the rate of unemployment at which involuntary unemployment is zero or nearly so. In the three economies considered here, unemployment rates of 3–4 per cent are frequently referred to as full employment rates of unemployment. However, this convention is not derived from any careful analysis of the nature of unemployment at 3–4 per cent or the historical record in recent times.[20]

The experience of the OECD economies during the 1960–73 'golden age' period is of assistance in this regard (Cornwall 1994, Table II.1). During this period the unemployment records of 18 developed capitalist economies fell into a high unemployment group of four and a low unemployment group of 14, with annual average unemployment rates of 4.7 and 1.5 per cent, respectively, and an overall average of 2.3 per cent. This suggests that for most of the OECD economies the unemployment rate must fall below 3 per cent before low rates of involuntary unemployment are encountered. In other words the common assumption of 3 per cent as the full employment rate of unemployment is not too low, and the data in Table 4.2 show no evidence of self-regulating tendencies in Canada, the United States or Britain.

Tables 4.3 and 4.4 also help to evaluate the beliefs that full employment is a natural tendency and that the danger today is excessive rather than insufficient aggregate demand pressure. Table 4.3 gives annual average rates of inflation and unemployment for the golden age and for the recent period

Table 4.3 Average annual rates of inflation (ṗ) and unemployment (U)

	1960–73		1983–93		1983–95	
	ṗ	U	ṗ	U	ṗ	U
Canada	3.3	5.0	4.1	9.8	3.7	9.8
United Kingdom	5.1	2.9	5.1	9.9	4.8	9.8
United States	3.2	4.8	3.9	6.8	3.6	6.6

Sources: R. Layard et al., *Unemployment, Macroeconomic Performance and the Labour Market*, Oxford: Oxford University Press, 1991, Table A3; *Economic Outlook*, OECD, Paris: OECD, December 1996, Tables A16 and A22; and *OECD Historical Statistics 1960–94*, Paris: OECD, 1996, Table 8.11. Data for 1983–93 allow comparison with data in Table 4.4.

Table 4.4   Alternative unemployment measures

	United States			United Kingdom			Canada		
	U–5	U–6	U–7	U–5	U–6	U–7	U–5	U–6	U–7
1983	9.6	12.6	13.9	11.1	13.1	13.9	11.9	14.3	15.7
1984	7.5	10.1	11.2	11.0	13.0	13.8	11.2	13.8	14.8
1985	7.2	9.6	10.6	11.5	13.3	14.1	10.3	12.9	13.8
1986	7.0	9.4	10.3	11.6	13.4	14.3	9.4	12.0	12.7
1987	6.2	8.5	9.3	11.1	13.0	13.6	8.7	11.1	11.7
1988	5.5	7.6	8.4	9.1	10.6	11.1	7.6	9.8	10.3
1989	5.3	7.2	7.9	7.4	8.7	9.1	7.4	9.5	9.9
1990	5.5	7.6	8.2	7.0	8.1	8.4	8.0	10.1	10.6
1991	6.7	9.2	10.0	8.6	10.3	10.6	10.3	12.9	13.6
1992	7.4	10.0	10.8	9.8	12.2	12.8	11.3	14.2	14.9
1993	6.8	9.3	10.2	10.3	13.1	13.8	11.2	14.4	15.2
Average	6.8	9.2	10.1	9.9	11.7	12.3	9.8	12.3	13.0

Source: US Bureau of Labor Statistics (1995).

during which support for greater CBI developed. In all three countries, inflation rates changed little but unemployment rates increased markedly in the recent period. If anything, recent data suggest a growing unemployment bias due to inadequate aggregate demand. What is of interest is the contrast between the changing inflation and unemployment record and the changing temper of the times as reflected in the views of economists, central bankers and government officials. In the early period, at least until the late 1960s, there were widespread fears that aggregate demand would prove to be insufficient. In the recent period these same groups have focused their attention on the dangers of excess demand and inflationary pressures, expressing little concern with unemployment. The actual inflation and unemployment performance lends no support to these concerns.

Table 4.4 reinforces this view. Along with the conventional measurement of unemployment, U–5, it shows two other measures.[21] U–6 includes involuntary part-time workers, both workers in full-time jobs who are on shortened hours because there is not enough work available, and those who have settled for part-time jobs because they could not find full time work. U–7 adds discouraged workers, that is, people who are available for work, but who have left the labour force or decided not to enter it because they believe that there are no jobs. Comparing U–6 and U–7 with the corresponding U–5 figures indicates that the conventional measure of unemployment substantially underestimates the true amount of involuntary unemployment and its associated welfare costs. When conventionally measured, average unemployment rates for the 1983–93 period are 9.9, 9.8 and 6.8 per cent, respectively, for the UK, Canada and the US, while the corresponding average U–7 measure of unemployment is 12.3, 13.0 and 10.1, increases of approximately 25, 33 and 50 per cent in the measure of economic slack. All of this points to the existence of a sizable reserve army of the unemployed and the general weakness of aggregate demand during the recent period.[22]

In summary, the unemployment data show little evidence that capitalist economies display full employment or low involuntary unemployment tendencies. The high involuntary unemployment rates indicate that since the early 1980s insufficient rather than excess aggregate demand has been the problem, a condition due to restrictive policies. Yet powerful groups have shown more concern to effect institutional change that would further restrain inflation than it has for change designed to reduce the unemployment problem.

10   Conclusion

Considering each foundation stone of the greater CBI argument, closer analysis fails to reveal convincing evidence to support the case for increased CBI. The econometric results offered by its advocates cannot withstand even the most elementary scrutiny, the theoretical models are based on implausible and internally inconsistent assumptions and the historical record gives little support for either the theoretical base or for some key tenets of the neoclassical counterrevolution that we identified as the temper of the times. Those advocating increased CBI are arguing for stronger anti-inflation policies and therefore, in effect, for greater unemployment, while either ignoring the real costs of their policies or maintaining that there are none. And it should be emphasized that this comes at a time when governments have been implementing restrictive fiscal policies in an effort to reduce budget deficits, both in countries hoping to enter the EMU as well as others, and when unregulated international capital flows and globalization create additional constraints on the introduction of stimulative policies. These provide reason enough for there being no danger of inflationary pressure.

What then are the reasons for mainstream macroeconomists' increased concern with inflation and for their advocacy of greater CBI? We argue that the reasons proposed rest on shaky foundations, and that greater CBI will merely increase the already high unemployment costs experienced today. Indeed, in an age of prolonged mass unemployment throughout the OECD, rather than asking why economists have placed so much emphasis on greater CBI, there is a more pertinent question. Why have they shown such reluctance to alter their perception of how capitalist systems work and the way this perception is formalized? To put it otherwise, why did the mass unemployment of the 1930s lead to a successful Keynesian revolution against the prevailing neoclassical orthodoxy while the mass unemployment of the 1980s and 1990s has as yet had no such profound effect on mainstream economic thought?

Notes

1. The idea of a belief system is captured to a large extent by Kuhn's concept of a paradigm (1970) or the 'hard core' of Lakatos's scientific research programme (Lakatos and Musgrave (eds) 1970).
2. Most of the CBI literature is formulated in terms of a long-run equilibrium output level rather than an equilibrium unemployment rate. However, it is generally understood that either form may be used. As examples of the vagueness in the definition of the equilibrium output concept, see the articles by Alesina and Gatti (1995) and McCallum (1995).
3. An additional alleged source of inflationary bias is the propensity of governments to deliberately foster inflation as a revenue-generating device.
4. Jenkins (1996) makes the same point, and provides regression results for an inflation equation that support the claims that there are omitted variables in the earlier work. Debelle and Fischer (1994) and Posen (1996) both report a positive relation between output loss and central bank independence.
5. This model is explained in full in W. Cornwall (forthcoming). Note that this is a downward-sloping Phillips curve.
6. This index is based upon several measures of the legal independence of central banks, and was chosen because it includes a broader group of countries than the other indices, as well as covering four periods, allowing for changes in the level of independence over time.
7. One equation can be derived from the other through the addition of some form of Okun's law relating output and unemployment.
8. A third policy model is that of monetary credibility in which credibility is modelled as an outcome of a repeated game between the central bank and the government. Credibility is treated as a possible favourable result of the adoption of either of the two policies mentioned in the text.
9. For the relevant characteristics of the unemployed and of unemployment, see Clark and Summers (1979); Main (1981); Hasan and de Brouker (1982); and Fortin (1996).
10. For one of the best-known examples of this form of neoclassical unemployment theory, see Layard et al. (1991).
11. In the absence of market clearing, there have been wide differences of opinion about the determinants of the NAIRU. Consequently, in a new stage in the evolution of equilibrium unemployment theory it is arbitrarily determined as a simple function of past actual unemployment rates. One approach is to fit a smoothly evolving trend to actual unemployment rates, the so-called Hodrick–Prescott filter. A second simply defines it as 'the average rate of unemployment around which the economy fluctuates'. See CEPR (1995 Ch. 3); and Mankiw (1994, p. 118 and Figure 5–1), respectively. Convergence to the equilibrium is ensured by assuming the kind of adjustment mechanisms employed in NAIRU models.
12. See Tobin (1993) for a recent appraisal.
13. In the Harrod–Domar model, an equilibrium growth rate exists but it is unstable, as there is no adjustment mechanism in the model to bring the rate of growth of demand into line with the 'warranted' and 'natural' rates of growth. Therefore the system is liable either to continuous inflation or continuous declines in output and employment. In the neoclassical unemployment models, there is a mechanism assumed to generate stability of the equilibrium but as argued in the text it is quite unrealistic.
14. This contradiction is evident even in equilibrium unemployment models that emphasize

market imperfections. These assume real-wage bargaining no matter how pervasive is involuntary unemployment. See Carlin and Soskice (1990, Ch. 6), and Layard et al. (1991).
15. See Dow (1990).
16. When discussing the segment of the long-run Phillips curve that is downward sloping, it should be understood that this negative relationship carries a *ceteris paribus* assumption. All the remaining right-hand-side variables are assumed constant. Also nothing said in the text is inconsistent with the long-run Phillips curve becoming virtually vertical at low rates of unemployment.
17. The fact that estimates of the equilibrium unemployment rate vary widely from one study to the next and that over time estimates mimic actual movements in the unemployment rate, that is, there may be hysteresis in the unemployment rate, further strengthens this conclusion.
18. Mention has already been made of the failure to define the properties of this equilibrium rate.
19. Friedman and Schwartz (1965) argue that if the Federal Reserve had intervened in the early 1930s and increased the money supply, much of the downturn in the real sector could have been avoided.
20. For the United States, the Clark and Summers (1979) study indicates that in 1969, when the unemployment rate stood at 3.4 per cent, 35 per cent of all the weeks of unemployment experienced during that year were experienced by people out of work for 26 weeks or more. This suggests that even at unemployment rates between 3 and 4 per cent, much of the unemployment is involuntary.
21. The U–5 measure corresponds closely to the OECD standardized unemployment rate; the 1983–93 average for each of these economies is the same, whichever measure is used. For definitions of U–5, U–6 and U–7, see US Bureau of Labor Statistics (1995).
22. There are no comparable data for the OECD economies before 1983 or after 1993.

Bibliography

Alesina, A. and R. Gatti (1995), 'Independent central banks: low inflation at no cost?', *American Economic Review, Papers and Proceedings*, **85**, May, 196–200.
Alesina, A. and L. Summers (1993), 'Central bank independence and macroeconomic performance: some comparative evidence', *Journal of Money, Credit and Banking*, **25**, May, 151–62.
Carlin, W. and D. Soskice (1990), *Macroeconomics and the Wage Bargain*, Oxford: Oxford University Press.
Centre for Economic Policy Research (CEPR) (1995), *Unemployment: Choices for Europe*, London: CEPR.
Clark, K. and L. Summers (1979), 'Labour market dynamics and unemployment: a reconsideration', *Brookings Papers on Economic Activity*, No. 1.
Cooper, R. (1994), 'Strategy and tactics of monetary policy, discussion', *Goals, Guidelines, and Constraints Facing Monetary Policymakers*, Federal Reserve Bank of Boston Conference Series No. 38.
Cornwall, J. (1994), *Economic Breakdown and Recovery: Theory and Policy*, Armonk, NY: M.E. Sharpe.
Cornwall, J. and W. Cornwall (1997), 'The unemployment problem and the legacy of Keynes', *Journal of Post Keynesian Economics*, **19** (4), Summer, 525–42.
Cornwall, W. (forthcoming), 'The institutional determinants of unemployment', in M. Setterfield (ed.), *The Political Economy of Growth, Employment and Inflation*, London: Macmillan.
Cukierman, A., S.B. Webb and B. Neyapti (1993), 'Measuring the independence of central banks and its effect on policy outcomes', *World Bank Economic Review*, **6**, 353–98.
Debelle, G. and S. Fischer (1994), 'How independent should a central bank be?', *Goals, Guidelines, and Constraints Facing Monetary Policymakers*, Federal Reserve Bank of Boston Conference Series No. 38.
Dow, J.C.R. (1990), *How Can Real Wages Ever Get Excessive?*, National Institute of Economic and Social Research, Discussion Paper No. 196.

Fischer, S. (1994), 'Modern central banking', in F. Capie, C. Goodhart, S. Fischer and N. Schnadt (eds), *The Future of Central Banking*, Cambridge: Cambridge University Press, 262–308.

Fischer, S. (1995), 'Central bank independence revisited', *American Economic Review, Papers and Proceedings*, **85**, May, 201–6.

Fortin, P. (1996), 'The great Canadian slump', *Canadian Journal of Economics*, **29** (4), November, 761–87.

Friedman, M. (1968), 'The role of monetary policy', *American Economic Review*, **58**, March, 1–17.

Friedman, M. and A. Schwartz (1965), *The Great Contraction 1929–1933*, Princeton: Princeton University Press.

Grilli, V., D. Masciandaro and G. Tabellini (1991), 'Political and monetary institutions and public finance policies in the industrial countries', *Economic Policy*, **13**, October, 341–92.

Hall, Peter A. (1994), 'Central bank independence and coordinated wage bargaining: their interaction in Germany and Europe', *German Politics and Society*, Issue 31, Spring, 1–23.

Hasan, H. and P. de Brouker (1982), 'Duration and concentration of unemployment', *Canadian Journal of Economics*, **15**, November, 735–56.

Jenkins, M. (1996), 'Central bank independence and inflation performance: panacea or placebo?', *Banca Nazionale del Lavoro Quarterly Review*, **49**, June, 241–70.

Kuhn, T. (1970), *The Structure of Scientific Revolutions*, 2nd edn, Chicago: Cambridge University Press.

Lakatos, I. and A. Musgrave (eds) (1970), *Criticism and Growth of Knowledge*, London: Cambridge University Press.

Layard, R., S. Nickell and R. Jackman (1991), *Unemployment: Macroeconomic Performance and the Labour Market*, Oxford: Oxford University Press.

Main, B. (1981), 'The length of employment and unemployment in Great Britain', *Scottish Journal of Political Economy*, **28**, June, 146–64.

Mankiw, G. (1994), *Macroeconomics*, 2nd edn, New York: Worth.

McCallum, B. (1995), 'Two fallacies concerning central-bank independence', *American Economic Review, Papers and Proceedings*, **85**, May, 207–11.

Nordhaus, W. (1975), 'The political business cycle', *Review of Economic Studies*, **XLII** (2), April, 169–90.

Posen, A. (1996), 'Declarations are not enough: financial sector sources of central bank independence', *National Bureau of Economic Research Macroeconomics Annual 1995*, Cambridge, MA:, MIT Press.

Rogoff, K. (1985), 'The optimal degree of commitment to an intermediate monetary target', *Quarterly Journal of Economics*, **100**, November, 1169–89.

Tobin, J. (1993), 'Price flexibility and output stability: an old Keynesian view', *Journal of Economic Perspectives*, **7**, Winter, 45–65.

US Bureau of Labor Statistics (1995), 'International unemployment indicators, 1983–93', *Monthly Labor Review*, August, 31–46.

5 Leadership and stability in key currency systems: a simple game-theoretic approach

H.-Peter Spahn

1 Introduction

This chapter studies some basic problems of the working of a key currency system. A two-country model provides the general framework of the analysis where the active part is played by the interaction of central banks. The first question is how leadership by some country is established and why other countries accept their subordinate position. Two approaches which might cause such a systematic asymmetry are investigated: a model by Eichengreen highlights different market structures as to money demand; the fact that sterling assets were used as a secondary reserve in the gold standard, however, did not suffice to constitute a stable key currency structure. Instead it is shown that monetary policy preferences are the decisive factors; the key currency central bank acts as a Stackelberg follower in terms of game theory. Whereas leadership in the gold standard depends on the priority attached to the preservation of external equilibrium at given exchange rates, the emphasis laid on price stability determines that currency which is chosen for intervention and reserve-keeping purposes in paper standard systems like the European Monetary System (EMS). Welfare of member countries is affected by supply and demand shocks emanating from the leading country. Paper standard systems differ substantially from the classical gold standard as they exhibit a marked restrictive bias. This result offers some further reason for the evident instabilities of the EMS in the past years.

2 A model of the gold standard

Consider a symmetric setting of homogeneous economies, that is, two countries of equal size and efficiency. The working and interaction of these economies can be expressed by a set of log-linear equations where an asterisk denotes a foreign variable:[1] the first equation shows aggregate supply, that is, the price level p determined by autonomous wages w and rising marginal costs; the second equation presents aggregate income y depending on autonomous demand g, the rate of interest r and the real exchange rate (the fixed log nominal exchange rate is normalized to zero); money demand is captured by the third equation and money supply by the fourth. Greek letters represent constant parameters.

$$p = w + \alpha y \tag{5.1}$$

$$y = g - \beta r - \varepsilon(p - p^*) \tag{5.2}$$

$$m = p + y - \sigma r \tag{5.3}$$

$$m = q - \mu i. \tag{5.4}$$

High-powered money m is backed by some amount of gold and otherwise created by discounting bills. Although any central bank in the gold standard is obliged to maintain a fixed internal exchange rate between notes and gold, the overall degree of coverage was below unity. Historically, central banks did not strictly obey the 'rules of the game'; there was some flexibility in the relation between the external and the internal counterparts of money creation. Both these items of the central bank's balance sheet are shown in equation (5.4) where $q < 1$ measures the share of the given world stock of gold (which as a constant is suppressed) held as the bank's reserve and i represents the discount rate, that is, its policy instrument.

A similar set of equations can be designed for the foreign country. In order to avoid trivial causes for asymmetries all parameters are of the same value in both countries. The interest parity condition provides for the equality of the market rates of interest $(r^* = r)$.[2] Foreign money supply is given by

$$m^* = (1 - q) - \mu i^*. \tag{5.5}$$

Both central banks[3] are assumed to minimize loss functions representing the goal of maintaining external and internal equilibrium. In the gold standard, the former was considered to be of greater importance. It is measured by some level $\bar{q} > 0.5$ in both countries; this implies that both central banks cannot attract the desired amount of reserves at the same time. This assumption is made by Eichengreen in order to catch the restrictive bias which sometimes is attributed to the gold standard.[4] On the other hand, the internal target (which has a relative weight a and a^*, respectively) is given by full employment $\bar{y} = \bar{y}^*$. This target is equivalent to price stability, if supply shocks are absent.

$$L = (\bar{q} - q)^2 + a(\bar{y} - y)^2 \tag{5.6}$$

$$L^* = \left[\bar{q} - (1 - q)\right]^2 + a^* \left(\bar{y} - y^*\right)^2 \tag{5.7}$$

The solution of the macro system[5] elucidates that monetary policies, that is, variations of the discount rates, by proportionally changing the market rates $r^* = r$ have a parallel influence on output and prices, but act adversely on the distribution of gold reserves:

$$\underline{r} = -\frac{1}{\beta}\underline{y} = -\frac{1}{\beta}\underline{y}^* = -\frac{1}{\alpha\beta}\underline{p} = -\frac{1}{\alpha\beta}\underline{p}^* = \frac{\mu}{2\Omega}(i+i^*) - \frac{1}{2\Omega} \qquad (5.8)$$

$$\underline{q} = \frac{1}{2} + \frac{\mu}{2}(i-i^*) \qquad (5.9)$$

$$\Omega = \beta(1+\alpha) + \sigma.$$

The two reaction functions which give the optimal answer of each player to any behaviour of its opponent exhibit a perfectly symmetric shape. Their positions and slopes depend among other factors on the policy preference parameters. If both players attach a lower weight to internal equilibrium these functions have a positive slope (Figure 5.1):

$$RF\!: \quad i = \frac{\Omega^2(2\bar{q}-1) + a\beta(\beta - 2\Omega\bar{y})}{\mu(\Omega^2 + a\beta^2)} + \frac{\Omega^2 - a\beta^2}{\Omega^2 + a\beta^2}i^* \qquad (5.10)$$

$$RF^*\!: \quad i^* = \frac{\Omega^2(2\bar{q}-1) + a^*\beta(\beta - 2\Omega\bar{y})}{\mu(\Omega^2 + a^*\beta^2)} + \frac{\Omega^2 - a^*\beta^2}{\Omega^2 + a^*\beta^2}i \qquad (5.11)$$

The ellipses reveal the central banks' loss levels. Moving from any starting point in a south-western direction increases output and prices in both countries. The home country gains on its gold stock if the combination of discount rates is changed in the north-western direction. If the cooperative outcome (*C*) is neglected the choice is between Nash (*N*) and Stackelberg (*S*, *S**). A Stackelberg solution emerges if one player – the 'leader' – chooses his or her optimal position on the reaction function of the second player – the 'follower' – who in turn confirms in a passive way the outcome of the game.

Obviously both countries gain if a Nash solution can be avoided. As long as each player attaches the same weight to the policy targets ($a = a^*$) *S* is an unstable solution because the home country would gain even more if *S** would prevail (Table 5.1). The general, somewhat ironic feature of the game is that both players would like the other to be the leader as the loss of each country is lower in a Stackelberg-follower position. The unsuccessful attempt of both players to urge each other into the leading position ends up in the Nash high-interest solution. Therefore some features have to be added to an otherwise symmetric model so that a stable leader–follower structure can emerge.

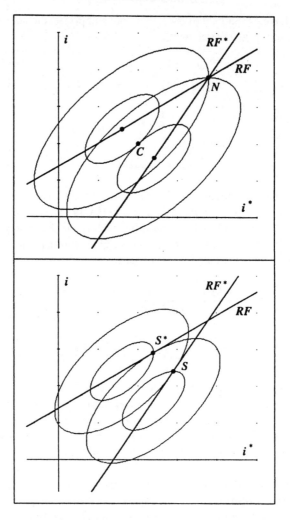

*Figure 5.1   Cooperative, Nash and Stackelberg solutions in a symmetric
two-country game*

3   Asymmetric games I: sterling as a reserve currency

Eichengreen (1987) exploits the well-known experience that financial assets
denominated in sterling served as a secondary currency reserve in the gold
standard. The foreign banking system used to back its home currency besides
gold with these assets, that is, accounts with London banks and British
bonds. Furthermore it is assumed – with some justification as to the historical
facts (compare Lindert 1969, pp. 48, 78) – that the demand for sterling

Table 5.1 Loss levels of both players in alternative Stackelberg solutions

Solution/loss	L	L^*
S	$\dfrac{a\Omega^2(2\overline{q}-1)^2}{a\Omega^2+(a^*)^2\beta^2}$	$\dfrac{(a^*)^3\beta^2(\Omega^2+a^*\beta)(2\overline{q}-1)^2}{\left[a\Omega^2+(a^*)^2\beta^2\right]^2}$
S^*	$\dfrac{a^3\beta^2(\Omega^2+a\beta^2)(2\overline{q}-1)^2}{\left[a^*\Omega^2+a^2\beta^2\right]^2}$	$\dfrac{a^*\Omega^2(2\overline{q}-1)^2}{a^*\Omega^2+a^2\beta^2}$

reserves increased in times of worldwide increases of interest rates. This demand function can be expressed as

$$f^* = f_0^* + \phi r. \qquad (5.12)$$

By dropping the constant f_0^* the foreign money supply (5.5) alters to

$$m^* = (1-q) + \phi r - \mu i^*. \qquad (5.13)$$

The share λ of f^* which is held as money (that is, not invested in sterling bonds) forms one part of the overall sterling money demand (5.3):

$$m = p + y - \sigma r + \lambda \phi r. \qquad (5.14)$$

Changes of the British discount rate now have a larger influence on gold flows compared to changes of the foreign rate, $|dq/di| > |dq/di^*|$. This is exactly what characterizes the specific power of the interest rate policy of a key currency central bank. Eichengreen furthermore argues that the asymmetric reaction of capital flows to interest rate changes tends to modify the shape of the reactions functions so that a stable Stackelberg solution with Britain as the leading country emerges. During a period of rising world interest rates, the Bank of England is not forced to counter interest rate increases abroad by similar adjustments at home as the direction of gold movements are biased towards Britain. According to Eichengreen, the home reaction function may reach a zero slope so that S turns out as the equilibrium solution which will be accepted by both players (Figure 5.2).

Unfortunately, Eichengreen reached this conclusion by means of a back-of-the-envelope analysis only. An algebraic examination and the inspection of loss levels show that in case of identical policy preferences ($a = a^*$) the

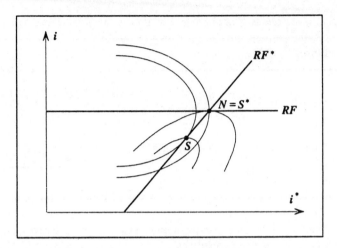

Figure 5.2   Eichengreen's asymmetric Stackelberg solution

foreign country would accept S because of $L_S^* < L_{S^*}^*$ but the home country would not as $L_S < L_{S^*}$ does not hold. Thus an agreement is precluded.

It is not disputed that the money demand effect may flatten the slope of the home country's reaction function. However, the same forces at work with respect to RF would make RF^* steeper so that a Nash solution will emerge. The economic reason for Eichengreen's mistake is to be found in his belief that an additional foreign demand for sterling reserves would shorten the money supply available for the British economy; indeed this seems to be straightforward from (5.14). This indirect restrictive monetary effect then would exert additional pressure on home prices and output so that the Bank of England could afford to ease its stance of monetary policy.[6]

The balance sheets of both central banks (Table 5.2), however, elucidate that if the foreign bank wishes to increase its sterling reserves it can do so only by shipping gold to England. In the foreign country, the quantity of money remains constant as only the structure of the central bank's assets will change (gold ↓, sterling notes ↑). On the other hand, the Bank of England increases its gold reserves by issuing additional notes which then are held abroad (gold ↑, notes abroad ↑). If the foreign central bank prefers to hold interest-bearing reserve assets ($\lambda = 0$) the acquired sterling notes are exchanged for sterling bonds (⇑) whereas the quantity of notes held by British non-bank sellers of these bonds rises (⇑). In no case any shortage of sterling notes emerges because the foreign demand for sterling assets leads to a parallel creation of money in Britain.

Table 5.2   Balance sheets of central banks in the gold standard

Bank of England		Foreign central bank	
gold ↑	notes	gold ↓	notes
bills and bonds	*– abroad* ↑	sterling reserves	
	– in Britain ⇑	*– notes* ↑	
		– bonds ⇑	
		bills and bonds	

4   Asymmetric games II: different policy preferences in the gold standard

The indisputable demand for sterling accounts and bonds as reserve assets does not suffice to establish a stable hierarchy of countries in the gold standard model. A second attempt to obtain such a result is made by assuming different policy preferences. There is some consensus that defending the external value of the pound was the overriding objective of British monetary policy.[7] Accordingly, it is now assumed that the relative interest in maintaining internal equilibrium is lower in Britain ($a < a^*$). By referring to Table 5.1 it can then be computed whether the twofold condition [$L_S < L_{S^*}$, $L_S^* < L_{S^*}^*$] for a Britain-dominated Stackelberg solution S is met. Again it turns out that this is not the case. The first condition holds only if $a > a^*$. However, this implies that S^* is a stable solution as [$L_S > L_{S^*}$, $L_S^* > L_{S^*}^*$] holds.

The origin of an asymmetric key currency structure may be explained by envisaging monetary policy before the establishment of such a system as an uncoordinated battle for attaining gold reserves by means of interest rate policies. If the Bank of England increases the relative weight of its reserve target the slope of its reaction function becomes steeper and the shape of the loss ellipse flattens out so that the point S – as indicated by the grey arrow – moves along the foreign reaction function to the north-east (Figure 5.3). As a tendency of rising interest rates, however, lowers output in all countries the 'weak' players – unable to neglect employment losses for political reasons – sooner or later had to give in. They recognized the existence of a superior strategy of accepting the hegemonic position of a 'strong' country and improved their economic situation by anticipating the path of interest policy pursued by the leading central bank, that is, by acting according to the dominant reaction function. By heading for point S^* they pursue an active Stackelberg-leader strategy which actually indicates a position of weakness. S^* is the best position which can be reached by both players given the setting of a non-cooperative game.

It is not paradoxical that the leading central bank in a key currency system should behave as a Stackelberg follower in terms of game theory. The very

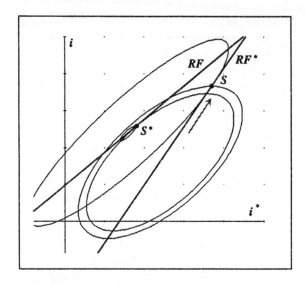

*Figure 5.3   The key currency bank as the Stackelberg follower in an
asymmetric two-country game*

behaviour that indicates dominance in the general setting of game theory
represents weakness in currency policy matters. The threat of a hard-nosed
central bank to pursue restrictive interest rate policies in favour of strengthen-
ing the currency leads foreign countries to orientate their monetary policies
by the signals sent out by that central bank. The essential prerogative of the
Stackelberg leader, that is, having the 'first move', means a voluntary subordination to a dominant player in a key currency system. A weak currency
country has to take into account the stance of monetary policy of the strong
currency country. On the other hand, the strong position of the leading bank
is characterized by pursuing its policy independently from interests and strategies abroad.

5   Asymmetric games III: Germany's price level as the nominal anchor of the EMS

The founding fathers of the EMS for obvious political reasons tried to cir-
cumvent the question as to which currency should play the hegemonic role.
The artificial ECU should serve as a substitute and represent the 'democratic'
content of the EMS treaty (in practice, however, it was used almost exclusively for official bookkeeping purposes). Interventions on the foreign exchange should be executed by both central banks involved.

   The working of the EMS can be analysed by assuming that central banks
hold home (*h*) and foreign (*f*) reserves which represent the basic component

of money creation. The money supply for the home country (say Germany) and the foreign country (say France) is given by

$$m = h + f - \mu i \tag{5.15}$$

$$m^* = h^* + f^* - \mu i^*. \tag{5.16}$$

As before i and i^* represent the active policy instruments,[8] whereas the h items are assumed to be fixed. The f items no longer represent a voluntary demand for reserve assets as in the gold standard model, but endogenous variables instead. The 'democratic' solution of the $n - 1$ problem was incorporated into an intervention rule:

$$df = -df^*. \tag{5.17}$$

The idea of a symmetric bearing of adjustment costs did not work for several reasons:

- If one country systematically achieves lower inflation it gains a competitive advantage which causes a disequilibrium in the current account.
- Countries which were exposed to reserve losses sooner or later had to replenish them by means of restrictive monetary policies.
- Just because the EMS treaty intended to maintain the general autonomy of national monetary policy countries who suffered from, say, a wage push abroad ($dp/dw^* > 0$) were free to sterilize the monetary impact of the enforced intervention. Any attempt to do so aggravated the reserve problem of the foreign central bank ($df^*/di < 0$).

Financial assets denominated in the currency of the country with the best price performance are in short supply as they are demanded for intervention purposes. The ensuing scarcity of that currency makes the rate of interest of that country to 'rule the roost' because it bears a liquidity premium (compare De Grauwe 1994, p. 105). The question of which central bank advances to be the hegemonic leader of the system thus again depends on economic policy preferences. Notice that, in contrast to the gold standard, the other member countries perceive the dominance of the key currency central bank as a restrictive feature of the system which, at least in the short run, leads to employment and welfare losses.[9]

The EMS is historically the first pure paper currency standard.[10] This has some far-reaching consequences:

- The key currency itself, and not some gold reserve, is the final reserve asset to settle a balance-of-payment disequilibrium and to maintain desired levels of exchange rates.
- Although for these purposes in most cases sterling accounts were used, the Bank of England acted under the threat of gold withdrawals and thus suffered from a liquidity problem. This is no longer true with respect to the Bundesbank.

The standard game in the EMS also can be characterized by the attempt of both central banks to minimize loss functions expressing economic policy preferences and market constraints. The Bundesbank is assumed to be interested in price stability only:

$$L = (\bar{p} - p)^2. \qquad (5.18)$$

As mark assets advance to the reserve medium there is no necessity for the Bundesbank to hold French currency,[11] that is, $f = 0$ in (5.15). The structure of the Bundesbank's balance sheet then expresses the general logic of any bank's reserve holding: only assets of a superior quality compared to the bank's own issued notes can serve as a reserve. The privilege of the key currency central bank is that its own currency is the reserve of the whole currency system.

Because of the obligation to sustain the value of the franc, the Banque de France is forced to keep some optimal quantity of mark reserves $\bar{f}^*$ (whereas h^* is suppressed in (5.16) in order to simplify); the employment target, possibly above the NAIRU, is $\bar{y}^*$.

$$L^* = (\bar{f}^* - f^*)^2 + a^*(\bar{y}^* - y^*)^2. \qquad (5.19)$$

The equilibrium values of the macroeconomic variables (in the most simple case where $w = w^* = g = g^* = 0$) are given by

$$\underline{r} = -\frac{1}{\beta}\underline{y} = -\frac{1}{\beta}\underline{y}^* = -\frac{1}{\alpha\beta}\underline{p} = -\frac{1}{\alpha\beta}\underline{p}^* = \frac{\mu i - h}{\Omega} \qquad (5.20)$$

$$\underline{f}^* = h + \mu(i^* - i). \qquad (5.21)$$

This solution reveals the standard wisdom of a fixed exchange rate system: in contrast to the gold standard now the monetary policy of the leading country alone is able to influence activity levels of both economies whereas (due to the $n - 1$ problem) foreign interest rate policy only has a bearing on the desired level of its reserves.

The Bundesbank attains its single target without any interference with actions taken by the Banque de France. As the German price level according to (5.20) is completely controlled, the home reaction function is a horizontal line determining the level of the rate of interest necessary to maintain price stability. The loss of the Bundesbank is zero. The zero slope of its reaction function thus indicates the hegemonic position of the Bundesbank.

$$RF: \quad i = \frac{h}{\mu} - \frac{\Omega \bar{p}}{\alpha \beta \mu} \tag{5.22}$$

$$RF^*: \quad i^* = i + \frac{\bar{f}^* - h}{\mu}. \tag{5.23}$$

The Banque de France, on the other hand, is forced to follow German interest rate policies in order to defend the franc's parity on the foreign exchange. The French employment target in (5.19) actually cannot be controlled by the Banque de France. The French welfare loss depends mainly on the difference between the output target and the actual output level as determined by German monetary policy. Again, the weak country pursues a Stackelberg-leader strategy; because of the specific form of the Bundesbank's loss function, however, the S^* solution corresponds formally with the Nash solution (Figure 5.4).

6 Supply and demand shocks in the gold standard and in the EMS

Modern paper standard systems like the EMS – in relation to the gold standard – are less able to absorb supply or demand disturbances which emanate from the leading country. In order to compare the two systems more easily, the reason for the leadership role in each case is emphasized, that is, we assume an extreme interest in external equilibrium in Britain ($a = 0$ in (5.6)) and a perfect neglect of the foreign exchange in Germany (as already has been expressed in the corresponding loss function (5.18)).

If the Bank of England is interested only in the desired level of gold reserves it optimizes the difference of the two discount rates, neglecting their levels. The reserve target then is attained on any point of the British reaction function. This has a remarkable implication for the scope of foreign monetary policy: the French central bank has to accept that its reserve target cannot be reached, but it can choose the level of discount rates so that the desired output level can be achieved; this holds true regardless of any shocks which may occur. On the other hand, the EMS shows the reverse case: the French reach their reserve target but have to bear output losses if the Bundesbank aims at zero inflation in spite of high employment targets abroad or in cases of supply and demand shocks at home (Table 5.3).

Table 5.3   Loss levels in the S* solution

System/loss	L	L*
Gold standard	0	$(2\bar{q}-1)^2$
EMS	0	$a^*\left[\bar{y}^* - \dfrac{\bar{p}}{\alpha} + \dfrac{w+\alpha(2\varepsilon w^* + g - g^*)}{\alpha(1+2\alpha\varepsilon)}\right]^2$

The first row in Figure 5.4 shows the starting point in both systems, the second a supply shock, the third a demand shock, each emanating from the leading country. It is quite obvious and can be proved by simple algebra that the immediate reaction of monetary policy in the leading country in all cases is far more restrictive in the EMS. This in turn enforces a corresponding sharp increase of foreign interest rates as well and leads to large income and employment losses abroad. Because of rising welfare losses French politicians might decide to give up the fixed exchange rate. In general, therefore, the probability of a breakdown of a paper standard system when hit by a shock from the leading country is relatively large. The reason for this instability of the key currency system is quite obvious: in the gold standard the leading central bank does not react to an increase in prices as such, but only if inflation leads to a loss of gold reserves. Because the Bank of England thus did not pursue stabilization policies in the modern sense of the term, the member countries of the gold standard were not exposed to monetary restrictions as has been the case in the EMS.

7   The problem of internal and external equilibrium in the key currency country

If the Bank of England supported the stability of the gold standard by pursuing the goal of external equilibrium and if the Bundesbank undermined the stability of the EMS by fighting inflation at home, two obvious questions come up:

1. Why has it been possible for the Bank of England to neglect the target of internal stabilization? The simple answer is twofold: the problem of unemployment was relatively unimportant from a political point of view; and the trend of the price level was, if anything, falling, that is, the problem of inflation simply did not exist (Figure 5.5). Both peculiarities changed in the interwar period. Democracy and the increasing power of the unions precluded a continuation of a monetary policy strategy which had its only target in maintaining the equilibrium of the foreign ex-

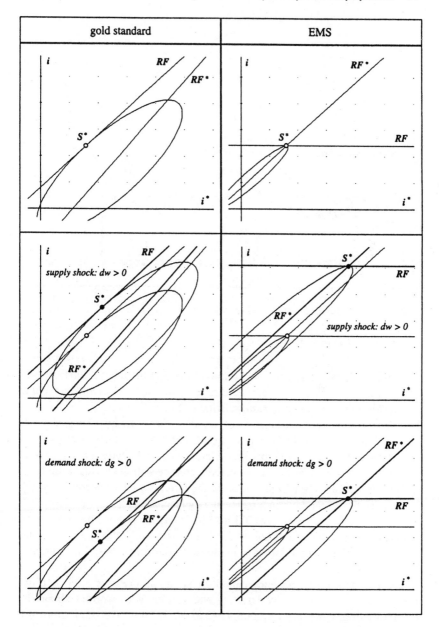

Figure 5.4   Effects of supply and demand shocks in the key currency country

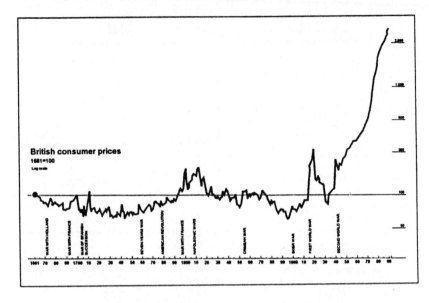

Source: *The Economist*, 22 February 1992.

Figure 5.5   The history of inflation

change market given the old and new parity of the pound. Interest rates
could not be increased any further and nominal wages did not come
down quickly enough to restore British competitiveness.[12]

2.   Why could the Bundesbank not stabilize the EMS by giving a larger
    weight to the target of external equilibrium? Why not optimize external
    stability by choosing an optimal relation of interest rates and an optimal
    level of interest rates for collective internal stability? This would not
    work because of the implications of the famous $n - 1$ problem: if the key
    currency central bank in a paper money standard took care of the stabil-
    ity of exchange rates it would lose its influence on income and prices.
    Thus some other institution (a foreign central bank? the unions?) would
    have to take over the job of providing the nominal anchor of the system.

   The idea that a key currency central bank should preserve price stability
can already be found in Wicksell (1898, p. 190) who worried about the
instability of any monetary system when exempted from the restrictions of a
gold standard. A casual inspection might suggest the proposition that it
makes no difference whether monetary policy controls the price of a single
good (gold) or the price of a bundle of goods (GDP). Experience of key
currency monetary policy after the demise of the gold standard reveals that it

makes a substantial difference: whereas the gold price can be stabilized on the foreign exchange market, general price level stability can only be enforced by restrictive activities on the goods and labour markets. Therefore, monetary policy comes into conflict with private and political employment interests. The quantity theory of money as the scientific foundation of practical monetarism has good reasons to play down this problem by resorting to the hypothesis of a direct link between money and prices.

However, it was just the fight for price stability in Germany which led to the breakdown of the fixed exchange rate agreement in the EMS. The general conclusion is that any paper standard system in contrast to a gold standard system suffers from a fundamental instability which has its origin in the centre of that system itself. A paper standard cannot provide a stable international monetary system if the key country's price level – which serves as the nominal anchor of the system – has to be stabilized by means of restrictive interest rate policies accompanied by a negative spillover on all member countries. This is the basic reason why modern key currency systems do not work. Thus there is at least some logic in the transition to a European Monetary Union.

Notes

1. The architecture of the model is basically the same as in Eichengreen (1987); see also Eichengreen (1984).
2. Neglecting expected exchange rate changes can be justified by virtue of the traditional 'restoration principle' (McKinnon 1993) according to which any short-term deviation from the once established exchange rate had to be reversed by means of economic policy actions. Market agents therefore expected a return to the previous level of the exchange rate and their activities supported the adjustment process (stabilizing speculation). The conclusions drawn in this chapter do not change, however, if expected exchange rate changes – leading to $r^* = r + \delta (p^* - p)$ – are taken into account.
3. Central banks are assumed to act according to policy preferences. Questions referring to the degree of independence of central banks from governmental orders cannot be tackled in this chapter (see, for example, Doyle and Wheale 1994).
4. Eichengreen's formulation of the central banks' preferences as contained in (5.6) and (5.7) can be criticized because missing the reserve target in both directions gets the same weight. A reformulation which attaches a smaller weight to an overshooting leads to an increase of the level of interest rates; this modification has no bearing, however, on the problem of leadership. Choosing different reserve targets $\bar{q}$ for each country does not alter the main conclusions of the model as this resembles the case of attaching a different weight to the goal of external equilibrium, which will be analysed below.
5. Constant supply and demand parameters have all been set to zero.
6. 'If in response to a discount rate increase abroad, the domestic central bank responds in kind, the increase in interest rates world-wide will provide an incentive for the foreign country to augment its stock of interest-bearing foreign exchange reserves. The supply of money available to domestic residents will be correspondingly reduced [sic!], requiring domestic money demand to decline to the level of supply through the reduction of prices, output and employment' (Eichengreen 1987, p. 23).
7. 'In deciding whether to change Bank Rate, the Bank of England ... looked almost exclusively at the size of its reserve. ... On the other hand, the Bank was little sensitive to the state of trade in Britain' (Sayers 1957, p. 61).

8. In practice, the most important central bank's interest rate in Germany is no longer the discount rate but rather the rate charged in repurchase agreements with the commercial banking sector.
9. Relative price stability, of course, is not a sufficient condition for establishing a leading position of a currency in a fixed exchange rate system. In the early 1990s, inflation was lower in France than in Germany. However, the attempt of the Banque de France to take over the leading position in the EMS by successively lowering French interest rates only intensified the speculation against the franc when the Bundesbank decided to keep German rates constant. Market agents considered the disposition of the French economy as one of repressed inflation so that monetary instability was expected to resurrect when the monetary control would no longer be exerted by the Bundesbank.
10. The Bretton Woods system was only a half-way abandonment of a metal-based key currency system (a full treatment of all three systems is given in Spahn 1996).
11. The actual large amount of dollar holdings are neglected as they have no role to play in the game under consideration.
12. Compare Eichengreen (1984), Bernanke (1993). The irony is that the US advanced to the key currency country because they attached a high value to the goal of internal monetary stability; otherwise they would have had to respond to the rise in gold reserves by lowering interest rates which in turn would have alleviated the British predicament.

References

Bernanke, B.S. (1993), 'The world on a cross of gold – a review of *Golden Fetters: The Gold Standard and the Great Depression, 1919–1939*', *Journal of Monetary Economics*, **31**, 251–67.

De Grauwe, P. (1994), *The Economics of Monetary Integration*, 2nd edn, Oxford: Oxford University Press.

Doyle, C. and M. Wheale (1994), 'Do we really want an independent central bank?', *Oxford Review of Economic Policy*, **10** (3), 61–77.

Eichengreen, B. (1984), 'Central bank cooperation under the interwar gold standard', *Explorations in Economic History*, **21**, 64–87.

Eichengreen, B. (1987), 'Conducting the international orchestra – Bank of England leadership under the classical gold standard', *Journal of International Money and Finance*, **6**, 5–29.

Lindert, P.H. (1969), *Key Currencies and Gold, 1900–1913*, Princeton: Princeton University Press.

McKinnon, R.I. (1993), 'The rules of the game – international money in historical perspective', *Journal of Economic Literature*, **31**, 1–44.

Sayers, R.S. (1957), *Central Banking after Bagehot*, Oxford: Clarendon.

Spahn, H.-P. (1996), 'Zinspolitik in Leitwährungssystemen – Goldstandard, Bretton Woods und EWS aus spieltheoretischer Sicht' [Interest rate policy in key currency systems – the gold standard, Bretton Woods, and the EMS], *Diskussionsbeiträge aus dem Institut für Volkswirtschaftslehre*, Universität Hohenheim, No. 120, Stuttgart.

Wicksell, K. (1898), *Interest and Prices – A Study of the Causes Regulating the Value of Money*, New York: Augustus Kelley (reprint 1965).

6 Coercing credibility: neoliberal policies and monetary institutions in developing and transitional economies

Ilene Grabel

(LDC's/   011 ESP P24
              016 ES2

1 Introduction

Nearly twenty years have passed since the economies of developing countries
began to be reconstituted along neoliberal lines. More recently, an ambitious
project of neoliberal economic reconstruction has been adopted in the former
socialist countries. Neoliberal economic policies and their institutional counterparts, such as autonomous central banks and currency boards, are presented by government officials and their Western advisers as the only *credible*
solution to the wide range of macroeconomic problems that are seen to
impede economic prosperity in the developing world and in countries under-
going a transition to capitalism.

Today, the notion of 'policy credibility' is invoked both casually and rigor-
ously as a salient basis on which to justify neoliberal economic policy and its
institutional corequisites (namely, 'independent' monetary institutions). Section 2 of the chapter discusses the practical implications of the incorporation
of the credibility criterion into economic debates in developing and transitional countries. In Section 3, I shall argue that the credibility criterion
presents a formidable obstacle to dissent and to serious consideration of
alternative economic programmes. This criterion has also been used to promote non-representative monetary policy-making institutions. In Section 4 I
conclude the chapter by offering two alternative criteria by which decisions
over economic policy and institutional governance could be adjudicated.

2 Credibility theory and application

In the following discussion I shall trace the use of the credibility criterion in
debates over the speed and character of economic reform programmes in
developing and transitional countries. I shall then examine the use of the
credibility criterion in an effort to privilege the creation of independent
monetary policy-making institutions.

Credibility and neoliberal economic programmes

The preoccupation with economic policy credibility emerged on the heels of
the failures of the ambitious neoliberal programmes in South America in the

late 1970s and early 1980s. By the mid-1980s, a consensus had emerged among neoclassical economists that despite the appropriateness of the neoliberal prescription, these programmes nevertheless failed to achieve their intended results because the policy community had not taken into account the *environment* in which these programmes were implemented (Grabel 1996a). This new focus on 'policy environment' is manifested in discussions of the appropriate macroeconomic preconditions for economic reform. One chief insight of the new revisionism is that careful attention must be paid to the question of whether economic reform programmes are deemed by the relevant economic actors to be *credible*.[1]

Today, the credibility criterion is centre stage in debates over economic reform in developing and transitional countries. In the transitional countries, 'shock therapy' rather than 'gradualism' is deemed by many to be the more credible reform path (Murphy et al. 1992; Sachs 1993).[2] Shock therapy is thought to send agents uniform, consistent information about the direction of the economy.

Unfortunately, the credibility and consistency of an economic reform programme is not easily assessed. At issue are the *perceptions* of economic actors concerning both the viability and effectiveness of the proposed policies and policy makers' commitment to sustain announced policies. The credibility argument depends on rather circular logic: economic policies are effective only if they are credible to private agents; but policies are deemed credible only if they are seen to be effective (Blackburn and Christensen 1989, p. 1).

The current preoccupation with credibility and consistency of economic reform programmes stems directly from the precepts of new-classical economics. In this approach, rational agents use the singular correct economic model and take into account all available information including the likelihood of policy reversal or collapse when forming expectations about the future.

How could economic policy be developed in this complex environment, in which the success of policy depends critically on agents' perceptions of its viability? There are essentially two choices: one could shade policy towards existing popular sentiments; or one could implement 'correct' policy, one that respected the economic fundamentals of neoclassical theory. The former option is ruled out of court on the simple grounds that 'incorrect' policy could not possibly retain credibility in the wake of the disruptions that would inevitably attend it. The latter, on the other hand, would induce credibility as it proved itself uniquely capable of promoting development and economic growth, even if it were to be unpopular in the short run. A correctly specified policy would therefore impel rational agents to act 'properly', at once achieving growth and the credibility necessary to sustain itself.

This theoretical insight about policy credibility has directly informed discussions of neoliberal reform programmes. The credibility of economic reform programmes is a precondition of their success. In developing and transitional countries, the responses of investors and decision makers in multilateral institutions are read as a measure of policy credibility. Hence, the infusions of domestic and foreign capital that often follow the adoption of neoliberal economic reforms are taken as evidence of the credibility of these efforts. For example, Chile's move to neoliberalism in the late 1970s and early 1980s was seen to be validated by foreign investors. By 1981, vast inflows of foreign capital (equal to 25 per cent of GDP), coupled with the celebration by the international business press of the Chilean 'miracle', conveyed credibility on the government's neoliberal reforms (Conley and Maloney 1995). The same dynamic played out following Mexico's 'rehabilitation' in the late 1980s and early 1990s (Grabel 1996b) and following the initial embrace of shock therapy in Poland and Russia (Gowan 1996).

'Credible' monetary policy-making institutions

These insights about credibility were soon elaborated in the context of consideration of optimal institutional structures, especially regarding the institutions that govern monetary policy (that is, central banks and, more recently, currency boards). The logic is straightforward: to be credible, monetary policy must be insulated from the vagaries of the political process, where short-sighted strategies often predominate. In the absence of political insulation, monetary policy can be manipulated instrumentally by governments seeking to garner political support. Aware of this possibility, the (rational) public will know that 'announced monetary policies may lack credibility because they are economically inconsistent or politically unsustainable' (Schmieding 1992, pp. 45–6).

Problems of monetary policy credibility may also arise if policy makers have a history of strategically reneging on policies they were previously committed to, in order to achieve a short-term political or economic objective. This is the problem of 'time inconsistency' (Kydland and Prescott 1977).[3] If a time-inconsistent monetary policy is implemented, the public is likely to sabotage the programme by engaging in behaviours such as capital flight which will ultimately engender a reversal of the initial policy. Monetary policy credibility (and hence, success) may also be threatened if monetary and fiscal policies are at cross-purposes, introducing the problem of 'Stackelberg warfare' (Blackburn and Christensen 1989, p. 27).

In the new-classical view, gaining the public's confidence in the technical abilities and the anti-inflationary resolve of monetary authorities in developing and transitional countries is no simple matter. In such countries, it is reasonable to expect that the public will have limited confidence in both the personnel of monetary policy-making institutions, and in the likelihood that the institution will be able to stay the course of politically unpopular policies. It is even reasonable for the public to question the longevity of new or reformed monetary policy-making institutions. These uncertainties may stem from the newness of the institutions themselves, from the legacy of high inflation and/or from the rapid turnover of personnel (Schmieding 1992, pp. 45–6). Staffing politically insulated monetary policy-making institutions with non-partisan technocrats is seen as a necessary condition for establishing policy credibility.

A 'credible monetary institution' may thus be defined as one that is able 'to use the instruments of monetary control without instruction, guidance, or interference from the government' (Henning 1994, p. 63). The hallmarks of these credible institutions are their willingness to implement and sustain correct policy, even in the face of short-term dislocations that they might induce. Freed from undue political influence, these autonomous institutions achieve credibility by demonstrating a steadfast commitment to the neoliberal agenda. Thus reassured, economic actors will rationally commit to behaviours that promote the success of neoliberalism and, thereby, the welfare of society.

Central banks   Independent central banks have recently been established in many Latin American countries – these include Argentina, Chile, Colombia, Mexico and Venezuela. In Asia, the Philippine central bank stands alone as the region's only independent central bank. In the transitional countries, independent central banks have recently been established in Albania, Armenia, Bulgaria, the Czech Republic, Estonia, Hungary, Poland and Romania (Loungani and Sheets 1995).[4] The rise of independent central banks reflects the widespread acceptance of the theoretical view that monetary policy credibility is strengthened by central bank autonomy. The IMF–World Bank also put pressure on developing and transitional country governments to establish independent central banks in myriad ways, including advising and training of bank officials.

The case for independent central banks follows rather directly from the general views (described above) on the prerequisites for credible policy. Central bank independence imparts a degree of credibility to monetary policy which cannot be achieved when policy is developed by elected politicians. This credibility stems from the political insulation of the institution. Armed with respect for the precepts of neoclassical economic theory, and protected by institutional barriers from political contamination, the non-partisan technocrats who staff independent central banks are able to pursue credible (and time-consistent) monetary policy in pursuit of an anti-inflationary course for the national economy (Blackburn and Christensen 1989).

Given the ability of independent central banks to carry out painful defla-
tionary programmes in developing and transitional countries, there is a rather
direct link between far-reaching neoliberal reform and efforts to reorganize
central bank governance. As Bowles and White (1994, p. 237) write:

> [A]lthough the case for central bank independence is primarily based on provid-
> ing lower inflationary outcomes, it also resonates with a wider agenda aimed at
> restoring 'discipline' and 'credibility' to economic decision-making in general.

Maintaining central bank independence is one way that the public and (domestic and foreign) investors can be assured that the central bank will be able
to pursue anti-inflationary monetary policy, and hence foster a favourable
investment climate.

A vast empirical literature seeks to substantiate the theoretical claims for
the anti-inflationary performance of independent central banks. Initial studies
focused on central banks in developed countries; these tended to confirm the
hypothesis (Alesina and Summers 1993; Blackburn and Christensen 1989).
More recently, efforts have been undertaken to substantiate these claims in
the context of developing and transitional countries. In a study of 12 transitional countries, Loungani and Sheets (1995) find that transitional countries
with independent central banks experience lower levels of inflation and greater
macroeconomic stability than do countries with dependent central banks.[5]

While central bank independence is now taken as a necessary step to
achieve credibility, it is not generally viewed as sufficient. Where central
banks are new institutions (as in the transitional countries) or where the
public has little confidence in these institutions (as in many developing countries), it may also be necessary to import central bank credibility by adopting
the actual operating guidelines of credible Western central banks or by importing central bank staff directly (Schmieding 1992, p. 55). Indeed, the
German Bundesbank Law has been adopted by the new Polish, Hungarian,
Czechoslovak and Bulgarian central banks (ibid., pp. 55–8 and fn. 59). But
not only can credibility be imported from abroad, it can also be 'enforced' or
'created' via externally imposed constraints on central bank operations. Such
constraints might involve conditioning foreign aid, loans and/or technical
assistance on the adherence to certain central bank operating practices (such
as a refusal to finance government debt) (ibid., p. 62).

The adoption of rule-based – rather than discretionary – monetary policy
may also enhance central bank credibility. These rules might take the form of
monetary growth rules or inflation targets. As before, this may involve importing credible rules from abroad. Obviously, central bank credibility will
only be enhanced by these constraints as long as the rules themselves do not
introduce time inconsistency or Stackelberg warfare, and as long as the

public is confident that the rules will not be breached. This introduces a game-theoretic dilemma in which central banks must search for increasingly credible means by which rules can be enforced. If the public does not find the central bank's commitment to policy rules sufficiently credible, then the central bank may seek to have these rules incorporated into the legal system of the country. If mere laws are not sufficiently credible, then a constitutional amendment might be pursued (a 'meta-rule') (ibid., p. 50). Perhaps because of these dilemmas, central bank reform efforts tend to side-step rule-based policy.[6] Instead, these efforts more modestly aim to establish institutional independence.

Currency boards   The impetus behind the creation of currency boards in developing and transitional countries is identical to that driving the creation of independent central banks. Currency boards represent another means by which monetary policy credibility can be created.

Historically, some 70 countries have created currency boards. Today, currency boards are operating in Lithuania, Argentina, Estonia, Hong Kong, Bermuda, Cayman Islands, Falkland Islands, Faroe Islands, Gibraltar and Djibouti.[7] Recent IMF reports (1996, 1997) use the success of existing boards as a basis on which to argue for their adoption elsewhere.

A currency board is a monetary institution which issues local currency that is fully backed by stocks of a hard foreign 'reserve currency'. By law, the local currency is fully convertible upon demand and without limit into the foreign reserve currency at a fixed rate of exchange. The rate of exchange between the local and the foreign reserve currency is inviolable: the IMF recommends that the exchange rate be written into the currency board's constitution (IMF 1996, 1997; Hanke et al. 1993). The reserves held by the currency board consist of low-risk, interest-earning securities and other assets payable in the reserve currency. The amount of foreign reserves held by the currency board must be equal to 100 to 110 per cent (as set by law) of the value of the local money stock.

From the perspective of new-classical theory, currency boards have much to recommend them. The credibility of the local currency may be enhanced via the direct link to hard foreign currency holdings. The public can thus be confident in the ability of the currency board to prevent debasement of the local currency. This confidence may prevent the public from engaging in currency substitution, destabilizing speculation against the local currency, and more generally, in actions that will undermine the stability of the domestic monetary system. Exchange rate stability may also buttress foreign investors' confidence in the domestic economy.

Currency boards complement the operations of independent central banks by providing another means by which the private sector can be assured that monetary management will proceed undisturbed by political pressure. Indeed, currency board credibility is seen to exceed that of independent central banks. This is because currency boards have responsibility for a very narrow set of tasks, while central banks (independent or not) have a broad range of responsibilities.

Currency boards help fill the 'credibility deficit' that confronts even independent central banks in countries where these institutions are new or where they have a poor track record. A recent IMF report on currency boards asserts that they offer a 'relatively effective way [for a country] to manage its currency in the face of limited central banking experience or low policy credibility' (IMF 1996, p. 179). Like central banks, they are to be autonomous – with their members drawn from the ranks of technocrats, economists and bankers, and appointed for multiple-year terms – to ensure that monetary policy is in the hands of an independent authority that does not have strategic incentives to veer towards an expansionary course.

Currency boards epitomize the credibility advantages of rule-based monetary policy; in all cases where currency boards have existed, they have operated in accordance with a strict set of simple, transparent rules. Hence, they possess even less scope for discretion than do independent central banks (IMF 1996, 1997). These legally (and in some cases constitutionally) binding rules, coupled with institutional independence, preclude currency boards from ceding to political pressures for monetary expansion. The association between currency board credibility and ('meta-') rule-based operations echoes previously discussed aspects of new-classical theory. As one prominent proponent of currency boards put it: '[al]though the rational expectations school has never considered in detail a currency board, the arguments ... lend support to the case for currency boards, since currency boards are rule-bound and have no discretion in monetary policy' (Hanke et al. 1993, p. 39).

As we have noted, rule-based policies are not *prima facie* guarantors of policy credibility. In countries where the rule of law may have meant little in the past, monetary rules that have a legal or even a constitutional basis may not themselves be credible. As with independent central banks, the credibility of currency board rules may be enhanced by introducing credible external mechanisms for ensuring compliance with the rules. This may involve efforts to import credibility by placing representatives of foreign central banks or multilateral institutions on currency boards, or by conditioning external financial or technical support on the compliance of the currency board with predetermined rules. Indeed, a model currency board constitution prepared for Russia by US consultants contains just such provisions for importing credibility. The proposed Russian currency board constitution 'includes a provision that a majority of the board of directors be foreigners. That will help prevent the government from bending the rules of the currency board' (ibid., p. 110).

It should be emphasized that the contemporary appeal of currency boards may derive from the complementarity between board operations and neoliberal economic reform. This complementarity is particularly evident when one considers the central role of efforts to promote reductions in government spending and increased external openness in neoliberal reform efforts. Given that currency board rules preclude the printing of 'fiat money' by central banks, currency boards provide a mechanism for ensuring that governments exercise fiscal discipline.

Currency board operations also complement neoliberal reform efforts that promote external economic openness. This is because currency board rules stipulate that the local money supply can only be increased following an increase in foreign exchange holdings. An increase in foreign exchange holdings may result from improved net export performance or from private capital inflows. Hence, expansion of the local money supply is predicated on the success of capital and current account liberalization.

3   A critical assessment of the credibility criterion

We now turn to a critical assessment of the use of the credibility criterion as a means of privileging neoliberal reforms and independent monetary policy-making institutions.

Credibility and neoliberal programmes

Recall that a key premise of the credibility criterion is that all agents in an economy uniformly derive their expectations about the consequences of an economic reform programme from the *same* correct neoclassical model (that is, the rational expectations hypothesis). If one rejects the notion that all agents rely on the same economic model, then it becomes apparent that the effects of an economic reform programme are exceedingly difficult to predict (compare McCallum 1983). If agents act on expectations formed under different models, then they will pursue behaviours that generate unpredictable macroeconomic outcomes, including outcomes that jeopardize the viability of the reform programme (Frydman and Phelps 1983). Thus, a rejection of the assumption of rational expectations complicates *ex-ante* judgements regarding the credibility of any economic programme.

But let us assume for the sake of argument that agents form their expectations rationally and that under *normal circumstances* economic agents could assign the identical, correct probability distribution to the likelihood of policy failure or reversal. This presumption is nevertheless implausible in the case of a *unique* policy reform such as a full-scale neoliberal reform. As Lucas (1973) notes, the non-recurrent nature of regime shifts affords no basis for applying past learning. Hence, agents might be expected to form diverse and inconsistent subjective probability distributions regarding policy reversal or collapse, and take actions that undermine the new policy (Conley and Maloney 1995; Frydman and Phelps 1983). These complications, which follow from the uncertainty of a regime shift, are simply ignored by those who argue for the credibility of neoliberal reform programmes.

But matters are more complicated still. Adjustments of expectations and behaviour in the wake of regime shifts occur in real time. In the process of adjustment, we must recognize the influence of any number of informational asymmetries and imperfections (Agenor and Taylor 1992). The behaviour of agents in the short run may very well generate economic outcomes that are inconsistent with long-term policy objectives. These complications are *seemingly* ignored by today's neoliberal policy makers and their Western consultants. Their implication, after all, is that policy design is a much trickier business than we may have thought.

Credibility and democracy I say *seemingly* ignored because they are in fact dealt with *implicitly*, and unfortunately, with severe undemocratic implications. This is indeed the most problematic aspect of the way in which the criterion of policy credibility has been incorporated in theoretical and policy debate. This criterion has been exploited to discredit and bar the implementation of all non-neoliberal economic programmes, including gradualist reforms in some transitional countries. We must examine this problem in some detail.

At first blush, it may seem that a proposition that states that credible policies are more likely to succeed is perfectly innocuous. But in the volatile political context in which neoliberal programmes were and are introduced in developing and transitional countries, this criterion has a malevolent import.

We can expose this malevolent face by reducing the credibility criterion for macroeconomic policy to a straightforward set of propositions. These propositions are quite simple, and yet they form the theoretical foundation of the new-classical approach to macroeconomic policy and institutions. The propositions may be stated as follows: (i) an economic regime (policy or institution) will garner credibility only to the degree that it is likely to survive; (ii) an economic regime is likely to survive only to the degree that it attains its stated objectives; (iii) an economic regime is likely to achieve its stated objectives only to the degree that it induces behaviours (in the aggregate) that are consistent with these objectives; (iv) an economic regime is likely to induce consistent behaviours only to the degree that it reflects and operationalizes the *true* theory of market economies; and (v) an economic regime reflects the true theory of market economies only to the degree that it is *neoclassical*.

The exclusionary, dissent-suppressing manoeuvre that has been undertaken here is captured in propositions (iv) and (v). *Alternative economic theories are summarily banned on the grounds that they could not possibly meet the unforgiving 'credibility' test, because they could not possibly be true.* Hence, policy regimes founded upon them must collapse, in part because of the inconsistent behaviours they necessarily induce. Writing on the intellectual maturation of the new-classical economics, Frydman and Phelps (1983, pp. 27–8) identify this aspect of new-classical economics as a barrier to intellectual pluralism. In their words, the 'thoroughgoing implementation of the rational expectations method in policy-making would entail the official promotion, or "establishment", of one model over others'. Indeed, so sure are policy makers and their advisers that neoliberal policies are necessarily best for all countries that IMF staff and advisers like Jeffrey Sachs travel the world prescribing 'a one size fits all' reform package (see Sachs 1994).

Notice the epistemological foundation of this perspective: governments and their Western advisers impute credibility to policies based on the purported truth of the theory from which these policies derive. In a deft manoeuvre, foreign advisers are presented as omniscient, benevolent figures issuing decrees for the betterment of citizens in the target countries. *Of dissent – in the academy or in the streets – the best that could be said is that it threatens to disrupt the credibility of the instituted policies by undermining confidence in them and inducing inconsistent expectations, thereby jeopardizing the entire 'liberal' policy regime.* In both these respects – the theoretical and the political – the credibility criterion bars the plurality of views and denies the value of dissent, both hallmarks of liberal democratic society.

Creating policy credibility   It should be acknowledged that in assuming the *exogeneity of policy credibility*, neoclassical theorists deny the significance of factors that are *endogenous* to all societies,[8] particularly class conflict and power, which significantly influence the likelihood of macroeconomic policy success, and hence, its credibility. In the particular case of the neoliberal experiments in developing and transitional countries, the credibility of these programmes is typically the result not of their exogenous properties – their presumed truth – but of their endogenous enforcement by domestic and foreign capital and the state, which have often repressed trade unions, abused human rights, stifled dissent, and relied on the support and financial resources of international and domestic elites, foreign governments and multilateral institutions. The credibility of neoclassical policies is secured, then, through the mobilization of political and economic power. Such power is critical given that a move to neoliberalism – let alone a transition to capitalism – requires a radical restructuring of economic and social life (Gowan 1995, p. 12; Burkett 1997).

From this perspective, the support of foreign capital in the form of inflows of direct foreign and portfolio investments or loans (or the threat of withdrawal) is critical because it *creates* policy credibility rather than signifies it. The importation of outside 'experts' plays the same role: the act of 'signalling credibility' should be understood to produce the effect of credibility rather than merely to reveal something that was already there, latent in the regime itself.

Recent events in developing and transitional countries exemplify these arguments about endogenous policy credibility. During the recent Argentine election the IMF, domestic and international capital and the state jointly acted to demonstrate the credibility of the government's commitment to neoliberal policy. In this case, policy credibility was secured via private and multilateral financial support (and the threatened withdrawal thereof) and through state repression of dissent against neoliberalism (Richards 1996).[9]

In the Russian case, the government has effectively used external financial support and political repression in order to signal to private investors that its commitment to neoliberal reform is credible. In the conflict between the imposition of neoliberalism and the popular will, the Russian government has opted for the former over the latter (Gowan 1996). More generally, Gowan (1995, 1996) and Amsden et al. (1994) note that throughout the transitional countries, IMF and World Bank financial and technical support plays a pivotal role in maintaining investor confidence in the longevity of neoliberal reforms.

Conversely, it must be acknowledged that non-neoclassical economic programmes are made *endogenously incredible* because those regimes that attempt to put them into place are often not able to curb the ability of domestic and international capital to engage in activities that undermine these programmes, such as capital flight or the withdrawal of external loans, aid, trade credits or technical assistance programmes. For example, the Polish, Hungarian and Czechoslovak governments in the early 1990s were forced by the IMF to abandon plans to pursue non-neoliberal economic programmes involving industrial development strategies and state-financing mechanisms. IMF and World Bank financial and technical assistance programmes to transitional countries stipulate that recipient governments could neither place restrictions on foreign direct investment nor encourage development banking. The Polish case is particularly dramatic in this regard: the terms of a World Bank loan agreement constrained the ability of the Polish Development Bank to issue direct, subsidized industrial loans. Moreover, these multilateral institutions have even barred transitional countries from pursuing gradualist reform or state capitalist models (Gowan 1995, 1996; Amsden et al. 1994).

I am arguing here that the way in which the credibility criterion is presently understood by neoclassical theorists and policy advisers reflects a particular vision of society. That vision is of a society marked by homogeneous and harmonious goals and expectations, and in which governments, to the extent that they can free themselves from interest groups, are able to implement policies designed to secure these goals. In short, it is a vision of society free of class and other social, economic and cultural conflicts. What is absent from this view is an understanding that in societies that are stratified by wealth, class and power, all economic policies are inherently biased in terms of their effects. Policies always serve some interests against others. Hence, policy credibility, in the context considered here, always means securing the wilful consent of some groups and the coercive acquiescence of others. This conflict-based view of policy is of course no less true of neoliberal regimes than of redistributive regimes. Credibility, in short, is founded on politics, not metaphysics.

Turning now to the empirical usefulness of the credibility criterion, the criterion has both dissent-suppressing and tautological attributes. As this criterion is presently employed, it precludes any substantive empirical refutation of the neoliberal programme. It can always be claimed *ex post* that the environment in which neoliberal programmes were implemented was not credible, and thus that the failure of the policies to achieve their intended results does not stem from flawed prescriptions. This is indeed the most commonly employed explanation offered for the failure of the neoliberal experiments in the Southern Cone[10] and for the difficulties encountered by the transitional countries.[11] As a consequence, this criterion precludes any meaningful empirical verification or refutation of the policies inspired by neoclassical theory.

Credibility and monetary policy-making institutions

A key advantage of independent institutions of monetary policy making is that their political insulation is seen to create the conditions whereby non-partisan technocrats can credibly pursue anti-inflationary monetary policy (in the case of central banks) and exchange rate stability (in the case of currency boards). Central bank and currency board credibility then necessitates that policy makers be unaccountable to the public in order to preclude capture by opportunistic politicians. Given the important distributional effects of monetary and exchange rate policy, a lack of accountability on the part of officials who make these policies raises important concerns about democratic practice. Why should efforts to secure investor confidence in the credibility of monetary and exchange rate policy dominate other important societal goals, such as the reduction of economic inequality?

Following from the above, we should see that the idea that independent central banks and currency boards are 'apolitical' is problematic. As economic institutions, independent central banks and currency boards 'do not exist "above" or "outside" politics but are embedded in a complex matrix of political forces' (Bowles and White 1994, p. 240). It must be recognized that

policy-making institutions that are structurally precluded from capture by
elected officials nevertheless operate in accordance with particularist interests. In the case of independent central banks and currency boards, investors
comprise the relevant interest group for which concerns about monetary and
exchange rate policy credibility are paramount. Thus, while neoclassical
economists would likely counter that the 'national economic interest' may be
served by pursuing monetary and exchange rate policies that appear to be in
investors' interests, the conflict-based view of policy (and society) adopted
here forces a rejection of this claim.

4 Towards alternative credibility criteria
In view of the anti-democratic political and intellectual implications of the
contemporary use of the credibility criterion, the basis for two alternative
criteria are suggested below.

Democratic credibility: maximizing veto points
As argued above, the credibility of all economic policy regimes is inherently
endogenous. In this case, we must take account of the distribution of power in
society as we ascertain the credibility of any particular regime. One useful
way to think about this is in terms of what Tsebelis (1994) calls 'veto points'.
Under different social structures, different critical actors are better or less
able to 'veto' or influence policy success through their behaviour. Occupants
of important veto points enjoy a disproportionate ability to defeat a policy
regime that they oppose. We can say that under a neoliberal economic policy
regime, the business community and especially wealthy investors occupy the
most powerful veto points. To weight policy credibility as a fundamental
objective under such conditions merely rewards the wealthy for their privilege. In contrast, progressives ought to seek a social structure that transfers
meaningful veto authority to the least-advantaged sectors of the population;
then, and only then, should credibility be treated normatively as a valid
decision variable.

We may attempt to operationalize this (admittedly abstract) idea of democratizing veto authority by developing a progressive criterion for economic
policy credibility, termed here the 'principle of democratic credibility'. This
criterion does not reject the idea of policy credibility, but rather substantially
*broadens the range of potential policy veto authority while weakening the
truth standard against which policy credibility should be adjudicated.* Using
the principle of democratic credibility, only those economic policies that are
not apt to be vetoed by the least advantaged, were they to have the power to
do so, would be deemed credible. Using this standard, macroeconomic policies are not deemed true and hence credible only to the extent that they
operationalize one theory of the economy – that attributed to neoclassical

theory. Rather, this agnostic standard allows for the credibility of a range of alternative economic programmes, provided that these programmes are validated by the broader citizenry. Using this criterion, heterodox or expansionary economic programmes would not be ruled exogenously incredible; instead, their sabotage by the self-fulfilling actions of elites and the Western policy community would be seen as an illegitimate exercise of political power in defence of particularist interests. Exposing the endogeneity of policy credibility in this way might serve to enable more effective resistance to these behaviours.

One should note that this standard alone does not in any way guarantee that only progressive economic policies will be implemented. This is why other complementary criteria for adjudicating economic policy must be pursued alongside this one. For example, such additional criteria might focus on the determination of whether economic policies are guided by egalitarian or redistributive goals.

Adjudicating the democratic validation of macro policy regimes is of course a complicated matter, one that is necessarily tied to culturally-determined understandings of enfranchisement and democracy. Such determinations are additionally complicated by the class-based nature of society. At a minimum, this determination should reflect the views of those groups such as the poor and other often disenfranchised populations. As radical as this standard might appear, *it is neither stronger nor more restrictive than the credibility criterion employed today.* Indeed, unlike the authoritarian neoclassical criterion, which determines *in advance of all debate* the direction of policy changes, this flexible standard allows for dynamic pragmatic adjustments, reflecting a collective learning by doing, as a normal outcome of governance. Moreover and finally, against the neoclassical vision, a democratic approach would embrace and emphasize a range of higher criteria to be used in the specification of macro policy, such as respect for human and labour rights.

On the matter of creating what are seen as credible monetary policy-making institutions – that is, independent central banks and currency boards – it is clear that this trend flies in the face of the principle of democratic credibility. Indeed, the very credibility of independent central banks and currency boards stems directly from their insulation from the population and the degree to which technocrats are able to exert unilateral control over decision making. By contrast, democratic central bank and currency board representation requires those major social and economic groups that are demonstrably affected by monetary and exchange rate policy, and who may have divergent interests *vis-à-vis* policy, to have some means to influence policy direction.[12] This view necessarily rejects the notion that all constituencies in society ultimately benefit from one particular 'good' monetary and exchange rate policy. Rather, given the wide-reaching distributive effects of monetary and exchange rate policies it is critical that the goals and implementation of policy be debated in order to take account of the divergent agendas or needs of different constituencies.

Of course, the desire to ensure democratic accountability and widen representation of social constituencies by increasing the veto points over monetary and exchange rate policies runs up against the problem that, if these are taken too far, the institution loses its 'credibility' in the eyes of financial communities and markets. This necessarily raises the broader issue of what are the appropriate goals of central banks and currency boards. As Arestis and Bain (1995) argue, these goals should be broadened to include more than controlling inflation and maintaining exchange rate stability. If, for instance, a central bank or currency board operated in a manner consistent with Keynes's views it would be subordinate to the government as part of the institutional structure ensuring public control over private agents in the economy (ibid.).

The principle of fallibility in policy formulation and monetary management
A second criterion for assessing macro policy formulation and the governance structure of monetary policy-making institutions follows directly from the foregoing critique of the credibility thesis. I call this the 'principle of fallibility' in policy formulation and monetary management.

The principle of fallibility begins with the presumption that the premises on which economic policies are founded are necessarily inherently imperfect. I have alluded to some of the difficulties in this regard in the previous discussion of the complexity of such a seemingly straightforward concept like credibility, which is undermined by differences among agents' expectations and so on. Thus it follows that the outcome of macroeconomic policy cannot be predicted with certainty in advance of implementation. The principle of fallibility therefore simply calls for humility on the part of national leaders and their advisers.

The recognition of fallibility has clear implications for the content of economic policy and the conduct of monetary and exchange rate policy, especially if one takes seriously traditional liberal and left concerns about economic inequality. The fallibility criterion requires that economic policy makers and monetary authorities adopt a conservative standard for policy design that might *not only* target the improvement of the economic circumstances of the most disadvantaged groups, *but also* is likely to minimize the harm to the least advantaged, *in the event that a policy fails*. This standard is similar to the institutionalist criterion of minimal dislocation from economic policy, termed the 'fundamental principle of economics' (Foster 1981).

5   Conclusion

I have argued that the notion of credibility as developed within neoclassical theory has substantial anti-democratic effects. Despite the common conflation of economic liberalism and political democracy in popular and theoretical discourse, it is not surprising that neoclassical policy consultants continue to serve as chief counsel to authoritarian and demagogic regimes. Given that only neoclassical policies can survive the demanding credibility test, the suppression of dissent becomes an instrumental means towards the advancement of the common good.

In contrast, adoption of the standard of 'democratic credibility' would reinstate public debate and dissent as integral components of democratic policy making, especially in stratified societies. Moreover, recognition of the 'principle of fallibility' might induce humility among policy makers and encourage them to consider the possible adverse consequences of macro policy regime shifts and institutional reform prior to their implementation. Together, the adoption of these two principles would entail public debate over the distributive consequences of different types of macro policies and institutional structures, something which is generally lacking as a criterion for policy evaluation today.

Notes

1. Blackburn and Christensen (1989) and Persson (1988) survey the policy credibility literature.
2. By contrast, Dewatripont and Roland (1995) argue for gradualism because it introduces far less political opposition.
3. Persson (1988) surveys the time-inconsistency literature.
4. Whether legal independence translates into operational independence is an important consideration. For example, among the transitional countries, the Armenian, Hungarian, Polish and Romanian central banks are seen to have less operational independence than the Albanian, Bulgarian, Czech Republic and Estonian central banks (Loungani and Sheets 1995). In view of the problems with inferring operational from legal independence, Cukierman et al. (1992) develop several measures of central bank independence in a study of 72 countries (compare Maxfield 1994).
5. The findings of these studies have been challenged; indeed, a substantial body of empirical work finds that central bank governance neither accounts for observed price stability nor leads to positive economic outcomes (Bowles and White 1994; Cardim de Carvahlo 1995–96; Mas 1995).
6. However, currency board operations are rule based (see below).
7. Hanke et al. (1993, App. C) describes all current and past currency boards. Bosnia and Herzogovina is about to establish a currency board (IMF 1997).
8. Burkett and Lotspeich (1993) discuss endogenous policy specification.
9. In this election, President Carlos Menem was able to suppress popular dissent against neoliberal policies by promising that dire circumstances (such as investor flight) would necessarily follow any attempt to veer from the neoliberal course that he charted during his first term. Had he been defeated, his predictions might well have been confirmed in part because of the expectations of flight that his own campaign induced!
10. The other explanation offered is that these programmes were improperly sequenced (Grabel 1996a).

11. Gowan (1995) discusses Sachs' efforts to account for the disappointing early results of the transitional country reforms.
12. See Epstein's (1988) arguments for 'democratizing' the US Federal Reserve.

Bibliography

Agnenor, P.R. and M. Taylor (1992), 'Testing for credibility effects', *International Monetary Fund Staff Papers*, **39** (3), 545–71.
Alesina, A. and L. Summers (1993), 'Central bank independence and macroeconomic performance: some comparative evidence', *Journal of Money, Credit and Banking*, **25** (2), 151–62.
Amsden, A., J. Kochanowicz and L. Taylor (1994), *The Market Meets its Match*, Cambridge, MA: Harvard University Press.
Arestis, P. and K. Bain (1995), 'The independence of central banks: a nonconventional perspective', *Journal of Economic Issues*, **XXIX** (1), 161–74.
Blackburn, K. and M. Christensen (1989), 'Monetary policy and policy credibility: theories and evidence', *Journal of Economic Literature*, **XXVII**, 1–45.
Bowles, P. and G. White (1994), 'Central bank independence: a political economy approach', *Journal of Development Studies*, **31** (2), 235–64.
Burkett, P. (1997), 'Democracy and economic transitions', *Studies in Political Economy*, **52**, 111–36.
Burkett, P. and R. Lotspeich (1993), 'Review essay: *The Order of Economic Liberalization: Financial Control in the Transition to a Market Economy* (R. McKinnon)', *Comparative Economic Studies*, **35** (1), 59–84.
Cardim de Carvalho, F. (1995–96), 'The independence of central banks: a critical assessment of the arguments', *Journal of Post-Keynesian Economics*, **18** (2), 159–75.
Conley, J. and W. Maloney (1995), 'Optimal sequencing of credible reforms with uncertain outcomes', *Journal of Development Economics*, **48**, 151–66.
Cukierman, A., S. Webb and B. Neyapti (1992), 'Measuring independence of central banks and its effect on policy outcomes', *World Bank Economic Review*, **6** (3), 353–98.
Dewatripont, M. and G. Roland (1995), 'The design of reform packages under uncertainty', *American Economic Review*, **85** (5), 1207–23.
Epstein, G. (1988), 'Democratizing the Fed is a necessary first step', *Dollars and Sense*, **136**, 130–22.
Foster, J.F. (1981), 'Current structure and future prospects of institutional economics', *Journal of Economic Issues*, **15**, 943–7.
Frydman, R. and E. Phelps (eds) (1983), *Individual Forecasting and Aggregate Outcomes: Rational Expectations*, New York: CUNY Press.
Gowan, P. (1995), 'Neo-liberal theory and practice for Eastern Europe', *New Left Review*, **213**, 3–60.
Gowan, P. (1996), 'Eastern Europe, Western power and neo-liberalism', *New Left Review*, **216**, 129–40.
Grabel, I. (1996a), 'Financial markets, the state and economic development: controversies within theory and policy', *International Papers in Political Economy*, **3** (1), 1–42.
Grabel, I. (1996b), 'Marketing the Third World: the contradictions of portfolio investment in the global economy', *World Development*, **24** (11), 1761–76.
Hanke, S., L. Jonung and K. Schuler (1993), *Russian Currency and Finance*, London: Routledge.
Henning, C.R. (1994), *Currencies and Politics in the US, Germany, and Japan*, Washington, DC: Institute for International Economics.
International Monetary Fund (1996), 'Currency boards circumscribe discretionary monetary policy', *IMF Survey*, 20 May.
International Monetary Fund (1997), 'Currency board arrangements more widely used', *IMF Survey*, 24 February.
Kydland, F. and E. Prescott (1977), 'Rules rather than discretion: the inconsistency of optimal plans', *Journal of Political Economy*, **85**, 473–91.
Loungani, P. and N. Sheets (1995), *Central bank independence, inflation and growth in transition economies*, International Finance Discussion Papers, Federal Reserve System, No. 519.

Lucas, R., Jr. (1973), 'Some international evidence on output–inflation tradeoffs', *American Economics Review*, **63**, 326–34.

Mas, I. (1995), 'Central bank independence: a critical view from a developing country perspective', *World Development*, **23** (10), 1639–52.

Maxfield, S. (1994), 'Financial incentives and central bank authority in industrializing nations', *World Politics*, **46**, 556–88.

McCallum, J. (1983), 'Policy "credibility" and economic behaviour', *Journal of Post-Keynesian Economics*, **VI** (1), 47–52.

Murphy, K., A. Shleifer and R. Vishny (1992), 'The transition to a market economy: pitfalls of partial reform', *Quarterly Journal of Economics*, **107** (3), 889–906.

Persson, T. (1988), 'Credibility of macroeconomic policy: an introduction and broad survey', *European Economic Review*, **32**, 519–32.

Richards, D. (1996), 'The political economy of recent Latin American elections', mimeograph, Department of Economics, Indiana State University.

Sachs, J. (1993), *Poland's Jump to the Market Economy*, Cambridge, MA: MIT Press.

Sachs, J. (1994), 'Life in the economic emergency room', in J. Williamson (ed.), *The Political Economy of Policy Reform*, Washington, DC: Institute for International Economics, pp. 501–24.

Schmieding, H. (1992), *Lending Stability to Europe's Emerging Market Economies*, Tübingen, Germany: J.C.B. Mohr.

Tsebelis, G. (1994), 'Decision-making in political systems: veto players in presidentialism, parliamentarism, multicameralism and multipartism', mimeograph, Department of Political Science, UCLA.

7 Credibility: measurement and impacts. Central bank experience and Euro- (Europe) perspectives

Georg Erber and Harald Hagemann

ESP

F33 F36

1 Introduction

Credibility has become a common term in economic publications over the last couple of years (see, for example, Currie and Levine 1993), when one starts to assess possible outcomes especially of policy actions of governments and central banks (see, for example, Blackburn and Christensen 1989; Blackburn 1992; Cukierman 1992, 1995). But the notion of credibility is related to all kinds of human relations where contracts between economic agents comprise intertemporal exchange. The promised actions by economic agents have to be fulfilled according to an explicit or implicit contractual agreement. If behaviour expected because of a contractual relation is not effective at the time when it becomes due, people will start to reassess their own commitments and change their own behaviour accordingly. In Western democracies, the state takes care that commitments given to others in a legal contract can be enforced in cases of violation. But many contracts between economic agents have no legal foundation even if they are crucial for the people involved. The legal system invented by Western civilization as a protective measure against arbitrary violation of important commitments between different people or institutions is one of the outstanding social innovations of Western civilization. In contrast to national states, international agreements between states or international organizations like the World Trade Organization (WTO), the United Nations (UN) or the International Monetary Fund (IMF) face an enforcement dilemma, as the common controversies concerning violations of human rights, trade agreements and so on reveal again and again. The debate initiated by Theo Waigel, the German Minister of Finance, to establish a stability pact to find a way to enforce fiscal behaviour to maintain price stability after European Monetary Union (EMU) has been established is another example where sovereignty has to be given up by the single member states.

However, without successful intertemporal commitments between economic agents the perceived correspondence between agreement and behaviour by other people which is essential for stable human relations becomes weakened or may break down completely. The intertemporal nature of many contracts leads to an asynchronous flow of transfers between both parties concerning goods, services, money or property rights and makes it especially important that during this period the contractual framework is not dismissed or unilaterally changed. Trust which existed at the beginning will otherwise be replaced by distrust.[1] Without trust a prisoner's dilemma emerges, since if one cannot trust the commitment of the other side one has to take precautionary measures to hedge oneself against unwarranted losses. In common language this perception of human relations is expressed as well as credibility given to a person or an institution.

Societies differ in their attitude about how much given promises in an explicit or implicit contract will bind an individual or an institution to restrict their actions accordingly. The question how to determine credibility therefore also has a cultural dimension (see, for example, March 1988; Fukuyama 1995). High-trust societies are considered to have a comparative advantage compared to others where less-reliable social relations exist. Trust is considered to be a major ingredient of the social capital of a civil society (see, for example, Coleman 1988). High-trust societies could internalize substantial positive externalities of credibility because transaction costs between its members are substantially lowered. The superiority of democratic states in relation to others with a less solid legal framework is even considered to be one cornerstone of Western civilization compared to others (see, for example, Huntington 1993). The transformation of the industrial society to an information society which is currently under way makes it even more important that information exchanged between people can be trusted because information has become a major resource in addition to physical goods or personal services.

Lenin and Mao Tse-tung as revolutionary communists were very sceptical about credibility as a common virtue of a society, by remarking that trust is good but control is better. This, however, had severe repercussions on the Soviet Union or the People's Republic of China because control of people can only be exercised by an enormous control mechanism. The deterioration of a civil society where credibility, trust and reputation are not highly valued, can be observed in all kinds of dictatorships. The amount of resources wasted for a society could be quite substantial. But even in Western capitalist societies like the US, the UK or Germany there seems to be a tendency that an increasing share of GDP has to be devoted to the legal system because transactions between members of the civil society have become so diverse and complex. Some authors are therefore worried that this would lead to a kind of social sclerosis, that is, the term *Eurosclerosis* has been coined to describe institutional failures (see, for example, Olson 1982), which can only be corrected by countermeasures to reduce regulatory and legal constraints developed in the past, but have become defunct with social and technological change. Thatcherism started the process of deregulation, lean government and privatization of public utilities to overcome rigidities developed in the past by the legal system in Britain. That deregulation and regulation of contracts have both costs and benefits can be seen in the sequence of periods where one system is set against the other. Therefore how Western civil societies develop their contractual framework, whether it be legal or established by an unwritten system of trust, involves a delicate fragile search equilibrium.

It is not the intention of the present chapter to dig too deeply into the reasons of why and to what extent differences in credibility between various societies matter; instead we want to focus more closely on the issue of how we might develop some kind of objective measurement concept applicable to economic questions. This may seem quite ambitious because we do not expect to create a consensus between the community of economists that the way we do it is the way it has to be done, but on the other hand the present situation seems to us even more unsatisfactory. As Stanley Fischer once remarked: 'Credibility is a slippery concept which should not be overvalued' (Fischer 1994, p. 208). Nowadays, many authors use the terms credibility, trust and reputation without clarifying their exact meanings. They seem to assume that credibility is something which is self-evident. Either one has it, or one does not have it. The readers of books and articles or the audience of speeches will know if they agree with the author or speaker that someone or some institution has credibility or not. This points already to one important aspect of credibility. There is definitely a *subjective* element in it. People do not make the same interpretation about somebody else's behaviour. As during the last election in Britain, voters give credit to different parties by considering their promises about how they will run the economy, and this credibility assessment has become even more important when political parties appear to have the same or at least very similar aims. Nowadays there is hardly a party which does not accept that fighting inflation and reducing unemployment are crucial aims of their policy, but the differences lie in the number of people who believe that those proclamations are credible. An incumbent president or chancellor who for years declares that economic inequalities will be reduced, but fails to stop its increase will sooner or later lose credibility that the proclaimed aims are really the targets of his actual policy. This simple example illustrates one other important aspect of credibility. The revealed performance of an individual or institution in the past is pertinent to the credibility assessment by others. A reputation can be established according to the degree of credibility built up from past performance. Telling children that those who lied once will not be trusted afterwards is just a simple way of teaching children this fact.

In the present chapter we restrict our discussion of the measurement of credibility to the notion of rational credibility. As already mentioned, the differences in subjective perception between economic agents will basically lead to subjective measures of credibility. Taking this view as a starting point one has to begin with a model of how individuals arrive at their individual credibility assessment of economic events, just as utility theory has become the foundation of modern microeconomic theory of consumers or households. From this one has to proceed to aggregation procedures to formulate a credibility index which determines the credibility given by a group of persons to a certain activity. This line of reasoning is not followed here; rather, we are looking for a simpler way of credibility measurement which is much more common to macroeconomic theory, where aggregate economic relationships are assumed, for example, for consumption and income or investment and interest rates. What they lack in most cases is a solid microeconomic foundation (for attempts to close the gap, see, for example, Clower 1967; Phelps 1970). The advantage of macroeconomic theory compared to microeconomics, however, lies in the fact that by using these stylized facts of economic relationships as a starting point one ends up with much simpler models. Simplicity of a model might not be a sufficient condition to justify such an approach, but macroeconomics has been quite successful in constructing models which deal with complex economic relations and derive measurable quantities for the variables used. Without the definition of a GDP and its measurement, much of the current debate on economic policy would not be possible. Similarly, we disregard the microeconomic foundations of credibility measurement to arrive at a first concept of how credibility might become explicitly measurable. Since we derive a concept based on some model of credibility formation we call this kind of credibility rational, to distinguish it from other forms. Like Frank Knight, who made a distinction between risk and uncertainty where risk is based on a probability model while uncertainty is not, we define rational credibility as something where an explicit model of credibility formation has been formulated. Just as Muth (1961) and Lucas (1972) introduced the concept of rational expectations, to distinguish it from other forms of expectations, we want to stress by the term rational credibility that we exclude any kind of myopic perception of individuals leading to some kind of biases. One might have some reservations about starting with this restrictive form, but we think it is essential to keep things simple at the beginning before introducing more intricate aspects of credibility formation. Finally, we want to make reference to the game-theoretic dimension of credibility which gives an appropriate framework for formalizing credibility. Rational credibility is considered by us as a situation where symmetric information in a dynamic game prevails (see, for example, Rasmusen 1989).

2 Credibility

Summing up the previous remarks made with respect to credibility we have identified the following properties.

- credibility is basically *determined by individuals* with respect to certain contractual relations with other individuals or institutions;
- generally it is *determined by the individuals' perception* of a person or institution that it will fulfil commitments;
- differences between credibility assessments by individuals occur because they might use *different implicit or explicit models* and *different kinds of information* concerning the other actors in the contractual relation;
- *rational credibility* is based on explicit models and excludes myopic perceptions of individuals;
- if individuals use the same information for their credibility assessment as well as the same explicit model of *credibility formation* this will lead to *a dynamic game with symmetric information*;
- *credibility is accumulated over time by the revealed performance of the actor* to whom credibility is attributed.

Taking these aspects of credibility formation into account for a representative individual we shall now turn to the question of measurement concepts.

Measurement concepts

Measurement of credibility may take place by using different metrics. As in all other situations where one tries to measure something, one has to determine whether a nominal, ordinal or cardinal metric exists. As we know from the debate on utility measurement, one could argue that a cardinal metric does not exist for credibility measurement (see, for example, Debreu 1959; Houthakker 1950; or Marschak 1950), but we shall assume for convenience that a cardinal metric for a credibility variable can be established.

Furthermore one has to assign the attributes or respective variables to be measured. One might think of credibility measurement as using a single variable or a whole vector of variables, depending on the particular situation where credibility assessment is introduced. As a first starting point it will be much more convenient to assume that a single variable which also possesses a cardinal metric will be sufficient. Therefore, between the observable variable X and the credibility variable C a bijective mapping from X to C will exist so that each state measured by X will be attributed a unique value of C. We shall call this the *credibility function*.

$$C \leftarrow X. \tag{7.1}$$

The mapping from X into C should be a decreasing[2] function in X so that a higher value of X would lead to a lower value in C. This will lead to a complete ordering of the credibility variable with respect to X. However, we do not assume that this mapping should be a steady function. Furthermore, we assume for simplicity that we observe X at constant intervals of time so that we can use a time index to denote different moments of time. Since credibility is determined in this abstract setting by observing the single variable X over a certain period of time, we define a second mapping for a variable R which denotes the accumulated reputation with respect to X over a particular time period running from t equal to 0 to t equal to T.

$$R_T \leftarrow (X_0, X_1, \ldots, X_T). \qquad (7.2)$$

The variable R_T will therefore denote the state of reputation acquired by the revealed performance at time T. We shall call this the *reputation function*.

Since the variable X should express the commitment made by an actor or an institution and its actual performance X will just measure the difference between target value, X^a and actual outcome, X^r,

$$X \leftarrow (X^a - X^r). \qquad (7.3)$$

Let us start with a first simple version for an explicit model of determining the reputation function.

Cumulative stock approach   If one considers the reputation that a person or an institution has acquired after some time, we could design the process of getting a reputation as a learning process. People learn something about the performance of an agent or an institution by revealed behaviour and proclaimed targets. The simplest way to measure the revealed performance is summarized in a simple model by adding up the single values of the trajectory of the variable X. This might be appropriate if we assume that the actor him- or herself is unable to learn from past experiences and just reacts to the same causation process by the same reaction function. If, however, people were to adjust their strategies according to their past performance, the earlier assessments would be less valuable as information about the future performance of the agent than the more recent ones. The agent will then follow a closed-loop control mechanism instead of an open-loop control (see, for example, Chow 1975).

The problem is that generally one will have very little knowledge about how agents learn, so that an explicit model cannot be represented by a learning function. Instead, one might introduce in the reputation function some form of time-discounting mechanism so that past performance is written off as less informative than the more recent one. If we assume that learning is making progress at a constant rate, the discount rate will be constant as well measuring the learning speed of the agent. A simple version might be formulated similar to the way in which capital stocks are depreciated using the perpetual inventory method. The parameter η denotes the depreciation rate of reputation.

$$R_t = R_{t-1} + C_t - \eta \cdot R_{t-1}. \qquad (7.4)$$

Applying backward recursion to (7.4), one ends up with a relation which is consistent with our definition of a reputation function. We have given this form the name *cumulative stock approach of reputation measurement*.

This approach, however, seems to be quite incomplete in a sense that it might not detect significant changes in the variability of an observed trajectory of the variable X. Especially in the analysis of data from financial and money markets, research efforts have been intensified to include a mechanism which takes into account changes in the variability of a time series, by using measures of volatility.

Volatility measurement   That the variance of time series observed in money and financial markets fluctuates significantly has been observed, and has led to a more intense analysis of heteroscedasticity of stochastic processes in econometrics. A simple form to detect this for the exchange rates was created by the IMF by calculating time-varying variances for exchange rates and using them as volatility indicators (see Figure 7.1, and, for example, Branson 1985). Exchange rate volatility has been one crucial topic which has attracted substantial research input since the breakdown of the Bretton Woods system (see, for example, Krugman 1992).

In econometrics, a number of attempts to develop appropriate models for heteroscedastic error terms followed. Two distinct types of stochastic volatility models have become common in the literature, first the family of ARCH (autoregressive conditional heteroscedasticity) (see, for example, Engle 1982; Bollerslev et al. 1992) or GARCH (generalized ARCH) models, and second, the family of Bayesian vector autoregression models with stochastic volatility (see Shephard 1994; Uhlig 1997).

What makes these models so attractive in the context of credibility measurement? It is a common observation that credibility and reputation are not acquired and lost in a steady way. Many economic agents make their personal assessments on the effects of shocks with regard to the sustainability of actual economic policies. Some events might lead to abrupt changes in the policies of the central bank and the government, but also of companies to maintain their share prices on the stock exchange. In the theory of optimal

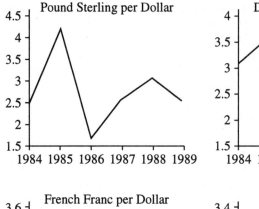

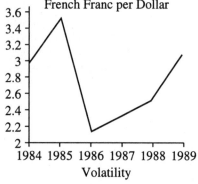

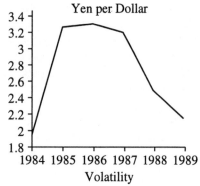

Volatility

	1984	1985	1986	1987	1988	1989
Pound sterling	2.40	4.14	1.67	2.56	3.06	2.53
Deutschmark	3.08	3.60	1.86	2.80	2.60	3.19
French franc	2.95	3.52	2.13	2.33	2.50	3.07
Yen	1.95	3.25	3.30	3.19	2.51	2.16

Notes:
Changes in currencies versus US dollar.
Volatility = standard deviation of monthly proportionate changes versus the US dollar in average exchange rates over the period.

Source: International Monetary Fund, cited in Orr (1992, p. 171).

Figure 7.1   Volatility of main currencies versus US dollar

control this can generate problems of time inconsistency (see, for example, Blackburn 1992; Currie and Levine 1993). If one assumes a framework of a model with forward-looking rational expectations of the other agents of the economy in an optimal policy model setting (see, for example, Lucas and Sargent 1981), then it might occur that under stochastic adverse shocks the time consistency of an optimal policy cannot be maintained and reneging on the policy after the occurrence of the shock becomes a superior solution (see, for example, Currie and Levine 1993). These effects can induce speculative bubbles (see Flood and Garber 1994). Loss of credibility therefore takes place under certain circumstances in a catastrophic or chaotic way (see, for example, Thom 1975; Zeeman 1977; Day 1994). As we now know from chaos theory, where an area of chaotic instability is called *cusp*, this might be due to certain non-linearities in stochastic or even deterministic processes. Therefore the stochastic volatility models hold some promise that they might catch these irregularities, also known as stochastic shocks, which have plagued econometric modelling over the last decades and led to a much more sceptical attitude of the public and policy makers towards econometric models as useful instruments for economic policy design.

In the following we shall present a sketch of what Bayesian autoregressive stochastic volatility models look like, and what their attractive properties for credibility measurement are. Consider a simple version of the model, given by (see Uhlig 1997, p. 60):

$$X_t^r = \rho \cdot X_{t-1}^r + \frac{u_t}{\sqrt{\sigma_t}} \text{ with } u_t \sim N(0,1) \tag{7.5}$$

$$\sigma_{t+1} = \frac{\sigma_t \cdot \delta_t}{\lambda} \text{ with } \delta_t \sim B_1\left(\frac{v+1}{2}, \frac{1}{2}\right) \tag{7.6}$$

where all δ_t's and u_t's are drawn independently, where $t = 1, \ldots, T$ denotes time and $X_t \in \mathbb{R}$ are data and observable, $\lambda > 0$, $v > 0$ are parameters, and $B_1(p,q)$ denotes the (one-dimensional) beta distribution on the interval $(0,1)$.

This type of stochastic volatility model can now be analysed in a Bayesian fashion. As is well known, Bayesian models are an appropriate way to model learning of probability distributions because one obtains the posterior density from a subjective prior density and the likelihood function of the data-generating stochastic process. This feature would fit quite neatly into the framework of the learning process whereby economic agents determine their credibility in a stochastic environment where the economic system under control of optimal policy agents, for example, to control inflation, has to deal with symmetric and asymmetric stochastic shocks, often leading to time inconsistencies of their respective optimal policies if certainty equivalence does not prevail. The advantage of the stochastic volatility model outlined above is that it overcomes a shortcoming of the Bayesian approach. To obtain posterior densities one has to assume that the prior density and the respective likelihood function of the data-generating stochastic process belong to a conjugate family of probability distributions. In most cases this requirement restricts the possibility of choosing a prior density and the generating objective stochastic process substantially and also has the effect that closed solutions for the posterior density often cannot be obtained. This makes it quite awkward to use such models in applied econometric modelling. The autoregressive stochastic volatility model given by equations (7.5) and (7.6), however, gives closed solutions for the posterior density calculation in a way that is well known from Kalman–Filtering theory. Therefore the stochastic learning process becomes much easier to handle in applied econometric modelling by avoiding the numerical evaluation of the posterior density. Since the autoregressive stochastic volatility model can be easily generalized to hold for multiple time-series models, this feature can be used in a multiequation econometric model as well (for further details, see Uhlig 1997).

We conclude that recent advances in the theory of autoregressive stochastic volatility processes open up a new agenda for a more realistic way to deal with credibility in an environment where economic agents face a stochastic environment which is influenced by symmetric and asymmetric stochastic shocks.

Next we want to study ways to model the asymmetric behaviour of economic agents with respect to winning, losing or regaining credibility. There seem to be some kind of hysteresis effects built into the adjustment process which become quite obvious after a major credibility shock has occurred.

Asymmetric adjustments after credibility shocks   The cumulative stock approach of building up a reputation does not include this asymmetric reaction with respect to credibility shocks. Adverse shocks due to unexpected volatility determined, for example, by (7.5) in our simple stochastic volatility model lead to hysteresis effects with respect to credibility assigned to the performance of an economic agent. Hysteresis attracted much attention in economics when economists tried to explain the persistence of high unemployment in Europe (see, for example, Cross and Allan 1988; Franz 1987) or trade deficits of the US (Krugman and Baldwin 1987). These approaches always applied hysteresis models to macroeconomic relations, but did not attempt to give them an explicit meaning concerning human behaviour. Here we shall try to assign the hysteresis effect to the adjustment process taken into account by economic agents to internalize mismatches between proclaimed aims and performances measured by the variable X. Let us assume that credibility assigned to the observed outcome X is given by

$$C_t = C_{t-1} + \alpha \cdot (X_t^a - X_t^r) \tag{7.7}$$

taking the definition in equation (7.3) into account. The current degree of credibility is therefore determined by the value of credibility of the previous period because of an adaptive expectation formation process plus the difference between the proclaimed value and the actually observed value of the target variable X weighted with a parameter α. The parameter α might account for individual or cultural differences. Therefore, the actual credibility value increases relative to the previous one if the actual value of the target variable falls below the proclaimed target value. The proclaimed target value is therefore a ceiling for the economic agent that he or she does not want to exceed; for example, when the governor of a central bank proclaims that the inflation rate should not exceed 3 per cent. An inflation rate lower than 3 per cent will increase the credibility given to the central bank by other economic agents as observers of the central bank that price stability could be maintained and vice versa if the inflation rate exceeds the threshold level of 3 per cent. The model presented by equation (7.7) therefore has to be adjusted if the proclaimed target is to be considered a floor rather than a ceiling. One implication of the model for credibility assignment is that if the proclaimed target values are too ambitious so that they are never matched by actual outcomes, this will significantly lower credibility and reputation in the long run. Reputation and credibility might even fall to a level where they become negative. A situation where distrust and a lack of reputation prevail makes it necessary that the targets have to be met over quite some time to reestablish credibility and reputation. Therefore the economic agent should be very careful in choosing his or her target values so that they are feasible and should not attempt to reach for the sky to accomplish the impossible. Central bankers are quite aware that even if it would be the ideal state that zero inflation might prevail in an economy, any attempt to proclaim this as a target might undermine the credibility of the institution if it is not attained soon. Therefore more realistic targets have become common to maintain credibility and accumulate reputation. During election campaigns politicians quite often try to make the voters believe, by setting very ambitious targets, that they can accomplish significant changes – like George Bush's 'Read my lips, no higher taxes' – but face a major credibility crisis if they become elected and cannot deliver what they have promised. The proclaimed target values should therefore be based on a realistic prediction of the economic agent that they are feasible within the economic system. We shall summarize this by the following simple equation

$$X_t^a = \beta \cdot \mathbf{Z}_t \text{, for } \forall\, t = 0, \ldots, T \tag{7.8}$$

where $\mathbf{Z}_t$ and β denote vectors of variables and parameters of an economic model to describe the economy. Taking equation (7.8) into account it is assumed that economic agents should choose their targets to be time consistent so that credibility cannot be endangered by a time-inconsistent policy design. Hysteresis might now occur if the proclaimed target value depends not only on the economic model given by equation (7.8) but also on the previous realization of the actual target variable.

$$X_t^a = \beta \cdot \mathbf{Z}_t + \gamma \cdot X_{t-1r}^r. \tag{7.9}$$

This is the simplest version of a model which generates hysteresis effects (see, for example, Giavazzi and Wyplosz 1985). Even if lagged values for previous realizations are introduced, this would not basically change the fact that hysteresis is present in the system. Substituting the variables given in equation (7.6) by the expressions from the equations (7.7) and (7.9) one obtains

$$C_t = C_{t-1} + \alpha \cdot \beta \cdot \mathbf{Z}_t - \alpha \cdot (X_t^r - \gamma \cdot X_{t-1}^r). \tag{7.10}$$

The value of the parameter γ determines whether hysteresis effects might occur in credibility formation. If $\gamma = 0$, no hysteresis effect will occur in the credibility formation, but when $\gamma = 1$, no unique solution of the policy problem is feasible. This leads to a situation of path dependency of the policy problem. Furthermore, it is important to distinguish between hysteresis effects and persistence effects. Persistence effects occur if the parameter has a value which lies inside of (0;1). It is interesting to notice in this context that the Maastricht criteria for monetary and fiscal stability were chosen by the member states of the community by taking into consideration only the average performance of the countries in the past years. That is an example of the assignment method described in the simple form given by equation (7.9) of our model.

Summarizing now the result of the three previous sections, which outline the formation of reputation by the cumulative stock approach using the perpetual inventory method in equation (7.4) and the introduction of the model of a Bayesian autoregressive stochastic volatility for the realization of the target values by equations (7.5) and (7.6) due to incomplete knowledge of the actual economic environment which is perturbed by stochastic shocks, we get, together with the equation for the credibility formation (7.10), a system which is able to produce asymmetric adjustment behaviour if hysteresis or persistence effects are present in the formation of policy targets.

The model of credibility and reputation formation, outlined here, has to be studied in greater detail by simulation experiments and has to be tested in the way that the parameters are obtainable by econometric estimation methods. This is, however, beyond the scope of the present chapter. Furthermore, future research should be directed to the question of how credibility and reputation variables have to be introduced in a macroeconomic model as explanatory variables so that a feedback relation between economic reality given by a macroeconomic model and credibility and reputation occurs. We hope, however, that we have made a step forward in the right direction by freeing the concept of credibility from being vague and moving in the direction of establishing a theory of rational credibility.

3 Central bank experiences and Euro perspectives

Since the transition to an EMU will make it much more difficult to signal economic agents that the policy assignment of respective target values is credible because the European Central Bank (ECB) has not acquired a historical record of its performance, the formation of credibility will have to apply other credibility-enhancing methods than the one outlined in the rational credibility formation model above. The European Monetary Institute (EMI), the European Commission, the central banks and governments of the member countries will have to convince the public inside and outside the EMU area that prudent monetary and fiscal behaviour will occur after the establishment of stage 3 of the EMU process, that is, the final fixing of the exchange rates between members of the EMU. The high unemployment still persisting in all potential member countries is a serious factor because it compels governments to stimulate their economies (see, for example, our previous study Erber and Hagemann 1996). This liability also worried the first President of EMI, Alexandre Lamfalussy, who has asked for more decisive measures by the EU governments to push forward structural reforms (see Fisher 1997). The tasks due to be accomplished by EU governments are related to major reforms in increasing labour market flexibility and reforms limiting the cost inflation of the welfare system which otherwise would be the main cause of accelerating public deficits in the EU (see, for example, Wetter et al. 1995).

The introduction of a single European currency is an essentially political exercise. Few things in economics or politics are ever black and white and the EMU will be no exception. Since none of the uncertainties emerging from the EMU are completely accountable in advance, in some sense it resembles a marriage contract where the partners lose some degree of freedom to act independently to maximize their personal benefits. Similarly, success or failure of the EMU will depend heavily on the commitment and evolutionary learning of its partners to maintain and develop the relation. Therefore a well-designed EMU is a good thing for reaping the benefits of a currency union: savings in transactions and information costs and the growth potentials of a fully integrated huge European market. The question is: will this EMU be well designed?

The question is whether it will be possible for international financial markets to place the same confidence in the Euro as they have in the DM given some member states which had few reservations about more inflation until a decade ago. An automatic transfer of reputation from the Bundesbank to the ECB is not possible. As has been argued before, the reputation of the Bundesbank has been built up over time because of its good track record in achieving a relatively greater degree of price stability than all other monetary authorities in the last four decades. This credibility of the German currency was created by the monetary policy of the Bundesbank, which nearly always repressed domestic inflationary pressure in its early stages and gave the DM the necessary reputation, relative to the other EMS currencies, to become the anchor of the EMS. The Euro, naturally, will not have such credibility from the outset.

The credibility of the Bundesbank is not only based on its independence and the collective commitment of public opinion in Germany to price stability (due to the negative experiences with hyperinflation and the subsequent currency reforms after the two world wars which led to a widespread expropriation of money wealth owners) but also on the long-run capacity of the German economy to create and maintain substantial trade surpluses based on the ability of German industry to improve its international competitiveness without supporting currency devaluations. Credibility is not an all-or-nothing matter but a continuous variable. The Bundesbank could keep its anti-inflationary reputation in the wake of the breaking down of the Berlin Wall and German unification when expansionary fiscal policies, strong wage pressures, an investment boom, the unacceptability of real appreciation by inflation, and the failure of the EMS to allow for an upward realignment of the DM gave it little choice but to raise interest rates to a level sufficiently high to keep inflationary pressures at bay. Long-term interest rates increased from about 7.5 per cent to 9 per cent in the time from late 1989 to spring 1990 with the real rate of 6.2 per cent reaching its historical peak in summer 1990, when financial markets became fully aware of the tremendous amount of capital required for the rebuilding of the East German economy. The Federal Republic of Germany, which had been one of the greatest net exporters of capital in the world in the second half of the 1980s and into 1989, mutated to a net importer of capital from 1991 onwards. German events clearly were driving realignment expectations and eventually led to the breakdown of the ERM in the period between September 1992 and summer 1993.

This could have been prevented if the partners had allowed a unilateral appreciation of the DM in 1990 as an appropriate German response to the

German unification shock. This would have permitted the European partners to maintain lower interest rates at a time when their economies were moving into a recession, whereas the German economy experienced a *Sonderkonjunktur* due to the released pent-up demand from East Germany. Instead of the positive growth stimuli caused by lower interest rates they suffered from high interest rates and appreciation in real terms which were the consequence of their continuing to peg their currencies to the DM as if stage 2 of the EMU had already been reached. Thus the European partners, who benefited from Germany's rapidly rising imports which resulted in a swing in the balance of payments in current accounts from a historical record surplus of about 107 billion DM in 1989 to a deficit of about 30 billion DM in 1991, on the other hand suffered from the high interest rates in the wake of German unification which slowed down growth. Nevertheless, the keeping of the old parities within the EMS was unsustainable, since German unification had caused the need for an upward realignment of the DM – which was recognized rather early by the best representatives of standard economic theory (see, for example, Basevi 1991) – and real appreciation via inflation was not tolerable for the Bundesbank. This led to the collapse of the EMS in the two crises of September 1992 and of August 1993, which basically reflects the problems any fixed exchange rate system faces when no timely realignments are made despite greater differences in inflation performance. Since, with the exception of the Dutch guilder and the Belgian franc, all other currencies were devalued, in fact a widespread unilateral realignment of the DM became effective but in a particularly unlucky and costly way. In contrast to the other central banks who had hoped to continue the import of anti-inflationary credibility from the Bundesbank by remaining pegged to the DM but lost a greater part of their reputation and were forced to regain credibility, from the perspective of international financial markets, the Bundesbank was able to keep its reputation in the troubled waters after German unification. The Bundesbank proudly referred to the fact that when it had raised the key discount and Lombard rates to a maximum of 8 and 9.75 per cent, respectively, directly after the Maastricht summit in December 1991, rising short-term rates directly affected by monetary policy were afterwards associated with falling long-term rates, signalling the continuously high anti-inflationary stance of the Bundesbank. So from the experiences with the EMS since the 1970s, it may be concluded (Goodhart 1996, p. 242): 'Building monetary union in Europe on the basis of an expanding DM area would have been economically the least cost method of proceeding'. For this alternative strategy towards EMU, Goodhart gives the following rationale:

> There would then have been no transitional costs at all for the largest country in Europe, the country standing to receive the least economic benefits from EMU.

> There would then have been no problems about credibility, or nomenclature. Rather than having to go through the complex task of creating new, and untried, institutions, it would have allowed an evolutionary approach to EMU, and one that built upon monetary foundations, the DM and the Bundesbank, universally proclaimed to be the most successful in Europe. (ibid.)

In contrast to Goodhart's idea of an expanding Deutschmark area, we find the alternative strategy of starting the EMU without Germany, because 'the problem of the Maastricht strategy is that it does not help to overcome the German reluctance for entering a monetary union with countries that have experienced more inflation in the past' and 'the easiest way to have Germany in the European monetary union is to let it wait outside for a while' (DeGrauwe 1995, pp. 488 and 490). While it will be difficult to convince not only governments but also economists about the second part of the statement, the 'strategy' of starting EMU without Germany, an idea which has also been strongly supported by Franco Modigliani in the recent debate in Italy, has in common with the alternative of an expanding Deutschmark area that, from a political point of view, it is thinking the unthinkable – although for very different reasons. Since it was the basis for a sounder integration of unified Germany in Europe other countries, notably France, have no interest in a monetary union without Germany. On the other hand, for many European partner countries one major rationale of the Maastricht Treaty was to restrict the dominant position of the Bundesbank and to retain some authority over the common monetary policy. Since EMU is primarily a political exercise, the alternative strategies can be equally dismissed for reasons of political unrealism.

Things look quite different from the viewpoint of 'pure' logic. In contrast to the dominant role of the pound sterling in the gold standard system and the dollar in the Bretton Woods system, the central position of the DM in the EMS, which originally was intended to function as a symmetric system, was not shaped by institutional design but as a result of market forces. The accumulated stock of credibility which was built up by the Bundesbank over many years gave the DM the necessary reputation relative to other currencies to become the anchor of the EMS. It was also the reason for other countries to peg their currencies to the DM – as Austria since July 1981 and the Netherlands since March 1983 did with great success, and to a certain degree even Belgium since 1990 (although the Belgian franc has not yet reached the same status of a hard currency as the Dutch guilder or the Austrian schilling). But these are the only currencies which did not devalue against the DM in the two EMS crises of September 1992 and August 1993. In some sense it can be said that the Dutch guilder has become the strongest DM after German unification, and the designation of Wim Duisenberg to become first president of the new ECB seems quite natural. From the viewpoint of credibility the

Austrian case is particularly revealing, since the decision of unilaterally fixing the schilling to the DM was made before Austria became a member of the EU. The Dutch, Austrian and to a certain extent the Belgian cases are also of special interest to those countries which will not qualify for the EMU from the beginning and for the relationship of the 'outs', who can peg their currencies to the Euro in an EMS II, to the 'ins'. The Austrian and the Dutch cases show that the strategy of unilaterally fixing their currencies to the DM substantially gained them credibility on the financial markets only from that time when the basic macroeconomic data showed a high convergence with the German one (for a detailed consideration, see Fischer 1997).

It is an important aspect of credibility that it is accumulated gradually but can also be depleted, gradually or rather suddenly. Whereas it will be very difficult to transfer the reputation of the DM to the Euro and to maintain and enhance the reputation of the new European currency, this would be a far more difficult task for the common currency in an EMU without Germany. At the beginning its reputation would be far lower and the accumulation of credibility would be a time-consuming process and would always be endangered whenever inflationary expectations reemerged. Nevertheless, a successful EMU without Germany is not completely out of the question. A necessary but not sufficient condition would be the creation of a non-inflationary environment through political independence of the central bank, an element which is an important ingredient in the alternative strategy proposed by DeGrauwe. Naturally, central bank independence is an essential requirement for any single European currency wishing to establish its credibility. From that point of view one of the first decisions of the new Labour government in the UK was quite important when the new Chancellor of the Exchequer, Gordon Brown, announced on 6 May a significant change in transferring the responsibility for setting interest rates from the government to the Bank of England.

4 Summary and conclusions

Credibility is emerging as an important concept in economics which has repercussions on its theoretical foundations using stylized models of rational behaviour. In the area of finance and money markets, in many respects the most advanced forms of markets, the importance of credibility, reputation and trust has been noticed much earlier. The ECB and its credibility to be an effective institution to guarantee price stability in the countries of the EMU have led to a particular debate on credibility and reputation. However, to be a useful and not a diffuse concept, credibility needs to become more specific to be operational. Therefore we have designed an explicit model for credibility formation. The main issues which are crucial for such a model are the ability to account for the cumulative nature of reputation, the asymmetric adjustment of credibility due to some kind of hysteresis effect, and finally the ability of the model to deal with stochastic volatility which is not under the control of the agent so that targets and outcomes can lead to problems of time inconsistency and path dependency. The proposed concept of rational credibility outlined in this chapter is therefore now open to be tested on its usefulness by different applications in empirical research.

Credibility for the new ECB from 1999 onwards – if stage 3 of the EMU starts as expected by most observers – will be enhanced if the independence of the ECB is accepted by all members of the EMU as it was agreed in the Maastricht Treaty. New interpretations could severely damage the credibility of the EMU. That central bank independence can be an important factor in raising the credibility of a central bank was confirmed in the UK when Tony Blair's new government made its commitment to the Bank of England. This will help to clear the path for the UK to become a member of the EMU even if it is not willing to become a founding member. Therefore, the recent debate concerning candidates for the future first president of the ECB, mentioning Duisenberg and Trichet, should not give rise to any suspicions that any of them would follow a loose monetary policy. As Rogoff (1985) has already proposed, a *conservative* president who is trusted to resist all kinds of political pressures to follow a loose monetary policy to appease governments, the European Commission or the general public when inflationary pressures on the Euro build up, might be another insurance against a significant credibility gap between the Bundesbank and the ECB. Furthermore, the statistical and technical foundations such as the TARGET system, as well as a monetary policy design built on a broad consensus of all participating countries in EMU, should be in place (see EMI 1996, 1997). As Goodhart (1996) suggested, an early final fixing of the exchange rates could reduce the temptation of single EMU member countries to devalue their currencies and thus would quite likely stop the associated speculative attacks on single currencies before an agreement of the final fixing of exchange rates has taken place. The ongoing debate on the fulfilment of the fiscal criteria of sufficient convergence between all potential member states has shown again the problematic nature of setting ambitious targets when even countries such as Germany, which was always proud to have kept *the holy grail of price stability* in the past, because of unexpected circumstances will most likely fail to be on target. Without such a targeting all kinds of creative bookkeeping going on now will have become useless. The more important aspects of sustainable price stability based on long-term sustainable fiscal policies (see, for example, Erber and Hagemann 1996), a sufficient level of employment and a welfare state and social system whose financial foundations are not as shaky as they are now in most EU countries, would be the more reasonable foundations for ensuring the long-term credibility of an ECB. If structural reforms do not take place they will become a major burden as many economists foresee (see, for example, Krugman 1997; Dornbusch 1996; Alexandre Lamfalussy or Michel Mussa, the IMF chief economist in recent statements at the EMI and the Bundesbank; compare Fisher 1997 and FAZ 1997). The ECB will then have to face a situation where a lack of sufficient structural reforms in most EMU countries will create substantial pressures for unsound and unsustainable fiscal policies, and the ECB will have to gain credibility by a restrictive monetary policy and will be blamed for it even if the problems are not caused by the Euro or the monetary policy of the ECB. This might happen even if all potential EMU member countries meet the Maastricht criteria in 1997. However, the ECB should not become the scapegoat for failure to institute appropriate policy reforms in the EMU countries.

Notes

1. Although both terms, that is, credibility and trust are highly synonymous, one has to make the distinction that people have (dis)trust whereas institutions can have credibility.
2. Decreasing because X will be the deviation between target value and actual outcome (see equation (7.3)), that is, the larger the deviation between the target value and the actual outcome the lower the credibility value.

Bibliography

Barro, R.J. (1976), 'Rational expectations and the role of monetary policy', *Journal of Monetary Economics*, **2**, 1095–117.
Barro, R.J. (1986), 'Reputation in a model of monetary policy with incomplete information', *Journal of Monetary Economics*, **17**, 101–22.
Barro, R.J. and D.B. Gordon (1983), 'Rules, discretion, and reputation in a model of monetary policy', *Journal of Monetary Economics*, **12**, 101–21.
Basevi, G. (1991), 'Eastern Europe, Germany and the EC: a framework for analysing their economic integration', in W. Heisenberg (ed.), *German Unification in European Perspective*, London: Brassey's, pp. 133–64.
Blackburn, K. (1992), 'Credibility and time-consistency in monetary policy', in K. Dowd and M. Lewis (eds), *Current Issues in Fiscal and Monetary Economics*, London: Macmillan, pp. 155–74.
Blackburn, K.M. and M. Christensen (1989), 'Monetary policy and policy credibility: theories and evidence', *Journal of Economic Literature*, **27**, 1–45.
Bollerslev, T.R., R.Y. Chou and K.F. Kroner (1992), 'ARCH modelling in finance: a review of the theory and empirical evidence', *Journal of Econometrics*, **52**, 5–59.
Branson, W.H. (1985), 'Causes of appreciation and volatility of the dollar', *The US Dollar – Recent Developments, Outlook, and Policy Options*, Kansas City: Federal Reserve Bank.
Branson, W.H. (1994), 'Comments on *European Exchange Rate Credibility Before the Fall* by A.K. Rose and L.E.O. Svensson', *European Economic Review*, **38**, 1217–20.
Chow, G.C. (1975), *Analysis and Control of Dynamic Economic Systems*, New York: John Wiley & Sons.
Clower, R.W. (1967), 'A reconsideration of the microfoundations of monetary theory', *Western Economic Journal*, **6**, 1–9.
Coleman, J.S. (1988), 'Social capital in the creation of human capital', *American Journal of Sociology*, **94**, Supplement, 95–120.
Cross, R. and A. Allan (1988), 'On the history of hysteresis', in R. Cross, R. (ed.), *Unemployment, Hysteresis and the Natural Rate Hypothesis*, Oxford: Blackwell, pp. 26–38.
Cukierman, A. (1992), *Central Bank Strategy; Credibility and Independence: Theory and Evidence*, Cambridge, MA: MIT Press.
Cukierman, A. (1995), 'How can the European Central Bank become credible?', paper pre-

sented at the CEPR/Irving Fisher Society Conference on 'What monetary policy for the European Central Bank?', Frankfurt am Main, 9–10 June.

Currie, D. (1997), *The Pros and Cons of EMU*, London: Economist Intelligence Unit.

Currie, D. and P. Levine (1993), *Rules, Reputation and Macroeconomic Policy Coordination*, Cambridge: Cambridge University Press.

Day, R.H. (1994), *Complex Economic Dynamics*, Cambridge, MA: MIT Press.

Debreu, G. (1959), *Theory of Value*, New York: Wiley.

DeGrauwe, P. (1995), 'Alternative strategies towards monetary union', *European Economic Review*, **39**, 483–91.

Deutsche Bundesbank (1997), 'Geldmengenstrategie 1997/1998' [Monetary Strategy, 1997/1998], *Monthly Report*, January, 17–25.

Dornbusch, R. (1996), 'Euro Fantasies', *Foreign Affairs*, 75, September/October, 110–24.

Engle, R.E. (1982), 'Autoregressive conditional heteroskedasticity with estimates of the variance of United Kingdom inflation', *Econometrica*, **50**, 987–1008.

Erber, G. and H. Hagemann (1996), 'Sustainable price stability for Europe: prospective effects of a European Central Bank on long-term growth and employment, lessons from the past: the EU countries and the EMS', *Vierteljahrshefte zur Wirtschaftsforschung*, **65**, 381–91.

European Monetary Institute (EMI) (1996), *Fortschritte auf dem Weg zur Konvergenz* [Progress on the Road to Convergence], Frankfurt am Main, November.

European Monetary Institute (EMI) (1997), *Annual Report 1996*, Frankfurt am Main, April.

Fischer, C. (1997), *Glaubwürdigkeit in der Währungspolitik. Die Strategie der einseitig festen Wechselkursanbindung in Österreich, den Niederlanden und Belgien* [Credibility in Currency Policy. The Strategy of Currency Pegs in Austria, the Netherlands and Belgium], Marburg: Metropolis.

Fischer, S. (1994), 'Comments and discussions', *Brookings Papers on Economic Activity*, No.2, 206–11.

Fisher, A. (1997), 'EMI chief sounds alarm on EU's "dismal" jobs record, annual report highlights worrying trend', *Financial Times*, 24 April.

Flood, R.P. and P.M. Garber (1994), *Speculative Bubbles, Speculative Attacks, and Policy Switching*, Cambridge, MA: MIT Press.

Frankfurter Allgemeine Zeitung (FAZ) (1997), 'Der Euro löst die Beschäftigungsschwierigkeiten nicht, IWF–Ökonom Mussa: Mit der Globalisierung steigt der Lebensstandard / Kein Patentrezept für Europa [The Euro does not solve the Employment Problem, IMF–Economist Mussa: Globalization Increases Living Standards/No Patent Recipe for Europe]', *Frankfurter Allgemeine Zeitung*, 9 May.

Franz, W. (1987), 'Hysteresis, persistence, and the NAIRU: an empirical analysis for the Federal Republic of Germany', in R. Layard and L. Calmfors, (eds), *The Fight Against Unemployment*, Cambridge, MA: MIT Press, pp. 91–122.

Fukuyama, F. (1995), *Trust – The Social Virtues and the Creation of Prosperity*, New York/London/Tokyo: Free Press.

Giavazzi, F. and C. Wyplosz (1985), 'The zero root problem: a note on the dynamic determination of the stationary equilibrium in linear models', *Review of Economic Studies*, **52**, 353–7.

Goodhart, C.A.E. (1996), 'The transition to EMU', *Scottish Journal of Political Economy*, **43**, 241–57.

Houthakker, H.S. (1950), 'Revealed preferences and the utility function', *Economica*, **17**, 159–74.

Huntington, S.P. (1993), 'The clash of civilization', *Foreign Affairs*, **72** (3), 22–46.

King, M. (1995), 'Credibility and monetary policy: theory and evidence', *Quarterly Bulletin*, Bank of England, **35**, pp. 84–91.

Krugman, P.R. (1992), *Currencies and Crises*, Cambridge, MA: MIT Press.

Krugman, P.R. (1997), '"Bringt es hinter Euch" [Complete it Now!], MIT–Ökonom Paul Krugman über Globalisierung, die Europäische Währungsunion und die Politik der Deutschen Bundesbank', *Wirtschaftswoche*, No. 18, 24 April, 24–9.

Krugman, P.R. and R.E. Baldwin (1987), 'The persistence of the U.S. trade deficit', *Brookings Papers on Economic Activity*, No. 1, 1–43.

Lucas, R.E. (1972), 'Expectations and the neutrality of money', *Journal of Economic Theory*, **4**, 103–24.

Lucas, R.E. and T.J. Sargent (eds) (1981), *Rational Expectations and Econometric Practice*, London/Boston/Sydney: George Allen & Unwin.

March, R.M. (1988), *The Japanese Negotiator, Subtlety and Strategy Beyond Western Logic*, Tokyo/New York: Kodansha International.

Marschak, J. (1950), 'Rational behaviour, uncertain prospects and measurable utility', *Econometrica*, **18**, 111–41.

Muth, J. (1961), 'Rational expectations and the theory of price movements', *Econometrica*, **39**, 315–34.

Obstfeld, M. (1996), *Models of Currency Crises with Self-Fulfilling Features*, Centre for Economic Policy Research Working Papers, No. 1315, London, January.

Olson, M. (1982), *The Rise and Decline of Nations, Economic Growth, Stagflation, and Social Rigidities*, New Haven/London: Yale University Press.

Orr, B. (1992), *The Global Economy in the 90s, A User's Guide*, New York: New York University Press.

Phelps, E.S. (1970), *Microeconomic Foundations of Employment and Inflation Theory*, New York: Norton.

Rasmusen, E. (1989), *Games and Information, An Introduction to Game Theory*, Oxford: Basil Blackwell.

Rogoff, K. (1985), 'The optimal degrees of commitment to an intermediate monetary target', *Quarterly Journal of Economics*, **100**, 1169–89.

Romer, D. (1996), *Advanced Macroeconomics*, New York: McGraw-Hill.

Shephard, N.G. (1994), 'Local scale models: state space alternative to integrated GARCH processes', *Journal of Econometrics*, **60**, 181–202.

Thom, R. (1975), *Structural Stability and Morphogenesis: An Outline of a General Theory of Models*, Reading: Benjamin.

Uhlig, H. (1997), 'Bayesian vector autoregressions with stochastic volatility', *Econometrica*, **65**, 59–73.

Wetter, W., H. Krägneau, P. Köhler and M. Weilepp (1995), *Ordnungs- und strukturpolitische Anforderungen beim Aufbau der Europäischen Wirtschafts- und Währungsunion* [Regulatory and Structural Policy Requirements for the Development of a European Economic and Currency Union], Baden-Baden: Nomos Verlagsgesellschaft.

Zeeman, E.C. (1977), *Catastrophe Theory. Selected Papers 1972–1977*, Reading: Benjamin.

8 The political economy of the European Central Bank

Iain Begg and David Green

1 Introduction

Under economic and monetary union (EMU) in the European Union, responsibility for monetary policy will shift from member states to the European Central Bank (ECB), acting in conjunction with the existing national central banks in what will be known as the European System of Central Banks (ESCB). Fiscal policy will remain a competency of member states, but will be constrained by new rules. Thus, the advent of the single currency will result in a far-reaching transformation of the machinery for the conduct of macroeconomic policy. How the ECB is controlled, interprets its mandate and interacts with the fiscal authorities will all be central to the economic performance of the EU, posing intriguing political economy questions which this chapter explores.

In particular, the provisions on the ECB and the ESCB in the *Treaty on European Union* mean that the monetary authorities will be granted much more independence than is enjoyed by other supposedly autonomous central banks. It will be able not only to decide how to run monetary policy, but also what targets to set itself. This contrasts with, for example, the arrangements in New Zealand where the government sets a target that the central bank contracts to meet, the US where the Federal Reserve has to pay attention to the level of employment, as well as price inflation, or the new arrangements in the UK in which the Bank of England is set a target range for inflation.

We argue that the degree of independence to be granted to the ECB will be such that it will be insufficiently accountable to democratic political institutions. The likely implications are that monetary policy will tend to be biased towards a 'stability' that could be over-austere, while fiscal policy will be institutionally fragmented and, as a consequence, prone to incoherence. In the absence of sufficiently powerful European Union-wide automatic stabilizers generated by the operation of the tax and benefits/grants systems this could result in an inappropriate macroeconomic policy mix which may prove damaging to European prosperity and integration.

Europe today is confronted by sluggish growth, persistent unemployment, and structural problems. Ironically, given the powers that the ECB will acquire to deal with it, inflation is quiescent and there are suggestions that the era of high inflation may have passed, to be superseded by a new epoch of price stability. All of this raises questions about the suitability of the policy framework envisaged under EMU. Indeed, the combination of *democratic and economic policy deficits* may lead to a 'responsibility vacuum' which could, in turn, be a further significant source of macroeconomic policy problems.

This chapter first explores the stated goals of the ECB and then outlines its powers and the way in which it will be controlled. A brief review of the major arguments underpinning the move to independent central banking is presented and the different degrees of independence enjoyed by some major central banks are elaborated. The possible implications for fiscal policy in Europe are explored and conclusions advanced.

2 Goals of the European Central Bank

The goals, functions and organization of both the ESCB and the ECB have been established by the *Treaty on European Union* (1992) and the accompanying *Protocol on the Statute of the European System of Central Banks and of the European Central Bank*. The inspiration for the monetary policy framework to be implemented under EMU is the German system, and there are strong parallels between the statutes of the ECB and ESCB and the Bundesbank acts. However, it can be argued that there are a number of respects in which the ECB will have greater independence even than the Bundesbank in its conduct of policy, and that in contrast to the position in Germany where there is a powerful fiscal policy counterpart in the form of the Federal government, the EU will lack fiscal policy coherence. In addition, the mandate given to the ECB and the ESCB owes much to German influence, in that it stresses price stability. Article 105(1) sets this out:

> The primary objective of the ESCB shall be to maintain price stability. Without prejudice to the objective of price stability, the ESCB shall support the general economic policies in the Community with a view to contributing to the achievement of the objectives laid down in Article 2.

Clear as this may seem, it should be noted that price stability is not defined. Is it zero price change – the logical interpretation – or a low rate of inflation? Bank of England Chief Economist Mervyn King (1996) has argued that a low *measured* rate of price inflation may well be consistent with true price stability because of shortcomings in statistics. The precise target has important ramifications, if only because the stricter target would be expected to require a significantly tighter monetary policy. Yet in the absence of firm guidance either in the *Treaty* or in 'instructions' from the political authorities, it will be left to the ECB to decide what the target should be.

Price stability may be defined with reference to the consumer or retail price index or to a nominal GDP deflator. Indices vary in their coverage and the extent to which they take into account changes in asset prices and the inclusion of such important expenditure items as mortgage interest. Furthermore, stability may be ascribed to achieving a particular price level or a particular rate of change and may, or may not take into account improvements in the quality of goods and services purchased.

The phrase 'without prejudice' is also critical because it stimulates a hierarchy of objectives. Only if price stability is attained can the ECB turn its attention to other economic objectives of the Community. Consequently, it should not 'trade-off' a little more inflation for a lot less unemployment if that were adjudged to be a feasible option.[1] The wording of the mandate also means that it will be for the ESCB to determine what weight to give to such important Community economic objectives as growth and regional balance (Arestis and Bain 1995, pp. 169–73). The centrality of these objectives to the *raison d'être* of the European Union is underlined by Article 2 of the *Treaty*:

> The Community shall have as its task, by establishing a common market and an economic and monetary union and by implementing ... common policies or activities ... to promote throughout the Community, a harmonious and balanced development of economic activities, sustainable and non-inflationary growth respecting the environment, a high degree of convergence of economic performance, a high level of employment and social protection, the raising of the standard of living and quality of life, and economic and social cohesion and solidarity among Member States.

The lack of operational specificity in the goals of the ECB/ESCB means that, in practice, the Governing Council and Executive Board will have a considerable degree of *goal independence*, a characteristic that plainly distinguishes it from other models for central banks. This confers almost unparalleled power on the ECB and will be highly significant as the operational independence of the ESCB and ECB have also been established by the *Treaty* and the *Protocol*. It seems that the ECB will readily fit Fischer's (1995, p. 205) description of a central bank which is 'too independent'.

There is an important difference between the situation in New Zealand – regarded as the key experiment of the 1990s in the theory and practice of monetary policy (see the chapter in this volume by Dalziel) and that which it is envisaged will pertain in the European Union. In the case of New Zealand, the Reserve Bank is set targets by the government operating through a Policy Target Agreement which is agreed between the Minister of Finance and the Governor of the Reserve Bank of New Zealand. In the European case, the ECB is established by treaty and will have the responsibility of interpreting the exact target to hit and the weight it gives to its specified objectives. The

ECB will be much more powerful in relation to other economic authorities than its New Zealand counterpart. This will be of even greater significance as the ECB is the only pan-European macroeconomic policy-making institution which is currently envisaged.

3 Control of the European Central Bank

That the ESCB and the ECB are to be independent of control by elected politicians is enshrined in the *Treaty*. Not only will the ECB be independent but elected politicians are, by the terms of the *Treaty*, debarred from even attempting to influence the ECB as Article 107 makes clear:

> When exercising the powers and carrying out the tasks and duties conferred upon them by this Treaty ... neither the ECB, nor a national central bank, nor any member of their decision-making bodies shall seek or take instructions from Community institutions or bodies, from any government of a Member State or from any other body. The Community institutions and bodies and the governments of the Member States undertake to respect this principle and not to seek to influence the members of the decision-making bodies of the ECB or of the national central banks in the performance of their tasks.

The *Treaty* also provides that all member states will have adopted legislation to ensure that their national central bank is independent. Most member states have now complied with this, although in several instances the degree of independence falls short of that which will be bestowed on the ECB.

There is no provision for the ECB's independence to be overridden in times of crisis by elected politicians. Furthermore, the reporting requirements are relatively light. It can plausibly be argued that there is a significant *democratic deficit* in these arrangements. The main reporting requirement is laid down in Article 109(b)(3) of the *Treaty* which provides for the ECB to 'address an annual report on the activities of the ESCB and on the monetary policy of both the previous and current year to the European Parliament, the Council and the Commission and also to the European Council'. In addition, competent committees of the European Parliament may call on Executive Board members of the ECB to testify. This is hardly onerous and shows that the main concern at the time of writing the *Treaty* was to take the control of monetary policy away from elected politicians *at any level*. This intention is further confirmed by the way in which the individuals who will control the ECB are to be appointed.

The ECB will be run by a Governing Council and an Executive Board. The Executive Board will be made up of six members, including the President and Vice-President. These members will be appointed by 'common accord of the governments of the Members States at the levels of the Head of State or of Government, on a recommendation from the Council after it has consulted the European Parliament and the Governing Council'. The Executive Board members will be appointed for one single, eight-year non-renewable term.

The ECB's Governing Council will be made up of the Executive Board plus the Governors of the national central banks. The Governors of the independent central banks of the member states are to be appointed for terms of five years or more. In general, voting on the Governing Council will be on the basis of one member, one vote. The exceptions are to do with matters concerning the capital of the ECB, the foreign reserve assets of the national central banks and the ECB and the allocation of monetary income of national central banks when the voting will be carried out by weights determined by how much each national central bank has subscribed to the capital of the ECB. On such matters the voting weights of executive board members will be zero.

4   Theory and practice of central bank independence

What strands of thinking and experience underpin the EU's decision to opt for an independent central bank with minimal accountability? In part, it is a question of politics.[2] German fears about inflation inevitably played a substantial part in ensuring that the ECB bore a close resemblance to the Bundesbank in its structure and mandate. Indeed, one of the ironies of the transition to EMU is the often articulated view from Germany that a move to EMU will jeopardize price stability.

At a *political level* Johnson (1996, p. 74) has summarized the view of many when he argued 'Democratic sovereignty over monetary policy has furthered the electoral ends of politicians, not the public interest in keeping inflation down', while Cukierman (1994, p. 1443) has argued 'the inflationary bias of policy arises precisely because of the way politicians operate'. Such forthright assessment, echoing the popular distrust of elected politicians, is reinforced in the UK by the argument that the ECB will be effective and credible because it is believed that 'The ECB should turn out to have greater credibility than the Bank of England because it will inherit the credibility of the Bundesbank' (Johnson 1996, p. 75).

Historically, the movement towards an independent central bank is the latest of three attempts to have some 'automatic', that is 'rule-based' protection against inflation. In the post-war period, European countries have tried to have three anti-inflationary anchors. First, there was a system of fixed exchange rates where all countries relied on the credibility of the hegemonic leading country. As Walter (1993, p. 66) has summarized 'a dominant role for the key currency country enables it to play a major role in world monetary affairs. It is often argued, for example, that the stability of the Bretton Woods system until the mid 1960s was due to an anti-inflationary monetary standard provided by American monetary policies'.

After the breakdown of Bretton Woods, the 'core' EU countries of the time sought to substitute Germany for the US as the key currency country. During this period, concerted attempts were made to tackle inflation by means of adopting specific monetary targets. It turned out that these attempts resulted in inflation being tackled more successfully than were the monetary targets met (Goodhart 1994, p. 1431). After the widespread abandonment of the attempt to meet monetary targets, the dominant view became that the way to deal with inflation was to allow the monetary authorities to use their discretion in framing policy. Part of this dominant view was that politicians could not be entrusted with monetary matters. Instead, policy should be executed by the monetary authorities, usually the central bank, who were to be given an unambiguous anti-inflation brief. The quality of work could be judged by the ability of the central bank to hit a publicly announced target. In this scenario, central banks enjoyed *operational independence* but not *goal independence*. A central bank was not to be independent *vis-à-vis* its goals but rather independent *vis-à-vis* its employment of instruments. In the case of the ECB it should be noted that precise terms of reference for 'price stability' have not been set. This will give the ECB considerable latitude.

Several studies have shown that in developed, industrial countries there has been a robust relationship between lower levels of inflation and the degree of bank independence in advanced industrial countries (for example, Cukierman 1992; Alesina and Summers 1993). According to a review published by the IMF (1996) recently there was a close inverse relationship between the index of central bank independence and inflation in the 1970s and 1980s. However, it should be noted that this is not an immutable economic law; as the IMF commented (1996, p. 129): 'For the 1960s and the 1990s, there is no clear relationship between the index of central bank independence and the rate of inflation' (for a more sceptical view, see Cornwall and Cornwall, in this volume).

The empirical case also turns on whether or not it is accepted that there is a relationship between inflation and growth and/or output. In this regard, Goodhart (1994, p. 1427) has rightly observed that the 'current enthusiasm for independent Central Banks rests importantly on general acceptance of the vertical longer-term Phillips curve; that there is no medium or longer term trade-off to exploit; that the best sustainable outcome that the monetary authorities can achieve is price stability'.

A further consideration to be taken into account will be the influence of specific cultural, historical factors. For example, Germany is particularly inflation averse because of experiences of hyperinflation before the war and post-war privation. The stability afforded by the policies of the Bundesbank may well have contributed to the success of the German economy since the war, and it is clear that the Bundesbank is a respected institution that

Germans will be loath to forgo. Equally reasonably, it can be argued that it was the deep-seated German business culture linked to the profoundly re-formed institutional relationship between employers and employees combined with the large pool of highly skilled labour which fuelled the German miracle. Indeed, the contribution made by the Bundesbank's relative independence may have been of secondary importance.

There are several strands of *economic theory* supporting the movement towards central bank independence. Mourmouras (1997) has recently surveyed the theoretical arguments underpinning the case for central bank independence. The theoretical case for central bank independence has been developed by an economic literature based on a game-theoretic approach. This literature has argued that the delegation of monetary policy to an authority which puts more weight on price stabilization than the rest of society will lead to a reduction in the inflationary bias in the economy and to gains in output and employment. However, as Eijffinger and De Haan's survey has shown (1996, pp. 13–15) central bank autonomy may lead to lower and more volatile rates of economic growth.

Other branches of economic thinking have also been pressed into service in support of the move to central bank independence. In New Zealand, agency theory and the theory of public choice have been influential (Scott 1996, pp. 11–12). The key feature of agency theory is to view the firm as a governance structure rather than as a single maximizing organization.

The theoretical case for independent central banking draws on several strands of literature. The lessons of 'institutional economics' were recognized to have implications for the public sector as well as the private sector. In particular, this focused on the implications of self-interested behaviour within the organization, asymmetric information and bounded rationality. The major lesson drawn for good governance is that the critical issue for the government is to act as a principal and contract efficiently with agents who will execute economic and social policy according to the contract drawn up. In matters pertaining to banking there have been fears that the central bank has, all too often, been 'captured' by the industry it has been attempting to regulate. This possibility, developed by public choice theory has provided another reason for establishing an independent central bank with a clear unambiguous brief.

In summary, the case for an independent central bank has been built up in an intellectual climate in which the dominant paradigm has been that the roots of inflation have been excessive monetary growth combined with fiscal indiscipline for both of which short-sighted, electorally self-interested politicians are held responsible. While we agree that price stability is highly desirable and that there is a robust case for vesting central banks with *operational independence*, this does not mean that the European Central Bank should be given the power to decide the relative weights of the various

European Union policy goals as well as the Union's monetary policy. After all, widespread social exclusion and high unemployment have been major, *if not the major*, economic issues in Europe in recent years. These problems have certainly been of greater concern than inflation.

5   The nature of 'independence' in the ECB model

There are many forms and degrees of central bank independence. There is justifiable concern that the provisions of the ECB and ESCB give too much power to unelected officials. To date, the debate has focused on rather high-level generalities contrasting an independent central bank with one which is controlled directly by politicians. In fact, the Bundesbank, the central bank with the greatest credibility in Europe, is not as independent as the ECB will be and it also has a more explicit duty to foster economic growth and development (see Table 8.1). As Deane and Pringle (1994, p. 338) have argued 'the proposed European Central Bank ... [is not] ... an ideal prototype for a future generation of central banks. Such a prototype should have a more specific mandate for a commitment to achieving financial stability, with the degree of accountability that a democratic political society ... requires'.

It may be that the move to create an independent European central bank has been overly influenced by the experience of institutions and arrangements which have been successful in the past without examining current conditions and likely future scenarios. While the problem of price inflation in Europe has not been 'solved' for all time it is certainly not at the top of the current policy agenda, nor is it in the United States or Japan. Instead, it is the issues of growth, employment creation, episodic financial instability and adjustment to unanticipated economic 'shocks' which are the major concerns. This puts a particular emphasis on the way in which monetary and fiscal policy combine to produce the overall macroeconomic policy mix.

Furthermore, transitional questions must be closely considered. It is important to get the political economy of the transition to a single money and an independent central bank right. This is no easy task. In the New Zealand 'laboratory', as the IMF (1996, p. 129) has noted, 'Increasing the independence of the Central Bank did not assure a costless disinflation: New Zealand underwent a large recession during its disinflation'. In Europe, it seems to be that the movement to meet the Maastricht criteria has been accompanied by a depressed level of economic activity, reinforcing fears that a single currency will be accompanied by a general dampening of European economic growth. As Kenen (1996, p. 22) has argued:

> With the exception of the UK every major EU country has undertaken to reduce its budget deficit in an effort to meet the fiscal tests set out in the Maastricht Treaty. This synchronized effect is worrisome. First it is likely to reduce aggregate

Table 8.1 Different degrees of central bank independence

	New Bank of England	Deutsche Bundesbank	Federal Reserve	European Central Bank
Framework	Instrument independence	Instrument and considerable goal independence	Instrument and considerable goal independence	Complete goal and instrument independence
Objective/ targets	Price stability (inflation 2.5% or less), support government growth and jobs policy	'Internal and external price stability', usually 0–2% inflation, stable D-mark	Price stability and maximum employment	Price stability first and foremost
Government powers	Can override Bank in emergency	Can override only by changing law	Can override only by changing Federal Reserve's terms of reference	Instructions or influence from Community bodies and member states prohibited
Supervises banks?	Yes	No	Yes	No
Board/ Council	Nine members: five from within Bank, four external appointments	Seventeen members: eight from central bank direct, nine from banks in *Länder*	Twelve-member Federal Open Market Committee	Six-member Executive Board plus the Governors of EU central banks
To whom accountable	Parliament	Public	Congress	Public – through Treaty?
Meetings	Monthly, one member one vote, minutes published after six weeks	Fortnightly, one member one vote, no minutes	Eight times annually, minutes published	At least ten times a year. Proceedings confidential

demand in the EU as a whole, adversely affecting output and employment and, in the process, making it harder for each country to reduce its own budget deficit. Second, it may adversely affect Europe's trading partners ... the 1999 deadline has forced too many countries to move too fast.

Although the ECB will have full autonomy over monetary policy, it has not been granted equivalent powers in some of the other areas, usually the province of central banks. There is, for example, concern that the lack of a European-wide body with competence in the area of banking supervision – a task that most central banks either take on explicitly or have close links to – could lead to a weakening of prudential control (Begg and Green 1996, pp. 397–9).

There is also a lack of precision on which body will be responsible for managing the EU's foreign exchange reserves and the exchange rate. The ECB will have considerable, albeit not exclusive, responsibility for European exchange rate policy but there is no guidance as to the policies, aims or the instruments by which it will operate. Deane and Pringle (1994, p. 334) have gone so far as to describe this as 'the obfuscation of Article 109'. This lack of clarity will give the ECB further opportunities to develop the degree of *goal independence* it enjoys. At the same time it highlights the asymmetry between the clear central control of monetary policy and the diffusion of responsibility for other economic policies.

6 Future fiscal policy in Europe

Fiscal policy under EMU will remain under the control of member states, but will be constrained by the rules on excessive deficits and the so-called no-bail-out rule. These have been reinforced by the agreement reached on a *stability pact* designed to curb the ability of member states to run budget deficits. These arrangements will mean that the scope will be much reduced for governments to engage in contra-cyclical macroeconomic policy, so that their ability to deal with 'asymmetric shocks' – unanticipated changes which affect only part of the monetary union – will be limited. An underlying reason for this is the strong belief in some quarters that the instruments of macroeconomic policy should be used mainly to ensure a stable economic environment, and that attempts by governments to pursue Keynesian demand management will inevitably prove to be counterproductive.

This approach to fiscal policy under EMU is open to challenge for a number of reasons. First, it can be argued that attention has to be paid to the policy mix. The experience of Germany in the period after unification illustrates the tensions that arise when fiscal and monetary policy pull in opposite directions. Under EMU, the likelihood of incompatibilities will be multiplied because not only will aggregate EU fiscal policy be the outcome of separate decisions by individual member states, but there will also be no formal means of reconciling it with monetary policy.

A second reason to question the provisions for fiscal policy is that some of the objections to Keynesian fiscal policy at the level of the member state are less persuasive at the EU level. Notwithstanding contemporary sentiment on the phenomenon of globalization, the EU as a whole is a fairly closed economic system, as indeed is the US. Thus, where individual member states are put off using fiscal policy to manage demand because cross-border flows contradict the policy, such policy shifts could prove much more effective at the EU level.

The credibility of the fiscal disciplines written into the *Treaty is* a third dimension of the EMU policy framework that warrants attention. The no-bail-out principle should mean that governments which borrow excessively will be penalized by the financial markets with higher interest rates. Central to this is how credible the rules are. Because of the strong mandate given to the ECB and the ESBC, member states will not be able easily, or at all, to pressurize the ECB so that a breach of the rule is unlikely.

By the same token, the various penalty provisions in the *Treaty* have the curious property that they are designed not to be used. As reaffirmed in the stability pact, a member state which 'offends' by persisting with fiscal deficits will be subject to escalating penalties, culminating in fines. This could, in theory, lead to the absurdity of a member state in deficit being obliged to aggravate that deficit by paying the fine. It is hard to imagine a British government, for instance, being prepared to pay up in those circumstances. And were it to do so, the ensuing political crisis would be awesome. Instead, the tacit understanding seems to be that the combination of peer pressure and common sense will bear so heavily on the delinquent member state that it will fall into line sooner rather than later.

What might this mean for the stance of fiscal policy? On the whole it will push governments to be fiscally more austere than they might otherwise be. At the same time, it should lessen the chances of fiscal policy being seriously at odds with monetary policy. It is interesting, nevertheless, to reflect on how a crisis would be resolved if a member state decided that domestic priorities – for example, a more growth-orientated policy implying running a deficit – ought to come first.

A further consideration is how the overall stance of macroeconomic policy in the EU will be set under EMU. The EU economy has struggled to emerge from the recession of the early 1990s and there is a growing acknowledgement that slow growth and unemployment are the main worries, rather than inflation. This suggests that the primary economic policy focus for the next few years in Europe should be on wealth and employment creation and tackling the threat to social cohesion posed by significant social exclusion. The trouble is that the ECB mandate makes it more difficult than it ought to be to pursue these objectives.

7 Conclusions

The ECB will have a degree of independence from political control greater than any existing central bank, a characteristic that will have far-reaching consequences for the conduct of macroeconomic policy under EMU. Although, in recent years, more central banks have acquired substantial independence in their operations, the ECB's independence is significantly greater because it has latitude in setting the goals of policy. Its remit is to ensure price stability, but it can make its own judgement on what constitutes such stability. In addition, its obligations to pay heed to other European Union policy objectives such as growth, employment and social cohesion are vaguely expressed and explicitly secondary to the aim of price stability.

This independence is accentuated by the relatively light reporting requirements and the terms on which the President and Executive Board of the ECB are appointed. Not only will the ECB enjoy operational independence, it will be subject only to light scrutiny by the democratic process. This, too, is likely to have implications for the conduct of macroeconomic policy as the ECB is under less pressure to take 'popular' decisions or to value what might be called 'objective functions' other than its own.

The arrangements for fiscal policy under EMU are much less satisfactory than for monetary policy and this may well result in an unsatisfactory policy mix (Doyle and Weale 1994). One element in this is the excessive deficits procedure and its offspring, the stability pact. These provisions should ensure that budgetary policies are disciplined in a way that guards against inflation, but they offer no latitude for dealing with deficient demand. In this sense, the arrangements will be asymmetric and could result in an excessively austere policy stance.

Because there will be no explicit coordination of fiscal policies of the member states, a related implication is that the overall fiscal policy may not add up to one that is either compatible with monetary policy or suited to macroeconomic conditions.

The potent combination of *democratic and economic policy deficits* may be a significant source of macroeconomic policy problems. As asset-price instability linked to macroeconomic policy developments is probably the most important source of financial instability generally (Crockett 1997, p. 34) the dangers to the European economy are considerable.

A further important conclusion is that the advent of the ECB implies a reassignment of more powers to the supranational tier than is either formally written into the *Treaty* or acknowledged in popular sentiment. The need for close fiscal policy coordination has not yet been reflected in the creation of institutions with powers over fiscal policy to complement those of the ECB over monetary policy.

As for the ECB and the ESCB, a possible proposal for reform would be that a more explicit contract should be negotiated between the member states and the ECB. This would have the virtue of making the goals of economic policy much more transparent and enabling the ECB to focus on hitting explicit targets defined by another body. The problem is likely to be that because the ECB/ESCB will enjoy instrument independence *and* goal independence there will be a substantial and widely perceived democratic deficit which will undermine the credibility of European economic institutions when adverse economic circumstances arise.

In part, this is because much unfinished business has been left. For example, the arrangements for prudential financial supervision or for the management of the EU's foreign exchange reserves are areas normally falling at least in part under the jurisdiction of a central bank. But they have, perhaps deliberately, been left somewhat vague in the *Treaty*.

Taken together, these various dimensions of the political economy of the ECB point to an increased risk of inappropriate policy. As the single, coherent policy-making body, the ECB could be portrayed as a scapegoat. Equally, the outcome could be a 'responsibility vacuum' in which the lack of an accountable body allows all sides to shift blame for misguided policies. Even for those who believe – and we do not go so far – that the role of macroeconomic policy should be limited to ensuring stability, this is a potentially alarming development.

Notes

1. Current fashion in macroeconomics is, in any case, unsympathetic to the notion that monetary policy can be used in this way, but fashions change.
2. Dyson (1994) gives a compelling account of the background.

Bibliography

Alesina, A. and L. Summers (1993), 'Central Bank independence and macroeconomic performance: some comparative evidence', *Journal of Money, Credit and Banking*, **25**, May, 1–14.

Arestis, P. and K. Bain (1995), 'The independence of central banks: a nonconventional perspective', *Journal of Economic Issues*, **39**, (1), 161–74.

Begg, I. and D. Green (1996), 'Banking supervision in Europe and economic and monetary union', *Journal of European Public Policy*, **3** (3), 381–401.

Crockett, A. (1997), *The Theory and Practice of Financial Stability*, Essays in International Finance, No. 203, Princeton, NJ: Department of Economics, Princeton University.

Cukierman, A. (1992), *Central Bank Strategy, Credibility and Independence: Theory and Evidence*, Cambridge, MA: MIT Press.

Cukierman, A. (1994), 'Central bank independence and monetary control', *Economic Journal*, **104** (427), 1437–48.

Currie, D., P. Levine and J. Pearlman (1996), 'The choice of "conservative" bankers in open economies: monetary regime options for Europe', *Economic Journal*, **106** (435), 345–58.

Deane, M. and R. Pringle (1994), *The Central Banks*, London: Hamish Hamilton.

Doyle, C. and M. Weale (1994), 'Do we really want an independent central bank?', *Oxford Review of Economic Policy*, **10** (3), 61–77.

Dyson, K. (1994), *Elusive Union: The Process of Economic and Monetary Union in Europe*, London: Longman.

Eijffinger, S. and J. De Haan (1996), *The Political Economy of Central Bank Independence*, Special Papers in International Economics, No. 19, Princeton, NJ: Department of Economics, Princeton University.

Fischer, S. (1995), 'How independent should the central bank be?', *American Economic Review*, **85** (2), 201–6.

Goodhart, C.A.E. (1994), 'What should central banks do? What should be their macroeconomic objectives and operations?', *Economic Journal*, **104** (427), 1424–36.

Grilli, V., D. Masciandaro and G. Tabellini (1991), 'Political and monetary institutions and public financial policies in the industrial countries', *Economic Policy: A European Forum*, **6**, 342–91.

International Monetary Fund (IMF) (1996), *World Economic Outlook*, October, Washington, DC: IMF.

Johnson, C.J. (1996), *In with the Euro out with the Pound*, London: Penguin Books.

Kenen, P. (1996), *Sorting Out Some EMU Issues*, Jean Monnet Chair Paper No. 38, Robert Schuman Centre, Reprints in International Finance, No. 29, Princeton, NJ: Department of Economics, Princeton University.

King, M. (1996), 'Monetary stability: rhyme or reason?', ESRC Annual Lecture, Swindon: Economic and Social Research Council.

Mourmouras, I.A. (1997), *Central Bank Independence: A Review of Theories*, Paper No. 360, London: Department of Economics, Queen Mary and Westfield College.

Scott, G.C. (1996), *Government Reform in New Zealand*, Occasional Paper 140, Washington, DC: IMF.

Treaty on European Union (1992), Luxembourg: Office for Official Publications of the European Communities.

Von Hagen, J. and B. Eichengreen (1996), 'Federalism, fiscal restraints and European Monetary Union', *American Economic Review*, **86** (2), 134–8.

Walter, A. (1993), *World Power and World Money*, Hemel Hempstead: Harvester Wheatsheaf.

9 The political economy of monetary policy: the effects of globalization and financial integration on the EU

Dorene Isenberg

F33 F36 E52

1 Introduction

For a short time in the post-Second World War era, 1950–1970, a 'golden age of capitalism' is said to have existed in the developed Western capitalist countries (Marglin and Schor 1990; Armstrong et al. 1991). In this era, the capital–labour accord acted like a peace treaty between the two most antagonistic sets of actors in the production process: workers and owners. As a result of this accord, unionized workers could be assured of increasing wages, steady employment, ample fringe benefits and decent working conditions. On the other side, employers could then expect a stable labour force, control over the production process, gains in productivity and no strikes. Peace did reign, for a while.

Gerald Epstein and Juliet Schor (1986 and 1990) have written extensively on the structure and macroeconomic and monetary policy of this period. Their programme, unlike most, has been to expand the understanding of how the financial sector worked and describe its interrelationship with the production side of the economy during this period. They have analysed, in particular, the role of central banks and the financial–industrial relationship in various countries and found that financial and monetary policy are tightly linked to the particular structural relations institutionalized in the labour, goods and financial markets.

Since the 1970s, the golden age of capitalism has given way to the 'global age of capitalism'. The peace accord is no longer in force, so the structural form that produced a high, but limited, level of certainty for the operational process of capitalism is gone. The new globalizing economy, which has experienced the rise of new capitalist regions, the proliferation of 'global' corporations, the internationalizing of financial markets along with rising levels of country and household debt, a continuing division into developed and still-developing countries, and an attempt to return to an at least minimally organized world via regional structures, such as the North American Free Trade Agreement (NAFTA) and the European Union (EU), have produced extended periods of stagnating growth, high and lingering inflation, violent recessions, and high and persistent rates of unemployment.

Globalization, while being the dominating theme in theory, policy and the press, is not the only force being expressed in this historical epoch. Regionalization, which at first sight appears to be counter to globalization, is an equally important force. Since the death of the Cold War, the bifurcated developed world has been restructured. Now, the great regional forces – the United States, Japan and Europe – are engaged in the process of putting a regional mark on capitalism. Given the interaction of these regional and international forces of integration, new questions about the evolving economies arise. What are the new labour–capital relations? How does industrial and financial capital interact? What is the impact of these changes on central banking and national monetary policies?

As a first and small step towards answers, this chapter provides a comparative analysis of the changing structure of production, financial relations, central banking structures and monetary policies in two countries in the European Union, Belgium and France. Section 2 describes the methodology that underpins this study and Section 3 outlines the political–economic structure of each country in the 1970s. Section 4 is a brief description of the policy. Section 5 describes the changes in each country's productive and financial relations and ties those changes into its central bank's monetary policy. The final section concludes the chapter.

2   The methodology

Epstein (1994), following upon his earlier work with Schor, constructed a political–economic econometric model of comparative central banking. It is an eight-countries structural model based on four actors and a set of structural behaviours. His economic actors are labour, industrial capital, financial capital and the central bank. The model is then presented as an IS curve and a political–economic curve, which is derived from mark-ups and capacity utilization. Using this model, Epstein analyses the relationship among monetary policy, the central bank and political–economic structure.

To better understand the forces producing the policies, a short explanation of Epstein's eight political–economic categories is necessary. Each of these categories reflects different types of financial, labour and industrial relationships which represent distinct configurations of power. On the financial side, industrial and financial capital can be related in an arm's-length relationship which is usually characterized by financial market domination. Or the capitals can be more closely related, and these relationships are characterized as bank intermediated. Epstein terms bank-intermediated relations, enterprise finance and market-dominated relations, speculative finance. On the production side, Epstein separates industrial capital and labour's relations into Kaleckian and Neo-Marxian structures. The Kaleckian relationship reflects an industry–labour connection in which an increase in capacity utilization produces a non-negative response in profits.[1] The Neo-Marxian relationship reflects a connection in which profits respond negatively to an increase in capacity utilization.[2] Finally, the central banks are divided into those that are independent and those that are integrated into the state's financing apparatus which is usually through the Treasury.

The possible combinations of these structures are most easily seen in pictorial form. Figure 9.1 is taken from Epstein (1994) and displays the different combinations as boxed triangles.

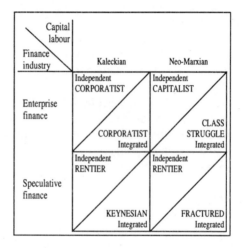

Source: Epstein (1994, p. 256).

Figure 9.1   A political economy model of comparative central banking

Epstein analysed eight countries, categorizing each into one of the eight political–economic classifications.[3] He then tested the set of countries to determine whether the political–economic structure had a determinant relationship to monetary policy. Interestingly, it did. Even more interesting was the discovery that central bank structure, dependent or independent, was the most important factor in determining monetary policy. Those countries with integrated central banks tended to have looser monetary policy, and those with independent central banks tended to have a tighter policy.

For this post-Peace Accord comparative study, Epstein's categorical designations will act as the starting point. Instead of an econometric analysis, this study will descriptively reanalyse the industrial, labour, financial, and central bank relationships of France and Belgium between 1970 and the early 1990s, and determine whether the changes in their political–economic structures have produced changes in their monetary policies. The current view is that globalized perfectly competitive markets have supplanted regulated markets. If this is the case, then the political–economic structures and monetary policies will have changed dramatically.

To lay the foundation for analysing the political–economic changes, the next section briefly revisits the political economy of Belgium and France at the end of the 'golden age'.

3 The golden age of capitalism, Belgium and France: structure and policy

Epstein and Schor (1990) and Epstein (1994) describe the structural relations and monetary policy of the 1970s and early 1980s. While all of the European countries were hit by the increase in oil prices in 1973 and 1979 and the mid-1970s' recession, each response was unique to its particular political and economic situation.

Belgium's economic classification in the 1970s and early 1980s was integrated corporatist. It operated with enterprise finance, an integrated central bank, and capital–labour relations dominated by strong unions that operated in a corporatist mode.[4] The integration of its central bank means that monetary policies implemented by the state were coordinated with the programmes agreed to by labour, industry and finance. Belgium in this rocky economic period had an appreciating currency and a negative balance of trade in addition to the internationally experienced stagflation and recession. It engaged in a monetary policy that was coordinated with an expansionary fiscal policy and focused on the rising value of the Belgian franc, so it was, effectively, a loose policy. By the end of the 1970s, inflation stood in the policy limelight. It was fought via high interest rates and a set of income and price controls that held wages to a growth rate that was less than inflation (Praet and Vuchelen forthcoming).

France with its integrated class struggle categorization experienced a tension between the capitals, finance and industrial, and labour. The integration of its central bank meant that both voices had to be acknowledged in the creation of economic policies, so the monetary policies implemented by the bank depended on which voice dominated at a point in time. France was not a country with a history of strong politically integrated labour unions, but the events of 1968 had moulded their weak voices into authoritative collective bargainers (Crouch 1993). These voices supported the state's expansionary monetary and fiscal policy regime in the mid-1970s, which fought the massive 1975 recession that occurred in the midst of inflation.

By the end of the 1970s, the expansionary policy had successfully fuelled economic growth, but inflation was emerging as a big problem. At this point the monetary and fiscal forces were turned to inflation fighting: interest rates rose and an incomes policy was established. This policy, however, favoured wages at the expense of profits which some analysts regard as the major reason for the lengthy inflationary disruption (Boisseau and Pisani-Ferry 1995).

In the 1970s and early 1980s, both countries were coping with the deepest recession since the Great Depression, and tenacious inflation. To fight these problems, Belgium and France used traditional Keynesian policies – monetary and fiscal – as well as incomes policies. The use of Keynesian policy, as opposed to monetarist, speaks to the overall power structure of the period: government-promoted economic growth and employment policies; and financial institutions regulated so as to support economic growth for labour and industry.[5]

On the international level, this subordination of finance to industry is manifested in the structure of the Bretton Woods agreement and its institutions. The agreement had been crafted at the end of the Second World War to stabilize the foreign exchange value of currencies and organize the trade and production in the war-devastated world economy. Eschewing market-determined currency values because of their potential volatility and deleterious effect on trade and international production, the world's major trading countries opted for fixed exchange rates. The fixity of these financial arrangements reflected the fetters that were constructed around financial markets at the international level and the extent to which financial capital was dominated by industry and labour.

For the most part, domestic financial markets also were highly regulated throughout the 1970s. Financial capitalists had to adhere to rules set up by the state which emphasized the financial sector's role of industrial financier – financing growth in the industrial sector. Additionally, there was the lingering widespread fear of the havoc that the financial sector could bring upon the whole economy. The Great Depression had passed, but the volatile unstable financial markets were still implicated for its onset, depth and duration. The prudential rules under which financial institutions and markets operated grew out of the lessons learned from these earlier débâcles. Most central banks in the developed world also reflected this structural restraint. These banks were integrated, not independent, so they coordinated their policies with governments' industrial policies. Financial capital was industry's handmaiden.

In addition to underlining the overarching power relations in this initial period, it is also important to note the domestic nature of the Keynesian policies. The monetary and fiscal policies were crafted and implemented to remedy national problems. While some of the national economic instability was internationally generated, the level of international integration was low at this point. The nation-state dominated consciousness and was the focus of policy making.

The economic problems encountered in the 1970s were plentiful. The old institutions and structures of the golden age continued to function and attempted to eradicate the new problems as they arose. By the 1980s, however, these institutions were no longer in control. New relationships were emerging that would define the new era of 'global' capitalism.

4 The transition: from golden age to global age

The oil crisis of the 1970s and the demise of the international monetary structure, which was initiated by floating the US dollar, crowned the beginning of the changing world economic order. In the numerous years since the float, most of the world's countries have been organized into a new international order based on market production. Developed and developing countries are intertwined in international production processes and trade which have been structured by international corporations more so than international governmental organizations (Hood and Young 1979).

The motivations behind this globally-scaled reorganization were to increase profits by decreasing costs of production and to promote efficiency. Both an increase in profits and in efficiency were linked to increasing the area of economic and social endeavour over which the market decision-making process rules.[6]

The internationalizing of market rule has been sequentially introduced. It started with goods and services and only much later did it expand into finance. In the 1950s, the corporations responded to the tariffed and barriered world of trade by cloning themselves: 75 per cent of foreign direct investment (FDI) was private (Hood and Young 1979, Table 1.1). Since trade was impeded, corporations expanded into other nations and produced for their new host markets (*The Economist*, 1995). As the effects of the General Agreement on Tariffs and Trade (GATT) spread through the developed trading world, trade barriers fell and the growth rate of FDI declined.

By the end of the 1970s, all the structures had been put in place for a take-off in international trade and production. As Hood and Young state, 'The existence of networks of foreign affiliates within multi-national corporations opens up the possibility of integrated production and marketing on a global basis' (1979, p. 24). The transnational corporation grew and spread in a regionally specific way. Europe, under the aegis of the European Economic Community (EEC), increased its intraregional investment activities as it increased its membership. Japan expanded its investments in Asia. The US had its largest number of new subsidiaries located in Europe, but it, more than the other developed countries, diversified its investments into Asia and Latin America as well (ibid., Table 1.5). These region-specific investments spawned the regional divisions in trade and production that continued into the 'global' era.

The 1980s and 1990s witnessed moves towards an internationalization of financial markets: financial deregulation and capital controls eradication. Financial capital began to flow more freely as the barriers came down. Within the European Community the Single Market Act was passed and the European Monetary System (EMS) was established, which prompted the EC nations to eradicate their capital controls. Britain's exchange controls were abolished in 1979. France initiated its financial deregulation in the mid-1980s. Belgium's financial structures and two-tier exchange rate stayed in place longer than they did in most European countries. They initiated their changes in 1991. Japan, unlike many of its neighbours, abolished its exchange controls in the same period as Britain.

As these international barriers were falling, the numbers of new assets created specifically for this internationalizing financial market were rising. In the 1960s, Eurodollars were introduced, while Eurocurrencies and Eurobonds were introduced in the 1980s. Along with these new assets came new and expanded markets for their sales. By the 1990s, all assets did not trade on all markets, but a major move towards financial market globalization had succeeded (Mussa and Goldstein 1993).[7]

Europe, given its commitment to a regional economic structure, the EC, piggybacked its move to regionalization on to an even greater commitment to international changes in the structure of markets. The meeting of the European Council at Maastricht in December 1991 ratified the Treaty on European Union. This treaty moved the treaty signers not only to political and social union, but also to monetary union. It provided for the eradication of all existing capital controls; the legal structure for the single currency; a European Central Bank (ECB) that would govern a system of national central banks; and a mandated monetary policy for the ECB – price stability. This new structure, the European Union, was an acknowledgement of the new international order.

These changes in market size, structure, and actors were all important to its reshaping. While the Peace Accord and the Bretton Woods agreement were still in effect, the Cold War divided the world, and the nation-state was the dominant governmental form and production space. As the next section shows, once the old structure faded away, the move towards international markets and regional governments produced new capital–labour power-sharing arrangements, financial structures and monetary policies.

5 The global age of capitalism: changes in the national political– economic structure

Belgium

Belgium, like other European countries, experienced the economic disorientation of inflation and then unemployed in the late 1970s and early 1980s. In Britain these disruptions resulted in a radical governmental change. The Conservatives were elected and Margaret Thatcher became Prime Minister in 1979. Unlike Britain, however, no radical change in government transpired in Belgium, so there was no electoral mandate to promote a change in policy making. None the less, a transformation did ensue. It came in the guise of inflation fighting, and it heralded a structural change in Belgian labour relations. These changes marked the move away from the 'social compact' that had characterized Belgian tripartite policy making in the post-Second World War era.

The Belgian trade unions had been categorized as corporatist and very strong. They were politically integrated into the national system of social and economic decision making; they had high density and coverage; they were integrated into and a product of the linguistic and regional cultures in Belgium; and they were the sole collective bargaining representatives for their members (Spineux 1990; Wallerstein et al. 1997). Through the 1970s, labour was co-partnered with capital and the state in shaping the growth path of the nation. At the end of the 1970s, however, the Belgians had an inflation problem that did not improve when the usual fiscal and monetary policy measures were applied. So in 1980 the government, without consulting the other social partners, decided to implement an incomes policy that would stop what it saw as a wage–price spiral (Crouch 1993). While the vestige of a tripartite system was saved by labour and capital's agreement to implement 'voluntary' wage restraints, this was the beginning of a weakened role for labour (Spineux 1990).

For much of the 1980s, the state controlled the collective bargaining process (Crouch 1993). All the partners in the tripartite process were still in place, but the state took it upon itself to dominate the process. After 1987, the state's statutory interference ostensibly subsided (Wallerstein et al. 1997). Then, in 1989 the state passed new legislation which gave it the power to abrogate any collective bargaining agreement that failed to maintain 'competitiveness' (Praet and Vuchelen forthcoming). With such a law in force the partnership could no longer be viewed as three sided; it was unilateral.

While the state initiated labour's excision from the tripartite decision-making process, industrial capital quickly joined hands with the state to demote its labour partner. When the state acted unilaterally in contract decisions, industrial capital resisted the process, but not the actions. Industrial capital seized the moment and pushed for a renegotiation of the 'social contract' that included more flexibility for them to restructure the workplace in response to technological change: they wanted greater flexibility in their management of the firm. They also wanted more collective bargaining at the company level (Spineux 1990). The aim of these changes was to shift power towards industrial capital in the negotiation process.

Industrial capital achieved its goals. More bargains over wages and working hours transpired at the company level (ibid.). Labour's voice was softened, but not absent. Belgian workers at the end of the 1980s were represented by some of the strongest labour unions in Europe (Crouch 1993; Wallerstein et al. 1997).

The result of the state's interventions, capital's push for flexibility and disaggregation, and labour's acceptance of these 'voluntary' incomes policies was the renewed profitability of the business sector and reignition of the economy's expansion. After experiencing a pretax rate of return in 1973 of more than 22 per cent, business profits bottomed out at 17 per cent in 1981. With the implementation of the 'voluntary' incomes policy, the pretax rate of return rebounded to almost 20 per cent in 1986 (OECD 1989). The incomes policy is also cited as the major source of the reduction of unit labour costs and production costs which enhanced Belgium's competitiveness. These changes are credited with laying the foundation for the surge in economic growth that Belgian industry experienced. Between 1987 and 1990 industry grew at the annual rate of 2.8, 5.4, 5.3 and 3.9 per cent, respectively, which surpassed the annual economy-wide growth rates (National Bank of Belgium 1991). Labour's surrender of income financed business's recovery.

Epstein did not categorize Belgium, but it is a bank-intermediated open economy with a large public sector debt. The banks in Belgium are universal financial intermediaries. They were heavily involved with the financing of both trade and government throughout the 1980s. Trade was most often financed by bank loans. Government finance required banks to purchase securities 'on tap', so they also played an important role in the capital markets.[8] The banks' historical involvement in both trade and government finance anchored them to industry and the state.

These relationships, however, underwent a transformation by the end of the 1980s. In 1975, banks accounted for 57.7 per cent of non-financial borrowers' finance while in the growth years of 1987–90, it was 40.1, 52.4, 49.6 and 34.5 per cent (OECD 1992b, 1996). After 1991, the banks also held a smaller percentage of government bonds in their portfolios, but continued to be important actors in the governmental finance process. These changes underscored the alteration in the industry–finance relationships. While continuing their activity in industrial finance, the banks were no longer engaged in industrial finance as their major venture. Other financial endeavours were competing for bank funds, and they received them. By the early 1990s, the Belgian industry–finance relationship was no longer intertwined as before, but banks still played a major role in industrial finance.

With the change in the finance–industry relationship has also come major changes in its competitive environment and focus. In preparation for the EMU and the Single Market before it, several financial reforms were enacted at the national and supranational level which impacted the sector. Supraregionally, the 1988 Second Banking Directive started smoothing the way for cross-border banking activity. By implementing home rule as the basis of bank regulation, the 'rules of the game' were standardized for an individual national player (but not across all the players), thus making inter-EC expansion easier. In addition, the even tighter financial integration that is due in the third phase of EMU – a single monetary policy and central bank for the whole of the European Union – has fostered national reforms marketizing the financial sector and inhibiting governmental control over finance. Specifically, new standardized government securities, linear bonds, were inaugurated; a secondary market for their trade was also created; an 'independent' central bank was introduced; direct access by the Treasury to central bank finance was prohibited; the central bank's use of credit controls was eradicated; and the two-tier exchange rate was replaced by a single exchange rate (National Bank of Belgium 1992).

The impact of these deregulatory reforms on the Belgian financial sector has been to increase its 'inward' internationalization and open up the domestic market to competition from foreign banks. Unlike Britain, the Belgian credit institutions were not positioning themselves to become an international financial centre. Instead, they were attempting to hold their domestic position in the face of falling national borders. While their strategy may have kept some new competitors from entering, others were not dissuaded. In 1985, there were only 61 foreign financial institutions operating in Belgium, but by 1992 that number had expanded to 73 (Pintjens 1994).

Another indicator of Belgium's increasingly internationalized banking environment is found on their balance sheets. In 1992, Belgian banks' claims on foreign countries accounted for 56 per cent of their total claim which in Europe puts them second only to Luxembourg in terms of the openness of their banking sector (ibid.). More than 50 per cent of their loans were made to borrowers in other nations. Given that borrowers go where the funds are, this openness could put Belgian borrowers in the position of being out-competed by foreign borrowers for their home resources.

Along with promoting the 'inward' internationalization of the Belgian financial sector, the regulatory changes encouraged the restructuring of the sector's mode of operation so that the 'customized' banker–client relationship could be supplanted by a 'standardized' market decision-making model.

The earlier-presented banking–industry loan statistics indicated their secular decline. The decline was more than stylistic; it symbolized the rising domination of standardized market finance.

What does all this mean for the structure of Belgium's political economy and monetary policy? The 1980s state coup in tripartite labour negotiations, the deregulation of the financial sector, the changes in the industry–finance relations, and finance's 'inward' internationalization all point to an altered political–economic structure and therefore, a change in monetary policy. The explicit motivators of these changes – EEC, Single Market Act, EMU – have promoted expanded use of market decision making and in the arena of politically determined decisions the prescription of appropriate macroeconomic positions, for example, 3 per cent deficit/GDP and 60 per cent debt/GDP ratios. The new political–economic balance of power and the mandated macroeconomic positions have produced both a tighter monetary policy since the 1980s and a rationale for the state's decision to usurp power in labour negotiations. Praet and Vuchelen state, 'More fundamentally, the strong currency policy also implied the necessity for the government to follow more orthodox fiscal policies and to intervene, if necessary, in the wage process' (forthcoming, p. 12). Since the state has been working with the central bank to produce Belgium's recent financial reforms, there is strong evidence that the ideology of 'perfect markets knowing best' is gaining ground and may soon rule the roost.

Inflation fighting and promotion of further European integration dominated policy-making decisions throughout the 1980s and 1990s.[9] In the earlier period, the 1970s and the early 1980s, Belgian monetary policy had focused on the stabilization of its exchange rate against its trading partners. The idea then was to keep the foreign 'pricing' of Belgian money, used to purchase Belgian goods, low and stable. While focused on the export side of the economy, the policy was aimed at stimulating domestic production. By the end of the 1980s, Belgian had joined the EMS and its monetary policy still focused on the exchange rate, except by then it was being used as an intermediate target. The ultimate goal was to stabilize prices – fight inflation. Monetary policy was turned on its head as the industry–labour relationship fell apart.

In 1990, at the suggestion of the central bank (still an integrated bank), the government decided to institute a hard currency policy by strictly pegging the franc to the Deutschmark. This policy was expected to provide anti-inflation credibility to Belgian interest rates and the franc, which in the long run would translate into lower interest rates and a stronger franc (OECD 1994).[10] Unlike the old policy, this one focused on the whole economy, not just a particular sector. Also unlike the old policy, it had deleterious short-terms effects: high unemployment. The year the peg was initiated, Belgian unemployment reached its low point, 8.7 per cent, but by 1994 it had trended upward, reaching 12.6 per cent (OECD 1995).

This follow-the-Deutschmark policy reflected the shift in the Belgian political–economic structure. With labour's demotion in the tripartite process, Belgium moved out of its integrated corporatist category. Even with the industrial relations institutional structures still in place, financial capital and the state were driving the monetary policy decision making, and neither of the other partners had the power to fight it. This power loss was not just the demotion of labour in the partnership. It was also the rise of the monetarist view of the market and the desire to be a full-fledged member in the emerging EMU.

The process of internationalization was also instrumental in the changes. Internationalism reflects different economic ideas in different historical periods. In this historical period, it internalizes the idea of market decision making, so the process of globalization has also been a force for marketization. The end result of these changes has been the decline of industry and labour's power and the ascendance of the financier's power and the will of the state. These changes in political economy provide the major explanation for Belgium's tighter monetary policies.

France

The 1970s witnessed French labour at its pinnacle of power in the post-Second World War period. Labour's gains after May 1968 solidified its collective bargaining position at the industry level, provided for legal recognition for national level bargaining, and produced limited tripartite talks (Crouch 1993). No one union or confederation of unions dominated France's labour relations, instead, it operated in a decentralized and pluralistic manner. While lacking the centralized union structure of Britain, Germany or Belgium, the two biggest unions, Confédération Générale du Travail (CGT) (50 per cent) and Confédération Française Démocratique du Travail (CFDT) (23 per cent), together represented about 73 per cent of the labour force in 1979. Through its employers' association, Conseil National due Patronat Français (CNPF), industry, too, was more organized than in previous periods. However, individual firms, in contrast to the CNPF, still dominated employer activity in bargaining. These institutional changes in labour and capital relations did not reduce the confrontational nature of their relationship. Epstein characterized this industry–labour relationship as Neo-Marxian.

The economic policy of the mid-1970s was expansionary, mainly recession fighting, and composed of an appropriate monetary and fiscal mix. Prime Minister Jacques Chirac's decision to fight the recession with expansionary policies shifted the distribution of income towards wages (Boisseau and Pisani-Ferry 1995). Labour's strength in this period, as well as the recession's heavy impact on GDP, worked together to move government into this growth policy.

During this period, the state had passed collective bargaining legislation, but no acknowledged confederated representatives for labour or industry endured after the 1970s' heyday. By the end of the decade a major change was under way, and workers moved towards the more 'reformist' unions (Segrestin 1990). By the early 1980s, labour had returned to its decentralized structure; industry returned to firm-level negotiations; and a general decline in the completion of successful contract negotiations ensued. The 'contested terrain' shifted from industry–labour tensions to tensions among the state, financial capital and the internationalizing market forces.

In this period, the mid-1970s, French monetary policy under Prime Minister Raymond Barre turned to inflation fighting and focused on exchange rate stability. Unlike Belgium, neither industry nor labour supported it. When Prime Minister Barre took France into the EMS in 1979, there was 'opposition from the union and [it] was not supported by the employers, because in the mind of many entrepreneurs, the memory of the successful devaluations of 1958 and 1969 was still present' (ibid., p. 4). Regardless of labour and business's missing support, the state strongly supported and acted on it.

This shift in Barre's policy was a domestic response to an internationally produced problem.

> For France international competitiveness has been a continuing policy preoccupation, particularly in the light of the perceived 'fragility' of the country's foreign trade . . . Similarly, a strong currency has been a long standing, if elusive, aim of macroeconomic policy making that runs through modern French economic history from Poincaré to DeGaulle and from Giscard to Mitterrand. (Boltho 1996, p. 91)

Barre adopted the tools of monetarism, but it can be argued that his government used only the tools, not the theory (Loriaux 1997, p. 134). The motivation behind Barre's policies was not to produce a more market-dominated internationalized France, rather, he was attempting to maintain the traditional role of the state in aiding in the economic development of the nation (Joint Economic Committee 1981).[11]

The best description for French political–economic relations in the 1980s is state dominated and the best description of its economic policies is a roller-coaster ride. First, the election of François Mitterrand's Socialist Party in 1981 raised expectations for a much larger role for the state in economic planning and for a better life for workers. Second, the 1982 recession hit hard as the state was nationalizing the big firms in industry and finance. Massive unemployment was then followed by wage, price and credit controls. Third, the franc was devalued and a new monetary policy, *franc fort*, followed. Fourth, President Mitterrand, Prime Minister Laurent Fabius, and Minister of

Finance Pierre Bérégovoy deregulated the financial sector and promoted innovations in financial assets and structures. Fifth, the economy expanded, Chirac became the Prime Minister with the parliamentary success of the right in 1986, and then, the Bourse crashed. The monetary policy was still the *franc fort*, but devaluations in the Exchange Rate Mechanism (ERM) followed the crash. In the meantime, Chirac was privatizing the nationalized industries. Sixth, most of the other countries in the EEC started the process of financial and economic deregulation in order to meet the criteria of the Single Market and the EMU. The monetary policy was still the *franc fort*. Finally, the franc was devalued in 1993, but remained within the EMS.

The obvious thread that runs through this period in France is the desire for a stable, strong franc. The needle that pulled the thread was the state, which drew its motivations from the changing world, the problems of the changing world, and its belief that it could and should guide the development of the French nation in all ways possible. Regardless of the politics of the government in power, after 1983, monetary policy focused on keeping the franc in the ERM and tightly pegged to the Deutschmark (Loriaux 1997).

As the current account deficit was growing more negative, this hard currency programme was implemented as a remedy. While it aided the export sector, the focus of the policy, it appeared to contradict the other policies of the Socialist government. In France, however, the central bank and the Treasury work closely together in setting the targets for national monetary and exchange rate policies and in determining how best to achieve them. Since policy making is coordinated, the often contradictory-seeming industrial and financial policies promoted by the state during this period need not be judged as schizophrenic. They are individual pieces of the state's strategic vision for the future.[12]

Other state policies, industrial and financial, were interwoven with the *franc fort*, so as to produce a new domestic economy that would be viable in an internationally competitive world market. Mitterrand's 1981 industrial nationalizations were a mapping of the state's vision of organization on to industry. Its 'set of measures operates through sectoral plans, organizing access to product markets and coordinating improvements in production processes' (Petit 1986, p. 396). This attempt at vertical integration stood in contrast to the mergers and acquisitions approach that was affecting industrial conglomeratizion in the US in this period. The objective in the French case was to solidify the links between final and intermediate producers so that the efficiency and international competitiveness of its firms and industries were enhanced (ibid. 1986). When the 1982 recession hit France, the plans could not be completed as desired.

Following upon the heels of he nationalizations was another controversial change implemented by the government. Prime Minister Fabius deregulated the French financial sector. The financial sector had long been highly regulated and seen as the mechanism by which the state achieved its monetary policies. The deregulations as Cerny argues, were 'part of a more comprehensive policy – not only deregulating markets but also modifying the *dirigiste* system itself. But these changes were also seen as imperative for maintaining competitiveness in a volatile and rapidly evolving international financial environment' (1989, p. 173). The state's modification of the *dirigiste* system was technical. New tools were used to achieve the same objectives, for the deregulation grew out of the logic of the nationalizations – maintaining France's international competitiveness. Finance Minister Bérégovoy maintained that deregulation would help industry by reducing interest rates on its investment borrowings. He claimed that interest rates fell by 2 per cent as a result of deregulation and it is widely accepted as fact that the deregulation was responsible for the reduction (ibid.).

The *franc fort* policy and its supportive monetary policies were maintained through the early 1990s. During the 1980s, France's balance of trade never returned to the black, but its export sector experienced strong growth. It's trading relationship with its other EEC partners especially flourished. Additionally, France experienced a strong and steady growth in FDI. These results, export and FDI growth, were aims of the state's policy. Both rising exports and FDI enhanced France's international competitiveness.

The French state's commitment to the *franc fort* was tested in the 1990s.[13] A recession began in 1991; the Maastricht Treaty was ratified in 1991, but barely accepted by the French public in 1992; and then market forces in the guise of speculators attacked the franc in 1993. The state in its support for EMU continued to promote the *franc fort*, which exacerbated the recession.[14] When it fought the recession by reducing interest rates in early 1993, France contested the decisions of the currency markets' speculators. Only with the help of the Bundesbank was the franc able to remain within the ERM and was the state able to maintain its policy stance. While the franc did not suffer the same fate as the pound and the lira, it was devalued and interest rates rose (Melitz 1995). After this speculative upheaval abated, interest rates did drop. Between 1992 and 1995, money market rates declined from 10.35 to 6.35 per cent. However, the state's target of increasing growth and reducing unemployment was not achieved. Unemployment, which had stood at 8.9 per cent in 1990, reached 12.4 per cent in 1994 and 12.7 per cent in 1996 (OECD 1996).

While not achieving all of its policy goals, the French state continued to be an economic actor through the early 1990s. Neither the internationalizing financial markets nor the regionalizing structures of the European Union kept the state from taking an active role in directing the growth path of the nation.

In France, liberalism gave the state a power it had previously lacked, that of making the franc a strong currency. Nor did the liberalization prevent the state, still under a Socialist government, from using its control over budget subsidies to implement a thorough and successful restructuring of industry. One must therefore be cautious in one's interpretation of French financial liberalization. It does not translate in any simply way into a withdrawal of the state from a role of active management of the economy. (Loriaux 1997, p. 160)

While the state has continued its *dirigiste* policy, its inability to stimulate a growth rate that would eradicate the high level of unemployment has meant that France's economic problems have been borne disproportionately by labour. Unlike labour's quiet period, 1975–92, strike activity has risen as the state's social welfare expenditures have fallen. At this point, increased strike activity is not indicative of restructured labour organizations or new labour alliances, but it does imply that labour does not accept the policy of competitive disinflation as a sufficient reason to continue with France's restrictive monetary and fiscal policies.

As labour has lost in this era of *dirigisme*, both the financial and the export sectors have gained. In the financial sector, not all the actors have profited from liberalization. Many of the financial intermediaries lost market share in the shift towards market-based instruments and structures. The bank directors, however, had been consulted by Finance Minister Bérégovoy prior to the liberalization. By using their suggested changes, the liberalization produced their return to profitability. While a return to profitability was a short-term goal, the longer-term goal – restructuring in the mode of the German banking system – has begun. As far as the gains for the export sector are concerned, the consistency of the state's promotion of a hard currency policy and the earlier dedicated credit policies which had provided non-market based loans to it, are responsible (ibid., pp. 134, 148–9). The credit allowed cheap, unfettered production and expansion to ensue. These sectors were the winners because the state's plan for producing economic growth centred on them.

The controlling actor in the determination of French monetary policy has undergone little alteration in the 'global age of capitalism'. The French state has remained an important economic actor dominating industry, finance and labour since the 1970s, and some would argue throughout the post-Second World War period (Loriaux 1997; Cerny 1989). The state's partners, however, have changed over this period. The 1970s Keynesian demand-management and credit policies reflected the state's link with labour and industry. The 1980s switch to a 'hard' currency exchange rate policy indicated that the state had taken a new partner, finance. Even with these partner changes, France's internationally competitive position has been at the centre of the state's policy.

As witnessed by decreases in strike activity after 1975, labour did not contest the state's policies until the *franc fort* was forged with EMU. While labour has begun to vocalize its dissatisfaction with the post-EMU policies, industry remains divided (Boisseau and Pisani-Ferry 1995). French finance capital, on the other hand, led the way for many of the reforms that the EMU has promoted, and it has also been a staunch supporter of the *franc fort*. Financial capital has also been a strong proponent of policies that would mesh the economy with the international financial markets. These policies have often fitted in well with the state's, and therefore the central bank's, views, which have been focused on France's domestic situation in an internationalizing world.[15] The French state in organizing its economic system so as to keep its distinctly national character, maintain a strong welfare system, and be a competitive actor in the international economy has also produced policies that accord more with financial capital's desires than with labour's.

6   Conclusion

The Keynesian demand-management policies of the 1960s and early 1970s were symbols for the dominant class forces within the political–economic structure of that time. The tight monetary policies, financial de- and reregulations, and decisions for 'hard' currencies in the 1980s and 1990s are also symbols of the forces dominating the political economy in this time. Clearly, the policies have changed, but as the study of Belgium and France has shown, it does not necessarily mean that the globalizing marketplace its the only and dominant force in determining those policies. While labour and industrial capital are no longer calling the tune, to which the state and its dependent central bank dance, it is also the case that the force pressing for globalizing change in these economies is not just an ethereal supporter of international markets or financial capital. The state and financial capital have acted as forces working to integrate the economy into an internationalizing market, but at the same time to maintain national character, the domestic interests of those within its boundaries, and, especially in France, the state's role as an economic actor.

In Belgium's case, the state began advancing the policies of financial capital early in the 1980s by dethroning the reigning powers – labour and industrial capital. Once the tripartite contract decision-making process had been blown apart, there was a power vacuum into which finance and the state moved. The state represented financial capital's views when it promoted financial deregulation and independence for the central bank. However, these policies were not attempts to internationalize the economy. Instead, they promoted the 'inward' internationalization of financial intermediaries and markets. Rather than replacing its financial institutions with markets or enticing multinational financial institutions to replace domestic ones, domestic institutions became active in international lending. The state, realizing what a small open economy Belgium is, understood that the process of internationalizing and regionalizing could swallow it.[16] Its response was to promote regionalization via the European Union, which would represent European, if not necessarily Belgian views, and to engage in 'inward' or domestic internationalization.

France presents an even stronger case of domestic internationalization. When the 1970s tenuous labour–industrial capital industry-level bargaining process broke down, the decentralized pluralism of French unions and industry reemerged. The state, historically an important economic actor, stepped into the void along with financial forces representing the internationalization process. Like Belgium, the internationalization process in France was shaped into a domestic form. The 'hard' currency policies aided the export and financial sectors while the state's other monetary and industrial policies aimed at making other sectors competitive at the international level.

Just as the internationalization process and financial capital have not completely overtaken the monetary policy decision-making process, it is also the case that labour is not completely outside the power bloc. The success of Britain's Labour Party and France's Socialist Party in the 1997 elections and the increased strike activity in France, Germany and Belgium indicate that labour cannot be discounted completely. However, as Epstein, drawing on the work of James Crotty (1993) says, 'As financial deregulation and international financial integration expand, it may become less possible for labor or industrial capital to influence central bank policy, and therefore we are less likely to see a Keynesian coalition emerge' (1994, p. 268). It may be impossible for a Keynesian coalition to emerge, the new economic structures have produced new political–economic forces. It is not, however, impossible for a new coalition for the new era to emerge. Maybe a labour–finance coalition and accord is the answer for a progressive future.

Notes

1. This Kaleckian result derives from the stability of the mark-up and the capacity to generate particular industrial relations. A corporatist capital–labour relationship or one like that in the capital–labour accord – interindustry relations are structured and stable, capital controlling the introduction of technology and the production process – would work. In both of these relationships, wages are set by contract, and then any surplus achieved in an expansion of production, again by agreement, go to capital.
2. The Neo-Marxian capital–labour relationship is institutionally associated with decentralized, contestational union structures. Epstein's distribution of income in this structure is based on a cyclical view of economic activity. When output is increased near a business-cycle peak, the result is increased wages for workers. Labour markets are tight at this point in the cycle, so workers can use their combined power to win wage increases at the expense of increased profits for capital (Epstein 1994, p. 242).
3. The countries that he analysed were Britain, Canada, France, Germany, Italy, Japan, Sweden and the United States.
4. Since Epstein's data were not available for Belgium, this classification is based on institutional data, such as the tripartite labour contract negotiations and contract decision making.

5. Even the independent Bundesbank held to Keynesian monetary policy. In a recessionary period, monetary policy was loose, causing interest rates to fall. During inflationary periods, monetary policy was tight, interest rates rose, and the bank relied upon the unions to hold wages in check, which they did.
6. Dore (1996) notes that efficiency is not necessarily linked to a more equitable distribution of income. The idea of economic convergence, which should lead to efficiency enhancement, benefits the owner of capital.
7. Mussa and Goldstein detail the various indicators of a completely integrated, globalized financial market. They find along with others in their survey that financial markets have not yet achieved complete integration.
8. In 1991 Belgium underwent a monetary reform. The 'on tap' issue of bonds was replaced by a competitive auction fashioned after that of the US Federal Reserve. Until then, government securities had been customized to the needs of the purchaser. Now, they are standardized and under the purview of market institutions (Praet and Vuchelen forthcoming).
9. Integral to this enhanced vision of integration was the vision of borderless states through which capital would flow without hindrance. The Single Market Act had already modified the existing treaties so as to allow the free flow of goods, but capital's free flow could still be impeded at the level of the state. While the Maastricht Treaty did not go into force until the end of 1991, its mandate for the free flow of capital was pre-dated by the 1988 European Council Directive which inhibited the use of capital controls. Capital's free flow was important to inflation fighting in the new 1980s' mode – monetarism. So, the European Community's political environment in the late 1980s incorporated the market link to anti-inflationary monetary policy even before Maastricht was signed (Bakker 1996).
10. The rationale behind such a decision rested on the idea of a credibility anchor, a currency which was seen as non-inflationary. By following the movements of the currency anchor within a small band-width of deviation, the 'follower's' resolve to maintain a low-inflation position would be acknowledged and not only would the following currency be stronger, but its interest rate would also have decreased by the decrease in inflation (Burdekin et al. 1994).
11. For a contrasting vision of these events, see Boltho (1996).
12. Numerous comments have been made about the crazy conflicting policies of the French government, but unless one actually believes that the state is schizophrenic, its actions must derive from some plan or strategic vision (Cerny 1989; JEC 1981).
13. Instead of calling it *franc fort*, it is now known as competitive disinflation (Banque de France 1991).
14. A counter interpretation holds that France's *franc fort* is the price it had to pay to show Germany that it had the fortitude necessary for EU leadership (Boisseau and Pisani-Ferry 1995).
15. The Bank of France was given its independence in 1994. This structural change could produce a new liaison between the central bank and financial capital, but the political–economic impact can be determined only in the future.
16. Belgium had a two-tier foreign exchange market, which it refused to surrender until the Maastricht Treaty outlawed it. There was a floating rate for capital transactions which took place on the free exchange market, and a fixed rate for current account transactions which took place on the official exchange market. This financial structure insulated the export sector from exchange rate risk.

Bibliography

Armstrong, P., A. Glyn and J. Harrison (1991), *Capitalism Since 1945*, Oxford: Basil Blackwell.
Baglioni, G. and C. Crouch (1990), *European Industrial Relations*, London: Sage Publications.
Bakker, A. (1996), *The Liberalization of Capital Movements in Europe*, Dordrecht: Kluwer Academic Publishers.
Banque de France (1991), *Annual Report, 1991*, Paris.

Boisseau, de C. and J. Pisani-Ferry (1995), *The Political Economy of French Economic Policy and the Transition to EMU*, Centre d'Etudes Prospectives et D'Informations Internationales, Working Paper No. 95.09.

Boltho, A. (1996), 'Has France converged on Germany?', in S. Berger and R. Dore (eds), *National Diversity and Global Capitalism*, Ithaca: Cornell University Press, pp. 89–100.

Burdekin, R., J. Westbrook and T. Willett (1994), 'Exchange rate pegging as a disinflation strategy: evidence from the European Monetary System', in P. Siklos (ed.), *Varieties of Monetary Reforms: Lessons and Experiences on the Road to Monetary Union*, Boston: Kluwer Academic Publishers, pp. 45–72.

Cerny, P. (1989), 'The "little big bang" in Paris: financial market deregulation in a *dirigiste* system', *European Journal of Political Research*, **17**, 169–92.

Coakley, J. (1994), 'The integration of property and financial markets', *Environment and Planning A*, **26**, 697–713.

Coakley, J. and L. Harris (1992), 'Financial globalisation and deregulation', in J. Michie (ed.), *The Economic Legacy 1979–1992*, London: Academic Press, pp. 37–57.

Crotty, J. (1993), 'The rise and fall of the Keynesian revolution in the age of the global marketplace', in G. Epstein, J. Graham and J. Nembhard (eds), *Creating a New World Economy: Forces of Change and Plans for Action*, for the Center for Popular Economics, Philadelphia: Temple University Press, pp. 163–80.

Crouch, C. (1990), 'United Kingdom: the rejection of compromise', in G. Baglioni and C. Crouch (eds), *European Industrial Relations*, London: Sage Publications, pp. 326–55.

Crouch, C. (1993), *Industrial Relations and European State Traditions*, Oxford: Clarendon Press.

Dore, R. (1996), 'Convergence in whose interest?', in S. Berger and R. Dore (eds), *National Diversity and Global Capitalism*, Ithaca: Cornell University Press, pp. 366–74.

Epstein, G. (1994), 'A political economy model of comparative central banking', in G. Dymski and R. Pollin (eds), *New Perspectives in Monetary Macroeconomics*, Ann Arbor: Michigan University Press, pp. 231–77.

Epstein, G. and J.B. Schor (1986), *The Political Economy of Central Banking*, Discussion Paper No. 1281, November, Harvard Institute of Economic Research, Harvard University, Cambridge, MA.

Epstein, G. and J.B. Schor (1990), 'Macropolicy in the rise and fall of the golden age', in S. Marglin and J. Schor (eds), *The Golden Age of Capitalism: Reinterpreting the Postwar Experience*, New York: Oxford University Press, pp. 153–86.

Harmon, M.D. (1995), 'British unilateralism in a multilateral Europe: sterling in and out of the Exchange Rate Mechanism', *New Political Science*, **33–34**, 51–104.

Hood, N. and S. Young (1979), *The Economics of Multinational Enterprise*, London: Longman Group.

Ibrahim, Y. (1997), 'Britain shifting monetary policy to central bank', *New York Times*, 7 May.

International Monetary Fund (IMF) (1982), *International Financial Statistics*, Washington, DC: IMF.

International Monetary Fund (IMF) (1995), *International Financial Statistics*, Washington, DC: IMF.

Joint Economic Committee (JEC), US House of Representatives (1981), *Monetary Policy, Selective Credit Policy and Industrial Policy in France, Britain, West Germany, and Sweden*, Washington, DC.

Loriaux, M. (1997), 'Socialist monetarism and financial liberalization', in M. Loriaux, M. Woo-Cumings, K.E. Calder, S. Maxfield and S. Pérez (eds), *Capital Ungoverned*, Ithaca: Cornell University Press, pp. 120–61.

Marglin, S. and J.B. Schor (1990), *The Golden Age of Capitalism: Reinterpreting the Postwar Experience*, Oxford: Clarendon Press.

Melitz, J. (1995), 'French monetary policy and recent speculative attacks on the franc', *Economic Notes*, **24** (3), 619–34.

Mussa, M. and M. Goldstein (1993), 'The integration of world capital markets', in Federal Reserve Bank of Kansas City, *Changing Capital Markets: Implications for Monetary Policy*, Jackson Hole, Wyoming, 19-21 August, pp. 245–313.

National Bank of Belgium (1991), *Annual Report 1991*, Brussels.
National Bank of Belgium (1992), 'Reform of the money market and of the instruments of monetary policy in Belgium', Research Department, Mimeo.
Organization for Economic Cooperation and Development (OECD) (1989), *Economic Surveys, Belgium/Luxembourg, 1988–1989*, Paris: OECD.
Organization for Economic Cooperation and Development (OECD) (1990), *Economic Surveys. United Kingdom*, Paris: OECD.
Organization for Economic Cooperation and Development (OECD) (1992a), *Economic Outlook. Historical Statistics, 1960–1990*, Paris: OECD.
Organization for Economic Cooperation and Development (OECD) (1992b), *Banks Under Stress*, Paris: OECD.
Organization for Economic Cooperation and Development (OECD) (1994), *Economic Surveys. Belgium–Luxembourg, 1993–1994*, Paris: OECD.
Organization for Economic Cooperation and Development (OECD) (1995), *Economic Outlook*, Vol. 57, June, Paris: OECD.
Organization for Economic Cooperation and Development (OECD) (1996), *Bank Profitability: Financial Statements of Banks, 1985–1994*, Paris: OECD.
Petit, P. (1986), 'Full-employment policies in stagnation: France in the 1980s', *Cambridge Journal of Economics*, **10**, 393–406.
Pintjens, S. (1994), 'The internationalization of the Belgian banking sector: a comparison with the Netherlands', in D. Fair and R. Raymond (eds), *The Competitiveness of Financial Institutions and Centres in Europe*, Dordrecht: Kluwer Academic Press, pp. 301–11.
Praet, P. and J. Vuchelen (forthcoming), 'Monetary policy in Belgium: the difficult road to orthodoxy'.
Segrestin, D. (1990), 'Recent changes in France', in G. Baglioni and C. Crouch (eds), *European Industrial Relations*, London: Sage Publications, pp. 97–125.
Sisson, K. (1995), 'Change and continuity in British industrial relations: "strategic choice" or muddling through', in R. Locke, T. Kochan and M. Piore (eds), *Employment Relations in a Changing World Economy*, Cambridge, MA: MIT Press, pp. 33–57.
Spineux, A. (1990), 'Trade unionism in Belgium: the difficulties of a major renovation', in G. Baglioni and C. Crouch (eds), *European Industrial Relations*, London: Sage Publications, pp. 42–70.
Wallerstein, M., M. Golden and P. Lange (1997), 'Unions, employers' associations, and wage-setting institutions in Northern and Central Europe, 1950–1992', *Industrial and Labour Relations Review*, **50** (3), 379–401.

10 Same tune, different words? The reaction function of G7 monetary authorities*

Jagjit Chadha and Norbert Janssen

F33 ES2 ES8

The essence of central banking is discretionary control of the monetary system. The purpose of central banking has been defined in various ways: to maintain stability of the price level, to keep the economy on an even keel, and so on. ... The choice of purpose – the object of monetary policy – is not irrelevant to the choice of method: a community might hope more reasonably in some cases than in others to attain its ends by making the monetary system work to rule. And working to rule is the antithesis of central banking. A central bank is necessary only when the community decides that a discretionary element is desirable. The central banker is the man who exercises his discretion, not the machine that works according to rule. (R.S. Sayers 1957, 'Central banking after Bagehot')

1 Introduction

The abandonment of the US dollar's link to gold in August 1971 signalled the end of the Bretton Woods system. The world monetary system has subsequently operated with unbacked fiat money which may be, depending on one's view of monetary authorities, something lying in the space between an exciting breakthrough and a dangerous experiment. The loss of gold as an anchor for monetary policy has induced monetary theorists and practitioners to search for a new strategy to ensure price stability in the medium and long term. This development has stimulated a lively debate about whether monetary authorities should stick to a policy of rules or one of discretion to achieve their ultimate objectives (see Fischer 1990).

In addition, a large recent literature has grown up examining monetary authorities' *actual* behaviour. Of special note are the studies by Clarida and Gertler (1996) and Bernanke and Mihov (1996) which examined German monetary policy in the post-Bretton Woods era. The former paper found that German monetary policy involves management of short-term interest rates in a manner similar to a Taylor rule and the latter went further to argue that the 'Bundesbank ... seems to be better characterised as an inflation targeter than

* We thank seminar participants at the Bank of England, the 1997 annual conference of the Swiss Society of Economics and Statistics, the Post-Keynesian Study Group, Clive Briault, Erik Britton, Darren Pain and Paul Tucker for valuable comments. Martin Cleaves, Jayne Willis and Jenny Salvage provided excellent research assistance. The views expressed in this chapter are not necessarily those of the Bank of England. Any remaining errors are the authors' responsibility.

as a money targeter' (p. 32). This type of examination of monetary authorities' actions has also been analysed recently by Chadha and Janssen (1997) for the G3 and the UK who find that the differences in feedback rule are more apparent than real.

So it would appear, from the recent literature, that monetary authorities have followed a 'discretionary rule'. And if we examine the announced policy rules among the monetary authorities in the G7 economies since the end of Bretton Woods, we actually find discretionary use of rules: (i) there is a clear (money) feedback rule for the whole period articulated only in Germany, (ii) there have been relatively frequent changes in the stated policy rule in Italy and the UK, and to a lesser extent, in Canada and the US, (iii) there is no clearly stated feedback rule in the case of Japan and (iv) there has been a long period of fixed-but-adjustable exchange rates in France.[1] It does not seem obvious that a representative agent for the G7 economies in the period since the end of Bretton Woods would have had a clear idea of the representative monetary authority's feedback rule.

Evaluating how such a discretionary rule should be written down is one of the purposes of this chapter. One of the advantages of having a rule is that it should allow agents to observe, judge and even predict the monetary authorities' actions. A discretionary rule is likely to be difficult for agents on each of these three grounds. In some sense, the recent innovation of inflation targets may be seen as an attempt to formalize the *de facto* operation of discretionary rules. In the past, these monetary authorities have adopted formal and/or informal targets for nominal income, monetary aggregates, the exchange rate and inflation. We might therefore expect to find considerable variation in the importance of different variables in explaining changes in official interest rates both across countries and through time, especially if stated intentions equalled actual intentions. This proposition is examined in this chapter.

In order to examine the behavioural, rather than promised, differences, we endogenize the policy instrument (the official interest rate) and gauge its feedback from real and nominal variables. We assume that the set of feedback variables – the information set – is similar among the seven economies and examine whether the differences in observed weighting can be well explained by stated rules. Our objective is to analyse whether the extent to which central banks feed back from these variables *over the economic cycle* differs as a result of the authorities' announced policy rules. For example, whether money plays an important role in Germany and whether feedback variables display considerable parameter instability in the case of Canada, Italy, the UK and the US.

After the preliminary data analysis, we adopt the identified Vector Auto-Regressive (VAR) framework developed by Sims (1980) in order to examine the factors which explain fluctuations in the policy rate. Leeper et al. (1996), in their summary of the VAR literature, remind us that the VAR framework has generally found that a large fraction of the variation in monetary policy instruments can be attributed to the *systematic* reaction of monetary authorities to the state of the economy. We can use this finding to examine whether the differences in *systematic* reaction across monetary authorities can be explained by stated policy rules.

The structure of the chapter is as follows. We briefly describe the model for the chapter and the main characteristics of policy rates in Section 2. Section 3 presents variance decompositions for identified innovations in the policy rate with respect to the assumed information set. Section 4 presents the main conclusions from the chapter.

2   Methodology and data

We use the classic Mundell–Fleming–Dornbusch model to describe the interactions in each country's macroeconomy. This model can be used to motivate a policy rate reaction function which feeds off cyclical deviations of macroeconomic variables from trend. Equations (10.1) to (10.4) set out the basic model, with an expenditure shock, g, added to the goods market schedule.[2] Where equation (10.1) is a money demand function, equation (10.2) is the goods market schedule, equation (10.3) is the Phillips curve relationship and equation (10.4) is the uncovered interest rates parity condition.

$$m - p = \phi y - \mu i \tag{10.1}$$

$$y = \sigma(i - \dot{p}) + \delta(e + p^* - p) + g \tag{10.2}$$

$$\dot{p} = \pi(y - \bar{y}) \tag{10.3}$$

$$\dot{e} = i - i^*. \tag{10.4}$$

We can solve for the cyclical movement in the interest rate, i, where $\dot{p} = 0$, $y = \bar{y}$, $\dot{e} = 0$, $i = i^*$, as follows:

$$i = \frac{1}{\phi\sigma + \mu}\left[-m + p + \phi\delta(e + p^* - p) + \phi g\right] \tag{10.5}$$

Equation (10.5) shows that cyclical deviations in the nominal interest rate respond negatively to relative money demand shocks and positively to cyclical movements in the price level, the real exchange rate and real demand shocks. We make one simple addition to equation (10.5), and follow McCallum's (1994) suggestion, by including the long-term interest rate within our set of information variables. This addition could be interpreted as monetary authorities being concerned about stabilizing long-run inflation expectations.

We use quarterly data for Canada, France, Germany, Italy, Japan, the UK and the US over the sample period 1971Q1–1996Q4 to examine whether central banks respond similarly to (changes in) real and nominal variables over the economic cycle.[3] Data on official and long-term interest rates, 10-year government bond yields, real GDP, the CPI and the real exchange rate index are taken from the *International Financial Statistics* (IFS) datatapes. For Canada we use the bank rate as the official rate, for France, Germany, Italy and Japan the discount rate, for the UK the base rate and for the US the Federal Funds rate. Additionally, time series on broad money (M2+ for Canada, M3 for France, Germany and the US, M2 for Italy, M2 + Certificates of Deposit (CDs) for Japan and M4 for the UK) are taken from national central bank sources. Standard Augmented Dickey-Fuller (ADF) tests indicate that all these variables are I(1) except the policy rate series which are borderline I(0)/I(1).[4] In order to analyse official rate setting over the economic cycle in the G7 economies we detrend all data using the Hodrick–Prescott filter with λ set to 1600. The advantage of this technique is that all detrended series are stationary and this chapter can focus on the response in cyclical official interest rates to the cyclical component of a set of feedback variables. We deal with the question of robustness of the model to different exogenous impulses by varying the ordering in the VAR model in Section 3.

Table 10.1 provides some summary statistics on the policy rates. The coefficient of variation (column 3) shows that the policy rates in the seven countries have broadly similar variability. As a first pass through the policy rate data, we then estimate auto-regressive integrated moving average (ARIMA) models for official interest rates in the G7 countries. We find that all seven official interest rate series can be modelled with low-order ARIMA models which show similar autocorrelations and thus persistence of interest rates.[6]

We could interpret this finding as suggesting that the monetary authorities all practise some form of interest rate smoothing and that, in the face of domestic shocks, that monetary authorities set their interest rates in a similar manner. But could the similarity in the time-series properties of the policy rate be explained simply by the existence of widespread international shocks? Table 10.1 also shows that the residuals from the seven national official interest rate models are in general found to be significantly correlated.[6] This suggests that there is a strong role for the international transmission mechanism within the setting of policy rates and/or that common shocks are hitting these economies. But as the correlations are all less than 0.5 a large part of the similarity in the time-series properties of interest rates must result from domestic policy choices. To the

Table 10.1 Summary statistics, ARIMA weights and correlations between residuals from official interest rate

	Mean	Std dev.	Std dev./mean	ARIMA	Canada	France	Germany	Italy	Japan	UK	US
Canada	9.06	3.25	0.36	(2,1,1)	1	0.46	0.25	0.40	0.26	0.32	0.59
France	8.75	2.86	0.33	(2,1,0)		1	0.43	0.47	0.35	0.26	0.45
Germany	5.01	1.72	0.34	(3,1,0)			1	0.42	0.47	0.31	0.29
Italy	11.31	4.15	0.37	(2,1,0)				1	0.33	0.39	0.29
Japan	4.68	2.12	0.45	(2,1,1)					1	0.49	0.38
UK	10.02	3.19	0.32	(2,1,0)						1	0.36
US	6.79	2.56	0.38	(2,1,0)							1

Note: The mean is given for the first difference of the log in percent. The ARIMA weights are chosen with respect to sequential log-likelihood tests and tests for residual serial correlation. The correlations are contemporaneous.

extent that the real exchange rate is found to be an important channel of interest rate fluctuations then international transmission of shocks is important, and to the extent it is not then there must be common shocks in these economies responsible for correlations in interest rate innovations.

The data set includes broad monetary aggregates, real GDP, the price level, the expected price level,[7] long-term interest rates and the real exchange rate. The theoretical motivation arising from the Dornbusch model and the empirical observations in this section are used in the following section to examine the similarities in monetary authorities' preferences.

3   Empirical results

Vector auto-regressive models
An unconditional VAR model splits the variation in a list of time series into mutually independent components as follows. If $\mathbf{y(t)}$ is a $\mathbf{k} \times 1$ vector of time series, we can write:

$$\sum_{s=0}^{m} A_s y(t-s) = A(L)y(t) - \varepsilon(t) \tag{10.6}$$

with the disturbance vector $\varepsilon(t)$ uncorrelated with $\mathbf{y(s)}$ for $\mathbf{s} < \mathbf{t}$ and an identity covariance matrix. Assuming A_0 is invertible (10.6) can be solved to give:

$$y(t) = \sum_{s=0}^{t-1} C_s \varepsilon(t-s). \tag{10.7}$$

Expressions (10.6) and (10.7) are not unique, although they exist under fairly general conditions. Given a matrix $\mathbf{W}$ that satisfies $\mathbf{W'W} = \mathbf{I}$, that is, any orthogonal matrix, ε can be replaced by $\mathbf{W}\varepsilon$, $A(L)$ by $\mathbf{W}A(L)$ and $C(L)$ by $C(L)\mathbf{W'}$, which gives a new representation of similar form. The disturbances are orthogonalized by a Choleski decomposition which ensures that the covariance matrix of the resulting innovations is diagonal. The elements of C_s (which are a function of $\mathbf{s}$) are characterized as the model's impulse responses. The latter indicate how each variable component of $\mathbf{y}$ responds over time to each disturbance in ε.

Multivariate VARs
We present results for the multivariate VARs ordered as follows: real GDP, expected inflation, broad money, the real exchange rate, long-term interest rates and the policy rates.[8] The lag lengths in each VAR were chosen by the Akaike and Schwartz information criteria. We use recursive and *N*-step-ahead Chow tests to test for parameter instability but no significant ones were found.

Figure 10.1 shows the variance decomposition of policy rate innovations with respect to the identified shocks in the other variables. In the short run, of up to a year, the main explanatory variable for policy rate innovations is the policy rate itself. This suggests that a degree of interest rate smoothing is operated by the authorities – each of the variance decompositions start at more than 50 per cent at time 0 and settle at their long-run level at about 10–30 per cent by six to twelve quarters.[9] The only exception to this interest rate smoothing pattern is Italy, where in the long run discount rate shocks account for about 40 per cent of the variance in official rates. The other common thread is the relatively small role for identified shocks to the real exchange rate and broad money in all countries – less than 20 per cent in all countries and up to 20 quarters. The minor role for the real exchange rate suggests a greater likelihood of common shocks rather than internationally transmitted shocks. The broad money result suggests that identified money shocks play little exogenous role in explaining interest rate innovations.

Identified shocks to real GDP have a similar profile in Canada, Germany, UK and the US where the profile rises sharply to a peak of about a third to a half of the variation in the innovation of the policy rate at eight, ten and four quarters, respectively. The longer-run influence lies at about a third in the latter three countries. In the steady state, real GDP shocks explain about 15 per cent of the variance in official rates in Canada, France and Italy. Only in Japan are shocks to real GDP found to explain a negligible proportion of innovations in the policy rate, at less than 10 per cent at all horizons.

Identified shocks to expected inflation play a significant role in Canada, France, Germany, Japan and the US, particularly after six to eight quarters, and account for a quarter to a third of the variation in the innovations in the policy rate. After about two years, shocks to expected inflation are even more important in explaining the variance in Canadian and French official rates than are official rates themselves. In contrast, identified shocks to expected inflation in Italy and the UK explain less than 10 per cent of policy rate innovations up to 20 quarters. It is striking that these are also the economies that have experienced the highest average inflation rates over the sample period analysed. Identified shocks to long-term interest rates are not found to play an important role in Canada, Germany or the US. But in France, Italy, Japan and especially the UK, shocks to long-term interest rates explain at least 20 per cent of policy rate innovations, even at horizons over eight quarters. In the UK, shocks to the long-term interest rate play as important a role as official interest rates.

We have not imposed any directional restrictions on the VAR but in every case the sign of the impulse response (available on request) is found to be correct. This gives us some confidence that our approach has been sufficient to identify a plausible process driving official policy rates.

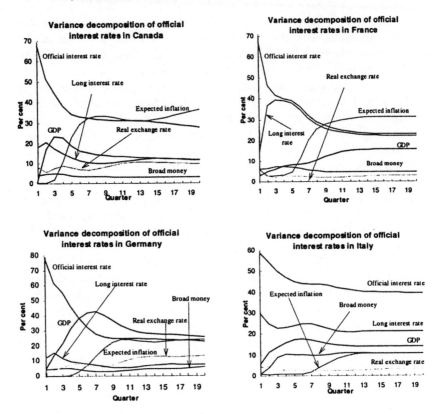

Figure 10.1   Variance decomposition of official interest rates in response to shocks to different variables in multivariate framework

The variance decompositions of cyclical innovations in official interest rates lead to the following tentative observations: (i) identified shocks to long and short interest rates explain short-term (up to a year) fluctuations in the policy rates;[10] (ii) identified shocks to the information variables have less than a proportionate impact on the level of interest rates (see Brainard 1967); (iii) the peak response of interest rates to GDP is typically at four to eight quarters; (iv) there is generally a lag of four to eight quarters for the peak response of policy rates to identified inflation expectations shocks; (v) only in the UK and the US are shocks to broad money found to be significant and then only marginally; (vi) where shocks to the real exchange rate play a significant role, in Germany and Japan, cycling occurs so the sum of responses is zero.

Given the attention to money in most monetary regimes, why is money found to be relatively unimportant in all the countries and particularly in

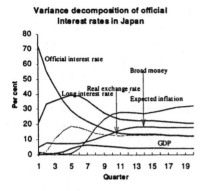

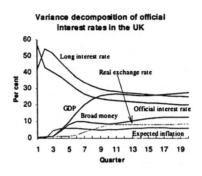

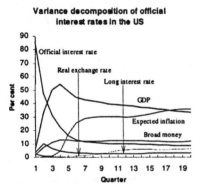

Figure 10.1 continued

Germany where a system of money targeting operates and in the other countries during their periods of money targeting? One explanation is that exogenous money shocks account for little of an economy's cyclical variation and
that the action lies in the endogenous part of money. Central banks may
actually realize this point and operate their stated rules on money with an
understanding of the need to decompose money growth into endogenous (that
is, those which may result from other variables in the model) and exogenous
elements (that is, those which are 'pure' monetary shocks). As pure monetary
shocks are rare, most of the information from money comes from its interaction with other variables.

Equally, the lack of importance of the real exchange rate could stem from
the increasingly well-demonstrated proposition that innovations to the real
exchange rate are largely real rather than nominal in nature – and therefore
more likely to reflect changes in the equilibrium real exchange rate rather
than monetary shocks driving the exchange rate temporarily away from equi-

librium (see Clarida and Gali 1994). Of course, in the case of real (or fundamental) shocks the need for offsetting monetary action through movements in the official interest rate is limited. We might also then suggest that the significant correlations in the ARIMA residuals presented in Table 10.1 are likely to result from common shocks rather than from international transmission of idiosyncratic shocks.

So if we were working back from the important identified processes driving policy rates, that is, on interest rate smoothing, real GDP, inflation expectations and not on broad money or the real exchange rate, why do monetary authorities not write down rules which describe their actual actions? Why have we not had rules which say 'we will move interest rates cautiously when real GDP and inflation expectations seem shocked away from trend'? Why do we have rules which talk about money targets, exchange rate targets or no rule at all? We do not know. But inflation 'targeting' with an intermediate target of the inflation forecast n years ahead, where real activity and inflation inertia variables explain movements in the policy rule (and the policy instrument),[11] may be a fair method of characterizing the actual operation of G7 central banks since the end of Bretton Woods. Of course, we may also be able to characterize such behaviour as being isomorphic to a nominal income target.

4   Conclusion

This chapter provides some further evidence that central banks respond to deviations from the trend of a standard set of macroeconomic variables when setting cyclical official interest rates. Since the adoption of fiat money, G7 monetary authorities have characterized their regimes with a variety of formal and informal targets: these have involved one or more of the following: money, exchange rate, inflation and nominal income. In previous work we suggested that such targets can be mapped into an interest rate reaction function which results from a standard Mundell–Fleming–Dornbusch model of the macroeconomy. In this chapter we find a (surprising) degree of similarity in the relationships between macroeconomic variables and the respective policy rates across the G7 countries: and, perhaps surprisingly, differences in responses between countries are not particularly well explained by stated monetary policy rules. This lack of transparency seems puzzling: why should central banks pretend that the information set on which they base their policy decisions is not diversified, when in fact it seems to be?

A common finding from the previous analysis of variance decompositions of official interest rates is that the monetary authorities in all G7 economies seem to operate, at least to some extent, a policy of interest rate smoothing. It is also striking that identified shocks to broad money have a limited role in explaining policy rate movements, in particular since monetary authorities in some G7 countries have adopted money targets at least for part of the period analysed in this chapter. In the majority of G7 economies, inflation expectations are found to explain a significant part of cyclical changes in official interest rates, although less so in Italy and the UK. Cyclical movements in GDP play an important role across the G7, except in Japan. It is also important to recall that no substantial evidence for parameter instability is found – this suggests little actual change in implicit feedback weights.

The above analysis also shows some differences in *cyclical* feedback by central banks. Most monetary authorities in the G7 incorporate financial markets' expectations when setting official rates, since long-term interest rates are significant, except in Canada, Germany and the US. The relatively minor role played by identified shocks to the real exchange rate seems to confirm the empirical view that such shocks are largely real in nature. The multivariate VAR results are robust to the choice of ordering of the variables.

Since the same identification structure was imposed on each country's VAR, the degree of similarity in *cyclical* interest rate setting across the G7 is perhaps not surprising. But the cross-country differences do not seem to match different stated policy rules. One interpretation of these results is that authorities tend to exercise some degree of discretion in the *cyclical* operation of their stated policy rules. Over most of the period examined, monetary authorities seem to have practised some form of state-contingent inflation target (or nominal income rule), rather than an intermediate target (for example, money targets). This observation is in line with the conclusions in Brainard (1967), who suggests that some form of eclectic monetary policy may be optimal in the face of uncertainty about shocks and the economy's structure. It should be stressed, however, that monetary authorities' interest rate reaction functions should probably be analysed within a structural model of the macroeconomy before such a proposition can be accepted more generally.

Notes

1. Of course, the ERM has operated since 1979 and Germany has been a member but as the anchor currency the external constraint does not bite in anything like the same manner as in France.
2. Where e is defined as the domestic price of foreign currency (so e rises if there is a depreciation), superscript * refers to foreign variables, dotted variables are defined as rates of change. This model is specified in mean deviation form so m corresponds to the cyclical component of money, p to that of the price level, y to real income, i to nominal interest rates and ϕ, μ, σ, δ, π are parameters.
3. The sample period for France covers 1978Q3–1996Q4 and that for Germany 1971Q1–1994Q4.
4. ADF test results are available from the authors on request.
5. The serial correlation and Chow break tests for these models are available on request.
6. With the number of observations we have, correlations of greater than 0.2 are significant at the 5 per cent level.
7. The expected price level is derived from the one-step-ahead ARIMA forecast of the price level.

8. The results are in general robust to the choice of ordering. Note also that the diagnostics on each VAR: serial correlation, heteroscedasticity, normality and Chow tests are available on request.
9. See Goodhart (1996) for some tentative explanations of this phenomenon.
10. This provides some support for the expectations hypothesis of the term structure of interest rates and for interest rate smoothing.
11. The short-run response of monetary authorities to economic shocks will ultimately depend on the relative costs of inflation and output volatility (see King 1997).

Bibliography

Bernanke, B.S. and I. Mihov (1996), *What Does the Bundesbank Target?*, National Bureau of Economic Research Working Paper No. 5764.

Blinder, A.S. (1996), 'Remarks at the Senior Executives' Conference of the Mortgage Bankers Association', *BIS Review*, No. 14, 1–15.

Brainard, W. (1967), 'Uncertainty and the effectiveness of policy', *American Economic Review*, **57** (1), 411–25.

Britton, A.J.C. (1991), 'Macroeconomic policy in Britain 1974–1987', *Economic and Social Studies*, National Institute of Economic and Social Research, **36**.

Buiter, W. (1984), 'Granger causality and policy effectiveness', *Economica*, **51**, May, 151–62.

Chadha, J.S and N.G.J. Janssen (1997), 'What monetary authorities do – an examination of reaction functions for Germany, Japan, the UK and the US', *Swiss Journal of Economics and Statistics*, **133** (3), 455–76.

Clarida, R. and J. Gali (1994), 'Sources of real exchange-rate fluctuations: how important are nominal shocks?', *Carnegie–Rochester Conference Series on Public Policy*, **41**, 1–56.

Clarida, R. and M. Gertler (1996), *How the Bundesbank Conducts Monetary Policy*, National Bureau of Economic Research Working Paper No. 5581.

Deutsche Bundesbank (1995), *The Monetary Policy of the Bundesbank*, October.

Fischer, S. (1990), 'Rules versus discretion in monetary policy', in B.M. Friedman and F.H. Hahn (eds), *Handbook of Monetary Economics Vol. 2*, Amsterdam: North-Holland, pp. 1155–84.

Friedman, B.M. (1995), 'The rise and fall of money growth targets as guidelines for US monetary policy', Paper presented at Bank of Japan Conference.

Fukui, T. (1996), 'Speech given to the Research Institute of Japan in Tokyo on 13 November 1995', *BIS Review*, no. 9, 1–15.

Goodhart, C.A.E. (1996), 'Why Do Monetary Authorities Smooth Interest Rates?', Financial Markets Group Special Working Paper, no. 81.

H.M. Treasury, *Red Book*, various issues.

King, M.A. (1995), 'Credibility and monetary policy: theory and evidence', *Bank of England Quarterly Bulletin*, **35**, 84–91.

King, M.A. (1997), 'The inflation target five years on', Lecture at London School of Economics, 29 October.

Leeper, E., C. Sims and T. Zha (1996), 'What does monetary policy do?', draft for Brookings Papers in Economic Analysis meetings.

McCallum, B.T. (1989), *Targets, Indicators, and Instruments of Monetary Policy*, National Bureau of Economic Research Working Paper No. 3047.

McCallum, B.T. (1994), *Monetary Policy and the Term Structure of Interest Rates*, National Bureau of Economic Research Working Paper No. 4938.

Neumann, M.J.M. and J. von Hagen (1993), 'Germany', in M.U. Fratianni and D. Salvatore, *Monetary Policy in Developed Economies, Studies in Comparative Economic Policies*, Vol. 3, Amsterdam: North-Holland, pp. 299–334.

Sayers, R.S. (1957), *Central Banking after Bagehot*, London: Oxford University Press.

Sims, C.A. (1980), 'Macroeconomics and reality', *Econometrica*, **48**, 1–48.

Ueda, K. (1993), 'A comparative perspective on Japanese monetary policy: short-run monetary control and the transmission mechanism', in K.J. Singleton (ed.), *Japanese Monetary Policy*, Chicago: National Bureau of Economic Research, pp. 7–29.

11 The independence of central banks: the case of Italy

Augusto Graziani

ES8   F33

1 Introduction

A widespread shift of opinion has taken place in most countries concerning the relationships between governments and central banks. Nowadays, the general opinion of both the experts and the man in the street is strongly in favour of a complete institutional and *de facto* autonomy of the central bank from the central government. The alleged motivation is that an independent central bank will ensure price stability, a task which a bank subject to the power of the government would be unable to fulfil.

The Maastricht Treaty moves in the same direction. According to Article 105, price stability is the main target of the European System of Central Banks. For this reason, the European Central Bank (ECB), to be established as the final outcome of the process of monetary union, will be totally independent from any government interference. It should, however, be mentioned that the Treaty, while declaring the bank as autonomous, contains no mention of any quantitative rule concerning the money supply.

In the dominant opinion a sort of divergence exists between the targets a central bank would reasonably pursue if left free to choose and the targets most frequently pursued by a government. It is generally agreed that any central bank, if left free to choose its own targets, as well as to use instruments of its own choice, would choose monetary stability as its first and foremost target. This is considered all the more true if the charter of the central bank itself prescribes price stability as a priority in the action of the bank. In the dominant view, it is also accepted that, in contrast, a government may pursue a number of different targets, all of which can be conflicting with monetary stability. A government may wish full employment in order to get a consensus from its voters; it may pursue a temporary increase in activity levels when political elections are approaching; it might use public expenditure in order to favour one or the other among the influential political parties. A sort of widespread agreement seems to exist that any government, if left free to pursue targets of its own choice, may well be tolerant towards inflation or even deliberately pursue inflationary policies. In fact, elegant theoretical models have been set up, in which the policy being actually pursued is the result of a game between a central bank, whose target function is price stability, and a government whose objective function includes political consensus and income redistribution and in the background a tolerant attitude towards inflation (Piga and Pecci 1997).

The idea that government intervention is by definition a factor of inflation has also been given the benefit of a theoretical framework. If we admit, as contemporary macroeconomics maintains, that the spontaneous actions of market forces produces full employment, deficit spending is no longer needed in order to reach equilibrium in the labour market. In such conditions, deficit spending becomes by definition a factor of demand inflation while price stability requires a balanced budget. Since, most of the time, governments are in favour of higher expenditure but against raising taxes, the only way a government can reach the desired targets beyond a certain level, is to finance expenditure either by issuing debt or by increasing the money stock. Both instruments, even if to a different extent and in different circumstances, require the cooperation of the central bank.

The conclusion is easily reached that if the central bank is an independent institution, then the bank will be free to pursue its spontaneous policy of price stability while the government will be unable to interfere and distort its action.

A similar way of reasoning, if consistent in itself, neglects a number of other complicating factors. The most intriguing of all is that in an open economy, with flexible exchange rates, the rate of interest is an instrument used for two main targets, being respectively *the control of liquidity* (and through it the control of the general level of prices) and *the control of the exchange rate*. Now in most countries the exchange rate policy is not entrusted to the central bank, being directly in the hands of the government. This creates a clear conflict between the independence of the central bank and the intention of the governments to keep for themselves decisions concerning the control of foreign exchange rates. Situations may arise in which the government might be in favour of raising the rate of interest in order to attract foreign capital and redress the balance of payments, while the central bank might be inclined to reduce it in order to stimulate the level of activity. The same problem is bound to emerge when the ECB is created. When monetary union is enacted, the national central banks will lose any power over the national exchange rates, since there will be no intra-European exchange rate left. It will then be in the power of the ECB to manage the exchange rates of the Euro *vis-à-vis* the non-European countries. So far as one can see, the ECB will be not only totally autonomous but also free from any democratic control, something which, as has been remarked, seems very far from the European political tradition (De Brunhoff 1996).

The reality of institutional facts, at least as they prevailed before the recent European drive in favour of a complete autonomy of the central bank, seems to confirm that the logic of economic policy imposes a coordination, if not a subordination, of the central bank to government authorities. The German Bundesbank is considered as the best example of separation between bank and government. Still, as has been correctly noted, the law of 1957 ruling the German Bundesbank states that 'representatives of the Government attend the meetings of the Council, may include points in the agenda and even require the suspension of a decision' (Pivetti 1996, p. 85; Giusso 1995, p. 73). The same law prescribes that the Bundesbank is obliged 'to support the general economic policy of the Government' (Article 12), with only possible exceptions in cases in which the action of the government conflicts with the fundamental task of the bank 'to safeguard the currency'.

However, in the German case, two more remarks should be added. The first one is the well-known fact that, after the great inflation of 1923, far beyond the independence of the central bank, price stability has become a common target of any government, reflecting an agreed priority of the whole German society (this remark goes hand in hand with similar remarks made in relation to the post-war monetary experience of the US, where, according to some, monetary stability was more the result of a political convergence than of the autonomous action of the Federal Reserve; Simonazzi 1992).

A further point is that not all agree on the fact that, in the second post-war period, Germany has actually given a priority to internal monetary stability. This is by far the dominant opinion (Bernanke and Mihov 1997), but it is by no means unanimous. Some in fact believe that post-war Germany has been pursuing primarily an external equilibrium, and that its aim has been to achieve a constant surplus in its balance of payments (Hagemann 1993a and 1993b; Thomasberger 1993). With this in mind, the German strategy has been defined as neo-mercantilistic (Ciocca 1979, p. 133). In order to achieve its goal, Germany has constantly been trying to keep the German mark undervalued in real terms. Up to 1991, the German rate of inflation had been extremely low in comparison to other European countries and the German mark should have been revalued much more than it actually was. In order to avoid an excessive revaluation of the mark, Germany, until the reunification of the country, had managed to balance the trade surplus by exporting financial capital.

Many attempts have been made to measure the degree of independence of single central banks in order to find out whether a correlation exists between independence and monetary stability. Grilli et al. have suggested a composite index obtained from a number of institutional factors, such as: who appoints the Governor and the Board of the central bank, how long does the appointment last, whether members of the government participate in the meetings of the Board, whether the law supports the bank in the event of conflicts with the government, to what extent and on what terms can the bank extend credit facilities to the government, who sets the discount rate, and other similar institutional arrangements (Grilli et al. 1991). Attempts made to find a correlation between the degree of autonomy of the central bank and monetary stability in single countries have given very doubtful results. In this connection, the suggestion has been put forward that, even when enjoying a complete formal independence, a central bank will unavoidably be subject to the political climate of the country and its decisions, even if taken in total freedom of action, will seldom contradict the general policy line of the government (Piga and Pecci 1997). In a more cynical mood, Malinvaud once remarked that it is hard to speak of a true independence of the central bank so long as its Governor, even if given a life appointment, can be fired any time at the discretionary will of the government (Malinvaud 1991).

2   The case of Italy: institutional setting and debate

The debate concerning the Italian central bank has soon taken up the typical features of a political debate, going far beyond mere technical considerations.

Greater autonomy for the central bank has always been a strong request of the circles connected with big industry and finance. In their view, the Bank of Italy has always been ready to finance government expenditure even at the cost of rationing liquidity to the private sector, whenever this was necessary in order to preserve monetary stability. The bank has been accused of channelling liquidity to government bonds, thus bringing about an almost complete atrophy of the financial market. In some cases, the acquiescence to the government has brought the bank to run a policy of easy money when, because of political reasons, the government considered it advisable to accommodate the unions and not to resist a wave of wage increases. Following from this, the main industrial circles now require that monetary stability be included in the Italian Constitution as a compulsory constraint to government action or even that strict guidelines concerning the money supply be explicitly stated. It has been recalled sometimes that the Italian Constitution (Article 47) includes the 'protection of saving' among the duties of the state, thus implying the duty of inflation targeting on the part of the government. It has been remarked, by contrast, that protection of saving can also be achieved through recourse to financial instruments such as indexed bonds. It has also been noted that when an inflation crisis is feared, the monetary authorities would do better to give priority to financial stability over monetary stability, since an increase in interest rates with a consequent chain of bankruptcies may damage savers much more than inflation would.

It should be added that the Bank of Italy has emphasized more than once that the only thing the bank can do is to control the money supply, which is just one cause of inflation. Other, and more powerful, factors of inflation, such as wage increases and excessive government expenditure, lie beyond the control of the monetary authorities (similar remarks have come from the Bundesbank).

The many followers of a strong movement in favour of structural and political reforms (a movement at present headed in Italy by the moderate Democratic left-wing party [Partito Democratico della Sinistra (PDS)] would pass a more benevolent judgement on the action of the Bank of Italy. They remark that, in the long years during which Italian government was in the hands of political parties having not only no respect for the economic limits of government expenditure and government deficits, but also largely open to corruption, the Bank of Italy was the only institution capable of preserving a rigorous line of action. The Bank of Italy was never openly dominated by single political parties, its recruitment policy was based on strictly professional criteria and its research unit was one of the few high-standard institutions in the field. The situation was such that the bank had to fill the gaps left open by the government and rightly became the only reliable leading authority in economic policy. Whenever the bank was forced to enact a monetary squeeze, this was due to the excess of money creation imposed by the government in order to finance public expenditure. For many years, unbalanced as the situation may have been, since the government was unable to preserve monetary stability, monetary policy as enacted by the Bank of Italy was the only consistent and seriously run policy in Italy. Past experience therefore suggests that the independence of the central bank should be preserved and increased.

Within the reform movement a more moderate view is gaining ground. In this view, the central bank should be given the status of an autonomous body as far as the choice of instruments goes. But the targets to be pursued by the bank should go beyond monetary stability and should be defined in a more general political framework involving the government, parliament, and in general all politically representative institutions. In fact, there are no clear reasons for putting decisions which affect the lives of all citizens in the hands of a body which is not elected by voters (Targetti 1995b).

According to this approach, the independence of the central bank should be inscribed into a general policy framework and be free from any strict quantitative prescription concerning the money supply. In addition to that, the independence of the central bank should be reconciled to the acceptance of multiple targets (not bare monetary stability) and the action of the bank coordinated with other aims, first of all with a strong employment policy (Fodor 1995).

In contrast to such moderate views, the extreme right-wing political parties insist on a complete subordination of the Bank of Italy to the government's decisions. Time and again attacks have been made on the Bank of Italy. The bank has been accused of having greatly damaged the national economy through mismanagement of the speculative attack brought in 1992 against the Italian lira, an attack which forced the lira out of the European Monetary System (EMS) and initiated a temporary breakdown of the EMS. The same right-wing circles have even accused the bank of improper management and possible corruption.

Over the last years, the institutional setting of the Bank of Italy has undergone a number of changes, most of them due to the introduction of the European common discipline. Ever since 1980, as a consequence of the so-called 'divorce' of the bank from the Italian Treasury, the bank has no longer had to buy the newly issued government bonds not subscribed in the market. Thus the monetary financing of government deficit has gradually been contained. In 1992, the bank was entitled to set the discount rate in total autonomy. Since 1993, the bank has no longer been obliged to advance to the Treasury up to 14 per cent of current government expenditure. Since 1994, European central banks have no longer been entitled to finance monetary government deficits.

This set of changes has resulted in substantially greater autonomy of the Bank of Italy. It should be remembered, however, that in principle the Bank of Italy has always enjoyed a formal independence. It is a joint-stock company, the stockholders being mainly savings banks. The Board of the bank is appointed by the shareholders' meeting and approved by the Cabinet. The Governor is appointed by the Board of the bank and is given a life appointment.

Of course, the borderline between formal and actual independence is debatable. As we shall see, in many cases the actual independence of the Bank of Italy has been far smaller than the mere institutional setting might suggest.

3   The case of Italy: the historical experience
A historical analysis of the independence of a central bank should point to specific cases in which a conflict between bank and government has emerged. This might allow an assessment as to what extent the bank has been able to put into practice its own policy even when this is in contrast to the views of the government.

The analysis that follows will show that, so far as the Italian experience goes, very few cases can be singled out in which a clear contrast between bank and government has emerged. In most cases, bank and government seem to have followed a common policy, and it would be difficult to discover whether this was the result of a common design or of one of the two agents overriding the other one. A few relevant cases of common action of bank and cabinet can be indicated briefly.

In 1947, Alcide De Gasperi headed the government and ran a policy of monetary stabilization with a view to fully integrating Italy into the western community. To support him he obtained the help of three well-known professors of economics, who were appointed members of the Cabinet, Gustavo Del Vecchio, Epicarmo Corbino and Luigi Einaudi, the last one being the most influential of all. As head of the newly created Ministry of the Budget, Einaudi, in the summer of 1947, enforced a severe monetary squeeze. Inflation was stopped, although at the cost of a long interruption of the post-war recovery (Hirschman 1948).

Fifteen years later, when the first serious waves of wage increases started, the political orientation of the government had changed radically. After 1959, because of the increasing political strength of the unions, the estimate of the trade-off between inflation and unemployment was revised, the political cost of unemployment being considered much higher than before. In the yearly report for 1962, published in May 1963, the Governor of the Bank of Italy (at the time Dr Guido Carli) declared that the bank had detected clear signs of inflation but that a monetary squeeze with a consequent unemployment crisis would have been on his part 'an act of rebellion'. Only in the second half of 1963, when the Italian exports were in clear trouble on the foreign markets and the balance of payments was showing a dangerous deficit, did the government take the decision to stop the expansion and the bank, for the first time since 1947, ordered a rapid monetary squeeze.

Carli was Governor of the Bank of Italy for 15 years (1960–75). Under his leadership, the bank acquired great power, mostly because of its well-established and continuous control of the whole banking system. The financial market was brought to an almost complete atrophy while the placement of government bonds with private savers and commercial banks was given top priority. The whole banking system, strictly controlled by the Bank of Italy, thus became a vital instrument of government action. However, the increasing power and independence of the bank went hand in hand with a closer cooperation between bank and government. In fact, the Governor of the Bank was regularly invited to attend the meetings of the Cabinet (Nardozzi 1994).

We now come to the one clear case of divergence between bank and Cabinet. In 1975, Carli resigned and Paolo Baffi was appointed in his place. In the 1970s, as a consequence of the very high level of monetary interest rates, the industrial sector was heavily indebted to the banking sector. There was the danger of financial collapse and, in order to ensure financial stability, the bank had to run a looser monetary policy than the strict target of monetary stability would have required.

The divergence between bank and Cabinet emerged on a different matter. The Bank of Italy is responsible for seeing that commercial banks adhere to the strict letter of the law. In order to do this, the bank enjoys inspection privileges with respect to the commercial banks and is entitled to examine each single document in their possession. In those years, the collusion between finance, political parties and sometimes even criminal circles, was already apparent and would increase over time through the 1980s and early 1990s. The new Governor gave clear signs of his intention to make use of his power in order to control the operation of commercial banks far more closely than his predecessor had done. This made the friction between bank and government inevitable.

In 1978, the Treaty for the establishment of the EMS was signed. The Italian government was in favour of it while the Governor of the Bank of Italy, Baffi, was highly sceptical about the possibility of Italy meeting the requirements of a regime of stable exchange rates. Italy, after obtaining an oscillation range for the lira of 6 per cent, against the 2.5 per cent band of the other countries, joined the EMS in March 1979. It should be noted, however, that Italy finally joined the EMS not because of a decision of the government in its own capacity but following formal approval on the part of parliament.

Although a case of clear divergence between bank and Cabinet, this is still one in which it would be difficult to determine the degree of independence shown by the central bank. Baffi, an avid supporter of the autonomy of the Bank of Italy, was soon induced to resign. Obscure manoeuvres forced the Governor to leave office in 1979 although it is not known who was responsible for these manoeuvres. Both the governor himself, and the Chief Executive of the bank, were indicted for embezzlement in the administration of a government-owned bank, an indictment that in the light of subsequent judiciary inquiries turned out to be totally groundless. Baffi was succeeded by Carlo Azeglio Ciampi, who held office until 1993.

In the following years, the Bank of Italy, as previously mentioned formally acquired greater independence. At the same time, some changes in the use of monetary instruments took place. The bank, along with all other European central banks, made decreasing use of the control of reserves while open market operations and variations in the discount rate were used to a greater extent.

The move towards greater autonomy of the bank was the result of a double policy choice. On the one hand the independence of the central bank was pursued in order to achieve greater monetary stability. At the same time, the full-employment target was forgotten. The first target was clearly indicated as an official policy line. The dropping of the second target was seldom mentioned and the increasing employment was officially interpreted as being in contrast to the government policy line and considered to be a consequence of external events. In fact the whole government policy was in itself consistent, to the extent that one target was given a priority and the second was actually dropped.

The new Governor took office when the inflation rate was reaching its peak (the general price index for consumption increased by almost 16 per cent in

1979 and by more than 21 per cent in 1980). The Governor quickly declared that fighting inflation was a top priority for the country. He invoked the adoption of an incomes policy and the monitoring of government expenditure, especially in relation to the monetary consequences of great public works.

As a firm believer in the working of external constraints, the Governor considered it important to keep Italy inside the EMS. The successive realignments of the European rates of exchange approved between 1979 and 1987 saw the Italian lira constantly devalued, but always by less than the inflation differential would have required. Since the real revaluation of the currency was creating difficulties for the balance of trade, capital imports were made attractive by keeping interest rates high. Starting with 1987, movements of financial capital were gradually made free and became totally free in 1990.

The policy of using capital imports for balancing the external payments was so successful that in 1990 Italy was able to give up the privileged oscillation band of 6 per cent obtained in 1979 and to accept the common band of 2.5 per cent. On the other hand, the policy of high interest rates produced a gigantic increase in the stock of government debt, mostly due to the accumulation of interest charges.

The Italian experience in the EMS, however, made it clear that running a monetary policy independent of the exchange rate policy is an almost impossible task. In the very period in which it was acquiring greater formal independence, the Bank of Italy was in fact losing actual autonomy because of the determination of the government to defend the position of the national currency inside the EMS.

In 1992, the situation became clearly untenable. In September 1992, the Italian lira left the EMS and became a freely fluctuating currency. It is of course debatable whether the decision was due to the violent speculative attack brought against the lira in the summer of 1992, or rather to pressures coming from the lobby of small and medium-sized exporting firms of Northern Italy. It is, however, a fact that the government resisted both speculation and vested interests until an agreement with the unions was reached, by which wage indexation was removed. The agreement was signed at the end of July 1992, and six weeks later the lira left the EMS.

In the following months, the monetary authorities had to face the hard task of reconciling a quick devaluation of the lira with internal monetary stability. Once more, monetary policy was subject to the constraints coming from the management of the foreign exchange rate. In spite of a rapid external devaluation (in April 1993, six months after the abandonment of the EMS, the lira had lost 30 per cent of its value *vis-à-vis* the German mark), monetary stability was preserved thanks to the unusually strong compression of aggregate demand. In 1993, for the first time since the war, aggregate consumption declined in real terms. Had it not been for the decision to preserve monetary stability in spite of the devaluation of the lira, monetary policy might have been far less restrictive. An increasingly independent central bank had to accept the implications of an exchange rate policy decided by the Treasury.

4   Concluding remarks

In a setting of general economic equilibrium, with well-behaved behavioural functions, it is possible to argue that all markets find a spontaneous equilibrium and that all relevant variables are market determined. In a similar setting, the only exogenous variable is the nominal stock of money. In an open economy, inflation targeting should aim at an inflation rate equal to the rate prevailing in the trade area to which the country belongs. If we can say that the level of money prices depends strictly on the quantity of money, we are in the presence of a one-target–one-instrument model and a solution should be available.

It is, however, highly doubtful whether it is legitimate to believe that the level of money prices depends on the quantity of money. It is certainly true that, as long as the velocity of circulation is constant, any increase in the level of money prices must be accompanied by a proportional increase in the nominal stock of money. But the increase in the money stock can be induced by factors, such as government expenditures or the level of money wages, which escape the control of the monetary authorities.

If the inflation rate exceeds the target level (let us say the rate prevailing in the trade area to which the country belongs) a problem of ensuring stability in the exchange rate emerges and the central bank, whatever its degree of independence may be, will give priority to the exchange rate target.

The target exchange rate may be defined in a variety of ways. When Italy left the EMS, the policy line of the government was to let the lira slip gradually *vis-à-vis* the German mark. The task of the Bank of Italy was to preserve monetary stability, a target pursued in order to exploit fully the benefits of devaluation. After 1996, the target was to realize a quick revaluation of the lira and once more monetary policy was subject to the requirements of the exchange rate policy.

Paradoxical as it may seem, the more autonomous the Bank of Italy is becoming on the formal and institutional level, the more its action seems to be dependent on goals set by the government.

Bibliography

Bernanke, B.S. and I. Mihov (1997), 'What does the Bundesbank target?', *European Economic Review*, **41**.
Ciocca, P. (1979), 'La politica economica della Germania Federale' [*The economic policy of Federal Germany*], in V. Valli (ed.), *L'economia tedesca*, Milan: Etas-Libri, pp. 27–39.

Ciocca, P. (ed.) (1987), *Money and the Economy*, London: Macmillan.

Ciocca, P. (1992), 'Il principio di autonomia nel Central Banking' [The principle of autonomy in central banking], *Quaderni di economia e finanza*, VI, No. 1, 5–22.

De Brunhoff, S. (1996), 'The European plan for the creation of a single currency', in G. Deleplace and E. Nell (eds), *Money in Motion. The Post Keynesian and Circulation Approaches*, New York: Macmillan, pp. 716–24.

Fodor, G. (1995), 'Sull' autonomia delle Banche centrali' [On the autonomy of central banks], in Targetti (ed.) (1995a), pp. 207–15.

Giusso, L. (1995), 'Riflessioni sull' autonomia della Banca Centrale' [Reflections on the autonomy of the central bank], in D. Velo (ed.), *L'autonomia della Banca Centrale*, Bari: Cacucci, pp. 65–76.

Grilli, V., D. Masciandaro and G. Tabellini (1991), 'Political and monetary institutions, and public policies in industrial countries', *Economic Policy*, 6 (2), October, 341–92.

Hagemann, H. (ed.) (1993a), *Probleme der Einheit* [Problems of the Unification], Marburg: Metropolis Verlag.

Hagemann, H. (1993b), 'On some macroeconomic consequences of German unification', in H. Kurz (ed.), *United Germany and the New Europe*, Aldershot: Edward Elgar, pp. 89–107.

Hirschman, A.O. (1948), 'Inflation and deflation in Italy', *American Economic Review*, 38, 598–606.

Malinvaud, E. (1991), 'Comment' on Grilli et al. (1991), *Economic Policy*, 6 (2), 392–4.

Nardozzi, G. (1994), 'Money and credit. Twenty years of debate in Italy (1970–1990)', *Banca Nazionale del Lavoro Quarterly Review*, No. 1, 3–51.

Piga, G. and L. Pecci (1997), *Indexation, Inflation, and Central Bank Independence*, University of Rome, Department of Public Economics, Working Paper.

Pivetti, M. (1996), 'Maastricht and the political independence of central banks', *Contributions to Political Economy*, 6 (15), 81–104.

Simonazzi, A. (1992), 'On the independence of the central bank. Reflections of the post-war U.S. experience', University of Rome, CIDEI, mimeo.

Targetti, F. (ed.) (1995a), *L'Italia e l'Europa dopo Maastricht* [Italy and Europe after Maastricht], a Supplement to *Economia e Banca*, VI (7–8).

Targetti, F. (1995b), 'L'unione monetaria europea: vecchi e nuovi percorsi' [European Monetary Union: old and new paths], in Targetti (ed.) (1995a), pp. 239–54.

Thomasberger, C. (1993), *Europaische Währungsintegration und globale Währungskonkurrenz* [European Monetary Integration and global currency competition], Tübingen: J.C.B. Mohr.

E31 E58 E43

12 Wicksellian norm, central bank real interest rate targeting and macroeconomic performance

Mario Seccareccia

1 Introduction*

As pointed out by Goodhart (1988), most central banks evolved originally out of the need to handle government debt as the fiscal agents of government, with the accompanying consolidation of note-issuing privileges within the hands of a single public institution largely being a byproduct of a desire to acquire the benefits of seigniorage. Over the last century, many central banks have also been entrusted with the social responsibility of regulating the financial system. As sole issuing agencies of high-powered money and lenders of last resort, central banks have acquired an important regulatory function, for instance, at the microeconomic level via the effective operation of clearing and settlement systems. More importantly, however, especially through the use of the discount window and bank rate policy, central banks have been entrusted historically with the macroeconomic demand management of the economy.

The object of this chapter is to show that, while mainstream economists have generally taken heed of the quantity theory of money as a theoretical framework that establishes a link between the quantity of money and the level of prices, historically those who have theorized about central bank behaviour have normally treated the quantity of money as an endogenous variable dependent on central bank discount rate policy. From this, there has ensued the well-known Wicksellian position that in order to control the rate of inflation, central banks must follow an appropriate bank rate policy that would secure equilibrium in the capital market by ensuring that the bank rate would always closely track the vagaries of the 'natural' rate of interest. However, because of the conceptual difficulties with the Wicksellian notion of the natural rate of interest, in the postwar period the revival of the Wicksellian norm for price-level stabilization arose out of an alternative formulation that replaced the earlier Wicksellian concept of the natural rate of interest with the Friedmanite one – the natural rate of unemployment.

* The author wishes to acknowledge the helpful comments provided by M. Lavoie, W. Mosler, A. Parguez, B. Vallageas and by various participants at conferences where this chapter was read. The usual disclaimer applies.

When this hybrid postwar Wicksellian model in favour of price-level stabilization was increasingly adopted by central banks beginning in the mid-1970s, the ultimate empirical outcome of this type of discretionary bank rate policy was twofold: it stabilized real interest rates and rates of unemployment at historically high levels. That is to say, the adoption of the Wicksellian mechanism of price-level stabilization, which remains the preferred choice of central bankers internationally (see, *inter alia*, Gavin 1990), inevitably results in a process of targeting real interest rates and unemployment at such inordinately high rates inconsistent with a socially acceptable level of macroeconomic performance.

2   The Wicksellian norm: a historical digression

Ever since the early nineteenth century, there has been much debate over the *modus operandi* of the central bank rate and, especially, on the impact of variations of the discount rate on macroeconomic variables. As described by Wood (1939), this debate was carried out historically at two different levels. First, the question had to do with the capacity of a central bank to set an appropriate bank rate so as to secure desired changes in the money supply, that is to say, the issue was regarding the nature of the causality between the bank rate and the money stock. At a second level of consideration, the question had to do with the traditional quantity-theory concern with the transmission mechanism between money and prices, whether it be through the bank's ability to control directly the money stock or indirectly by first altering conditions in the credit market through changes in the bank rate. Both of these concerns had been addressed in the famous debates between the Currency and Banking schools. Hence, early nineteenth-century loanable funds theorists such as Henry Thornton and Thomas Joplin subscribed primarily to the view that causality went from the bank rate to the money supply and not the reverse as, perhaps, others of the Currency School had defended (compare Eagly 1974, pp. 84–86; and Humphrey 1990a, pp. 40–52). Still others, such as Thomas Tooke and John Fullarton of the Banking School, completely rejected the view that the central bank could control any narrow monetary aggregate. These latter theorists questioned altogether the traditional belief that movements in the money supply would have a predictable effect on the level of prices and, indeed, they argued that the opposite was much closer to the truth.

As pointed out by Keynes when reviewing this vast literature in his *Treatise on Money*, the success of the Currency view, which refocused attention primarily on the need to control directly the quantity of money via central bank commitment to a commodity-money standard, did not stop some economists from analysing the causal mechanism along the lines of the earlier loanable funds theorists. In his *Treatise* (1930), Keynes recognizes:

> This notion, that an upward change in bank rate is associated with a diminished quantity of bank money, *either as cause or effect* ... so that the alleged association of high bank rate with falling prices follows directly from the usual quantity theory of money, runs, indeed, through all the later nineteenth-century literature on the subject. (Emphasis added; Keynes 1930, I, p. 168)

This is further reiterated in Hawtrey's *Art of Central Banking* (1932, p. 145) in which he points out that the generally-accepted theory during the nineteenth century relied on a causality going from the central bank's discount rate to the price level via its effect on the quantity of money. Therefore, even during what Laidler (1991) describes as the 'golden age' of the quantity theory, neoclassical economists showed strong concern with analysing the causal mechanism between money, interest and prices that focused on the causality going from interest rates to the money stock. The most celebrated of these neoclassical endogenous money theorists was Knut Wicksell who, perhaps, more than any other provided a coherent theoretical framework that could permit economists to address issues of monetary management of the macroeconomy and to appeal to central bank policy makers and bankers who, as pointed out by Myrdal (1939, pp. 14–15), had always subscribed to the view that the money supply was *not* directly a control variable.

Wicksellian loanable funds theory rested on his well-known two-interest rates analysis. Indeed, in his *Interest and Prices* (1898), Wicksell chose several terms to describe these rates. On the one side, we have the 'natural', the 'previous', the 'uncontrolled', the 'neutral', the 'natural real' and the 'natural capital' rate, while, on the other, we have the 'money', the 'market', the 'lending', the 'contractual', the 'loan' and the 'bank' rate of interest, to name just a few. While in his subsequent *Lectures* (1906) Wicksell was more careful in distinguishing these rates, for him there were two broad classes of interest rates in the economy that ought to be differentiated. In the first group, we find rates defined *in natura*, determined somehow independently of the monetary system, and reflecting the physical productivity of capital, whereas the latter group would include rates arising from the use of money or credit which are largely set by means of central bank discount rate policy. The first group of rates can be conveniently approximated by his concept of the 'natural' rate and the latter can be represented as the 'money' rate of interest.

A natural rate (ρ) is conceived by Wicksell (1898) as a pure commodity rate. It is the rate that would be established if commodity inputs in a productive system were lent or borrowed in kind; that is to say, it is 'the rate of interest which would be determined by supply and demand if no use were made of money and all lending were effected in the form of real capital goods' (Wicksell 1898, p. 102). Consequently, it is the rate that would equilibrate the market for capital goods if the latter were exchanged somehow outside of the monetary system proper; that is to say, it is '(t)he rate of interest at which *the demand for loan capital and the supply of savings exactly agree*' (Emphasis in original; Wicksell 1906, II, p. 193). The Wicksellian system is thus dichotomized into a real sector from which there emerges the natural rate and a monetary sector which is capable of supplying *ex nihilo* credit in excess of savings and which can therefore fix a money rate (i) independently of ρ. The reason for the relative independence of i from ρ has to do with Wicksell's presupposition of a high elasticity of the monetary system. In a highly developed credit economy, he argues: 'money ... is elastic in amount. Its quantity can to some extent be accommodated – and in a completely developed credit system the accommodation is complete – to any position that the demand for money may assume' (Wicksell 1898, p. 135). In this case, the demand for and supply of money tend to be 'one and the same thing' (Wicksell 1958, p. 76) with i being set largely at the discretion of the monetary authorities.

From this, it follows that since investment (I) is a function of ρ and saving (S) depends on i, then

$$I(\rho) - S(i) = \Delta M \qquad (12.1)$$

which suggests that whenever I exceeds S because of $\rho > i$, there would be net monetary creation (ΔM) which, under conditions of full employment, would bring about a cumulative process of inflation. In much the same way, a process of deflation would occur when $\rho < i$, and price stability would arise when $\rho = i$. This simple Wicksellian explanation of price movements can thus be summarized by the following equation:

$$\Delta P / P = \psi(\rho - i) \qquad (12.2)$$

with $\psi' > 0$. To the extent that ρ remains permanently above or below i, a steady-state rate of inflation or deflation will ensue that is determined by the coefficient ψ and, in which case, the price level would either rise or fall cumulatively.

Wicksell, however, did not think that such a simple steady-state solution would be attained. Indeed, he writes: 'But once the entrepreneurs begin to rely upon this process continuing – as soon as, that is to say, they start reckoning on a future rise in prices – the actual rise will become more and more rapid' (Wicksell 1898, p. 148). He thus recognized that, as soon as one introduces entrepreneurial inflationary expectations into his basic framework represented by equation (12.2), the rates of price change would themselves become time-varying values. In particular, as Robertson was to popularize later during the 1920s on the stimulative effects of inflation, Wicksell assumed that investment would be further spurred on by inflationary expecta-

tions over and above the entrepreneurial perceptions of the natural rate ρ, so
that equation (12.1) now becomes:

$$I(\rho, \Delta P^e / P) - S(i) = \Delta M \qquad (12.1')$$

where $\Delta P^e / P$ is entrepreneurial expectations of inflation. Assuming the simplest case of a positive linear relation between investment and $\Delta P^e / P$, equation (12.2) becomes:

$$\Delta P / P = \psi(\rho - i) + \gamma \Delta P^e / P \qquad (12.2')$$

where γ is a parameter representing the positive effect that inflationary expectations of inflation would have on investment (relative to S) and, consequently, on $\Delta P / P$. To understand the implications of introducing inflationary
expectations into his basic model, let us posit a simple one-period extrapolative
model of inflationary expectations found in Wicksell (1898, p. 97) such that:

$$\Delta P^e / P = \alpha(\Delta P / P)_{-1} \qquad (12.3)$$

From this assumption, equation (12.2') now becomes:

$$\Delta P / P = \psi(\rho - i) + \gamma[\alpha(\Delta P / P)_{-1}] \qquad (12.2'')$$

Once, say, a productivity shock occurs, that impacts positively on ρ and leads
to a deviation between the two rates, the price level would follow an explo-
sive path depending on the values of γ and α. While Wicksell himself had
little to say about the value of γ, he felt that the value of α was less than unity,
so that (barring a possible offsetting effect of γ) the rate of change in the price
level would normally tend towards a steady-state path asymptotically. At one
point, however, Wicksell actually alludes to what nowadays may be termed a
rational expectations possibility in which 'the expected rise in prices is each
time *fully* discounted' (Wicksell 1898, p. 148). In fact, much like the modern
re-discoverers during the 1980s of this Wicksellian solution (compare
McCallum 1986), he believed that such a system would be highly unstable
structurally and indeed indeterminate, since the price rise would become
infinitely large within each period. Except for this latter indeterminate outcome, Wicksell's specific autoregressive expectations version is depicted
graphically in Figure 12.1. In the diagram, the straight line diagonal traces
the steady-state solution when entrepreneurs' expected rate of inflation is
zero, while the non-linear curve describes the compounding effect of positive
or negative one-period autoregressive inflationary expectations, $\Delta P / P_{-1}$.

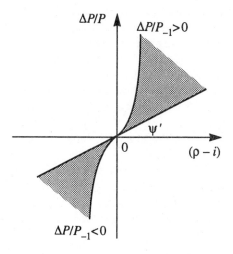

Figure 12.1   The Wicksellian process

Given the dangers of instability of the price level that can be inferred from his theory of the cumulative process, Wicksell suggested that the ultimate objective of monetary policy ought to be to preserve the value of money by maintaining the price level constant. Banks and, in particular, central banks ought therefore to follow a simple rule so as to prevent the money rate from progressively deviating from the 'uncontrolled' natural rate; that is, to raise the bank rate whenever prices are rising and to reduce it whenever prices are falling. The effect of adopting this norm would be to dampen price fluctuations and ultimately to achieve price stability. Consequently, periods of inflation or deflation would arise because of central bank inability to obey this simple rule owing to its relative passivity in moving the bank rate in the same direction as the natural rate (Wicksell 1906, II, p. 205). This Wicksellian view became widely held during the interwar era, as numerous disparate writers such as Fisher, Hayek, Hawtrey, Keynes of the *Treatise*, Mises, Myrdal, Lindhal and Robertson had adopted variants of this basic two-interest rate framework.[1]

An obvious problem now arises for banks that would wish to implement such a Wicksellian rule. Presumably, they would have to be able to monitor the movement of the natural rate; but how could such a rate be physically defined *in natura*? As Sraffa (1932, p. 50) had argued, and others such as Myrdal (1939, p. 50) and even the later Hayek (1941, p. 37) were to reiterate, there was no unique commodity rate that could be conceived meaningfully in barter terms except in the trivial case of a one-commodity world. For this reason, as both Nell (1967, pp. 386–94) and Rogers (1989, pp. 27–38) have argued, Wicksell's original concept of the natural rate succumbs to what was later to become the Cambridge critique of capital. This is probably why, in his *Lectures*, Wicksell himself was to redefine it in more subjective terms as the 'normal' rate. However, even if one were to define it purely as an expectation variable, as Myrdal (1939) had proposed, there exists no single 'perceived' rate but a whole vector of such individually-held subjective *ex ante* rates to which the bank ought to anchor its discount rate policy. For this important reason, it would seem, therefore, that an important pillar of Wicksellian theory did not rest on a sufficiently solid foundation to make his policy norm operationally useful.

Perhaps anticipating such criticism, already in his *Interest and Prices*, Wicksell defended the operationality of his bank rate rule and argued that it would be unnecessary for the banks actually to observe the movement of the natural rate. All that was necessary was to monitor the fluctuations of the price level. Wicksell (1898) points out:

> This does not mean that the banks ought actually to *ascertain* the natural rate before fixing their own rates of interest. That would, of course, be impracticable, and would also be quite unnecessary. For the current level of commodity prices provides a reliable test of the agreement or diversion of the two rates. The procedure should rather be simply as follows: So *long as prices remain unaltered the banks' rate of interest is to remain unaltered. If prices rise, the rate of interest is to be raised; and if prices fall, the rate of interest is to be lowered; and the rate of interest is henceforth to be maintained at its new level until a further movement of prices calls for a further change in one direction or the other.* (Emphasis in original; Wicksell 1898, p. 189)

Wicksell's general policy proposal could be interpreted as implying a very precise form of central bank reaction function, namely:

$$i = \delta_0 + \delta_1 \Delta P / P \qquad (12.4)$$

with $\delta_1 = 1$, and whose implementation would give rise to what Cottrell (1997) refers to as a phenomenological Fisher effect by ensuring a long-term real rate of interest equal to δ_0. Humphrey (1990b, p. 9) points out that a similar central bank feedback rule was later also defended by Cassel (1928, p. 528). Unfortunately, while the Wicksell/Cassel response to the theoretical conundrum of defining ρ is quite appealing, it presupposes that Wicksell's explanation of price-level movement in terms of his two-interest rates analysis is the correct one! As shown by Rogers (1989, pp. 113–27), this issue of the indeterminacy of the natural rate not only plagues the original model but all those postwar hybrid models based on concepts related to the Wicksellian natural rate.

Despite this obvious conceptual problem and the circularity of his reasoning, the celebrated Wicksell rule of price-level stabilization, as stated above, became fashionable among both monetary analysts and policy makers and came to be the cornerstone of central bank policy. This was particularly so during the early 1930s when countries that had abandoned the gold standard and adopted paper standards, sought alternative monetary norms. Jonung (1979, pp. 459–96), for instance, recounts how the Swedish central bank, the *Riksbank*, in 1931 became the first to subscribe officially to Wicksellian monetary policy and was technically to do so until the Second World War. In both Britain and Canada during the early 1930s, especially during the hearings of the Macmillan Commission (see Watts 1993, pp. 9–12) which, in the case of Canada, preceded the founding of the Bank of Canada in 1934, observers pointed to the success of the *Sveriges Riksbank* with its internal stabilization of the price level (compare Creighton 1933, pp. 50–53). Given the severity of the Great Depression, the political forces in place during the mid-1930s did not favour the adoption of the Wicksellian norm in support of a single objective, price stability, via interest rate policy. Within the Canadian experience, therefore, it is not surprising that the official preamble to the Bank of Canada Act of 1934 speaks not only of the goal of stabilizing the price level but also of the need 'to mitigate by its influence fluctuations in the general level of production, trade ... and employment' (quoted from Stokes 1939, p. 177).

The early postwar success of Keynesianism with the accompanying government commitments to full employment in most Western countries further weakened the support for the Wicksellian macroeconomic objective of price stability through discount rate policy. Most Western economies had achieved during the first two decades of the postwar period the twin objectives of high employment and low inflation not by fixing interest rates in accordance with the Wicksellian rule, but merely by pegging nominal interest rates at a sufficiently low level and keeping them stable at that level. The effect of what was essentially a low real interest rate policy was to foster the growth of private and public investment and the accompanying productivity growth (see Seccareccia 1995). Given the obvious success in terms of high growth and employment of this Keynesian low real interest rate policy, one would have assumed that the Wicksellian policy norm, which had become so popular among central bankers during the interwar era, would not have seen a revival during the postwar period. However, this was not to be so.

3 Hybrid Wicksellianism and the natural rate of unemployment

It may legitimately be argued that the return to hybrid forms of Wicksellian norms for price-level stabilization in the postwar period should be traced to the decision of the US Federal Reserve to abandon nominal interest rate

pegging and to return slowly to a discretionary discount rate policy after the
famous US Treasury–Federal Reserve Accord in March 1951, whose effect
was to begin to revive discretionary bank rate policy both domestically and
internationally in accordance with the previous Wicksellian framework, as
well as to push interest rates secularly upwards (compare Sylla 1988, pp. 31–
2; and Homer and Sylla 1991, pp. 387–93). However, it was not until the late
1960s and early 1970s that the economics profession was treated to what
turned out to be a well-articulated variant of the earlier Wicksellian formulation. Although unnecessarily modelled within a quantity theory framework,
the Friedmanite espousal of the natural rate of unemployment provided a
useful substitute to the earlier Wicksellian reliance on the two-interest rates
exposition of the inflationary process. Instead of the non-operational concept
of the natural rate of interest (ρ), in its place was proposed what at the time
seemed to be a more empirically-based concept of the natural rate of unemployment (U^*) and its later embodiment, the NAIRU. In many respects, it
could be argued that it is only when his earlier and less-celebrated restate-
ment of the quantity theory was recast in a hybrid Wicksellian dress did
Friedman's views achieve such prominence both within the economics profession and among central bankers internationally.

The natural rate of unemployment and its offspring, the NAIRU, have been
traditionally set within an inflation-augmented version of the Phillips curve
quite analogous to the earlier Wicksellian two-interest rates formulation dis-
played in equation (12.2′) above:

$$\Delta P / P = \phi(U - U^*) + \beta \Delta P^e / P \qquad\qquad (12.5)$$

where U is the measured unemployment, $\phi' < 1$, and $\beta = 1$. Friedman himself
in his original exposition of the theory pointed to its Wicksellian affinity,
when he wrote that his analysis 'could be translated fairly directly into
Wicksellian terms ... [with] its close counterpart in the employment market'
(Friedman 1968, pp. 7–8). Indeed, except for its obvious connection with the
Phillips curve, U^* serves a similar purpose to the earlier Wicksellian concept
of the natural rate of interest.

The literature on both the Friedmanite natural rate and the NAIRU is too
well known to necessitate much discussion.[2] It will suffice to say that, much
like Wicksell's natural rate of interest, the existence and/or uniqueness of
such concepts has been questioned by numerous economists both on theoretical grounds, especially with regards to the effects of hysteresis (see, among
others, Hargreaves-Heap 1980; Isaac 1993; and Akerlof et al. 1996) and on
empirical grounds relating to the sensitivity of the estimates to model specification, the definition of variables, and to the countries and sample periods
chosen for the econometric estimation (compare Setterfield et al. 1992; Rowley

1995; and Eisner 1996). However, the concern of this chapter is not with the theoretical and empirical basis of the natural rate hypothesis. What, rather, is of concern is the implication of implementing central bank policy within this hybrid Wicksellian framework.

Let us assume that the central bank is committed to the Wicksellian norm of price stability. Suppose, furthermore, that, regardless of the reason, there is a *perceived* positive supply-side shock on U^* as it is frequently believed by mainstream economists and policy makers to have occurred during the 1970s.[3] If we postulate a modified Wicksellian central bank reaction function of the general type depicted below:

$$i = \delta_0 + \delta_1 \Delta P / P - \delta_2 (U - U^*) \qquad (12.6)$$

with δ_0 and $\delta_2 > 0$ and $\delta_1 = 1$, then what would be the implication of the central bank's response to the perceived supply-side shock?

Before attempting to answer this question, however, let us first explain the nature of the reaction function being formulated. From the equation above, it is clear that the central bank would adjust nominal interest rates, i, either because U deviates from U^* and/or because $\Delta P / P$ is different from zero. Indeed, while $(U - U^*)$ and $\Delta P / P$ are interdependent in the Phillips curve framework (see equation (12.5) above), $\Delta P / P$ could increase for other reasons within the Friedmanite world, namely inflationary expectations. Hence, even in a steady-state world in which $U = U^*$, a commitment to the Wicksellian norm would involve a nominal rate of interest, i, changing in proportion to the rate of inflation, $\Delta P / P$, regardless of whether this rate of inflation is being fuelled by inflationary expectations or other cost–push factors, emphasized by advocates of NAIRU. Moreover, when $U = U^*$, our postulated reaction function becomes equivalent to the original Wicksellian form (see equation (12.4), above) which, as before, would secure a steady-state real rate of interest equal to the constant δ_0 in equation (12.6).

Let us now assume that there is a presumed supply-side shock. With the central bank acting on its perception of a rising natural rate U^*, the consequence of its action would be for the real rate of interest to move upwards in proportion to the coefficient δ_2. In this framework, therefore, as soon as the central bank believes that U^* is inching upwards, the effect would be to push up significantly the *ex post* real rate of interest as it seeks to bring the actual U into line with the higher U^*.

If we suppose, furthermore, that a key determinant of aggregate spending and the level of employment is the real rate of interest because of the effects it has on the value of private and public debt *à la* Domar (see Smithin 1994, 1996b, and Wray 1996), as well as because of the redistributive effect of real interest rates in favour of rentiers with a high propensity to save (compare Seccareccia 1988), we can depict this simple relation as follows:

$$U = \lambda_0 + \lambda_1(i - \Delta P / P) + \lambda_2 A \qquad (12.7)$$

where A is autonomous spending (independent of $(i - \Delta P / P)$) with $\lambda_2' < 0$ and with $\lambda_1' > 0$ and $\lambda_1'' < 0$ since U could only approach zero asymptotically as the real rate falls and/or becomes negative. From equation (12.7), it can easily be inferred that, as $(i - \Delta P / P)$ rises because of a perceived jump in U^*, the ultimate outcome would be to put upward pressure on the actual unemployment rate. Statistical evidence of such a non-linear positive relation between unemployment and real rates of interest is found in Figure 12.2. The scatter diagram describes the relation between the rate of unemployment and the real

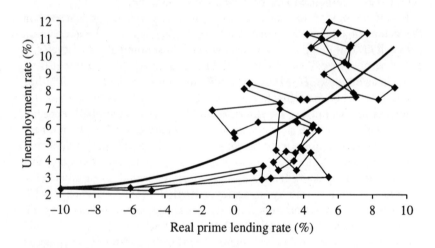

Note: The real rate was calculated simply as the nominal rate less the rate of inflation of the consumer price index in Canada. The diagonal non-linear least-squares line added to the scatter diagram was calculated as follows (with the t-ratios in parenthesis):

$$U_t = 4.56 + 0.44(i - \Delta P / P)_t + 0.22(i - \Delta P / P)_i^2$$
$$(8.98)\,(4.79) \qquad\qquad (1.49)$$

Sources: Statistics Canada, *Historical Labour Force Statistics* (Cat. no. 71–201); *Bank of Canada Review* (Selected Issues); and *Historical Statistics of Canada*, Ottawa: Statistics Canada, 1983.

Figure 12.2   Relation between the unemployment rate and the real prime lending rate, Canada 1946–1995

prime lending rate for Canada between the years 1946 and 1995. The simple least-squares line displays the degree of non-linearity of the bivariate relation, with deviations from the line probably being explained by the effects of other autonomous demand-side shocks (that is, fluctuations in the A term in equation (12.7) above) on the unemployment rate.

As long as the central bank's perception of a rising U^* persists, the outcome would be to stabilize both real interest rates and unemployment at significantly high levels. What is critical to our analysis is thus the central bank's *perception* of the Friedmanite natural rate or of the NAIRU. The original Wicksellian norm of price level stabilization through interest rate policy would merely peg *ex post* real rates at a given initial level δ_0. It is the central bank's presumption of a rising U^* in the hybrid Friedmanite version of the Wicksellian response process that brings about a discontinuous hike in the *ex post* real rates of interest and, accompanying it, a jump in the actual rate of unemployment in accordance with equation (12.7).

4 The implications of hybrid Wicksellian policies of price-level stabilization: some *prima facie* evidence

It is argued that this simple theoretical scenario described above regarding central bank perception of U^* depicts reasonably well the behaviour of central banks in both Canada and elsewhere since the mid-1970s. For instance, as early as in the 1972 *Annual Report* of the Governor of the Bank of Canada there was an increasing belief that the unemployment rate in Canada had undergone a significant structural shift, in part owing to the increased generosity of Canadian social programmes, especially the unemployment insurance system.[4] Although at the time this was not yet described as a shift in the natural rate of unemployment, as it was later to be interpreted (see Rose 1988, pp. 33–41; Burns 1991, pp. 39–51), U^* was perceived as beginning to move upwards so that actual unemployment was assumed no longer to bear the same relation to the rate of inflation as had previously been the case. Second, compounding this perception was the first OPEC (Organization of Petroleum Exporting Countries) oil price shock in late 1973, which had the effect of dramatically pushing up the rate of inflation to double-digit levels and further intensifying the unemployment problem in all Western countries.

Believing that the inflationary forces unleashed in the 1973/74 period had been the consequence of accommodative central bank behaviour that had led to an excessive expansion of the money stock (compare Sparks 1986, pp. 137–9), monetary authorities in both Canada and elsewhere began to redirect their policy in favour of price stability via the targeting of intermediate instruments, such as unborrowed reserves, M1, or M2 (see Friedman and Kuttner 1996). However, with the monetarist débâcle of the early 1980s which saw central banks being incapable of controlling monetary aggregates even within wide target ranges, monetary authorities had learned a hard lesson on the nature of endogenous money. However, since the abandonment of the targeting of monetary aggregates, central banks internationally have reasserted their commitment to the exclusive goal of price stability which in Canada has been widely interpreted to mean zero inflation (compare Lipsey (ed.) 1990; and York (ed.) 1990) and has entailed the drawing up of precise target ranges for the inflation rate since 1991.[5]

How can central banks achieve these inflation rate targets without targeting monetary aggregates? Within the Wicksellian world, the only effective instrument is the cost of advancing liquidity to commercial banks. For instance, within the present framework of zero-reserve requirements in Canada, it is essentially by setting short-term interest rates through the administering of the overnight rate which, in tandem with the bank rate, are the effective instruments of monetary and credit control (compare Clinton and Howard 1994; Duguay 1994; Thiessen 1995; and Bank of Canada 1995–96). Once short-term interest rates are set via the overnight rate, the ensuing effect on the money supply is thus presumed to have its impact on the labour and commodity markets, and eventually on the rate of inflation. Numerous critics have pointed out, however, that this transmission mechanism is highly tenuous and unspecified (compare Spotten and Rowley 1996). Yet, it is perfectly compatible with what we have described as the hybrid Wicksellian interpretation of the inflationary process cum the quantity theory that links money and prices.

The persistence of the Wicksellian interest rate mechanism of monetary control via an unofficial intermediate instrument, U (*vis-à-vis* U^*), together with central banks' strong commitment to price stability, has had the effect of maintaining both real interest rates and unemployment rates at historically high levels throughout the last two decades and, especially, after the second major OPEC oil price shock in 1979. By continually moving interest rates 'preemptively' (to use Macklem's (1997, p. 52) expression) to avoid 'excessive' labour market demand, central banks have continued to generate inordinately high rates of unemployment. Table 12.1 provides some useful descriptive statistics on both short- and longer-term interest rates, as well as on the unemployment rate for the postwar period in Canada. Regardless of whether the cutoff date for the first subperiod is 1974 or 1979, what is evident from the table is that there was a significant shift in both the mean and variance of the three interest rate series when, during the second subperiod, the Canadian monetary authorities had come to embrace fully the Wicksellian norm in favour of price stability. Hence, especially during the 1980s, the Canadian central bank had assumed that there was a rising NAIRU and, in accordance with the reaction function specified in equation (12.6) above, had followed a policy of combating inflation by continually pegging nominal interest rates above the actual rate of inflation by a wide and relatively constant margin.

Table 12.1   Five-year averages of real interest rates and unemployment in Canada, 1946–1995 (all relevant data in percentage terms)

Period	91-day TB	Bonds 10 yrs +	Prime rate	Unemployment
1946–50	–6.1	–3.9	–2.1	2.9
1951–55	–1.3	0.8	1.9	3.5
1956–60	1.5	2.5	3.5	5.6
1961–65	2.2	3.7	4.1	5.4
1966–70	2.0	3.0	3.2	4.4
1971–75	–1.8	0.5	0.7	6.0
1976–80	1.1	1.2	2.3	7.7
1981–85	4.8	5.6	6.3	10.5
1986–90	5.8	5.6	7.2	8.4
1991–95	4.3	6.4	5.5	10.6

Mean and variance for complete period and subperiods
1946–95

Mean	1.2	2.5	3.3	6.5
Variance	17.1	14.2	12.1	7.7
1946–74				
Mean	–0.5	1.2	2.0	4.5
Variance	17.1	14.7	12.0	2.2
1975–95				
Mean	3.6	4.4	5.0	9.2
Variance	2.7	2.8	7.1	2.7
1946–79				
Mean	–0.4	1.1	1.9	5.0
Variance	15.1	12.7	10.8	3.1
1980–95				
Mean	4.8	5.6	6.2	9.7
Variance	2.6	3.2	2.2	2.4

Sources: Statistics Canada, *Historical Labour Force Statistics* (Cat. no. 71–201); Statistics Canada, *Historical Statistics of Canada*, Ottawa: Statistics Canada, 1983; *Bank of Canada Review* (Selected Issues).

As these hybrid Wicksellian policies became fashionable in all the Western countries during the last two decades, the effects of these ant-inflation measures had similar implications internationally, that is, their adoption led to both an upward movement in real rates and unemployment gravitating around higher levels. Table 12.2 provides some descriptive statistics for the G7

Table 12.2   Mean and variance of the real discount and unemployment rates, G7 countries, 1951–1995

	1951–95	1951–79	1980–95
	Real discount rate (%)		
Mean	0.79	–0.11	2.77
Variance	12.75	13.20	4.49
	Unemployment rate (%)		
Mean	5.18	3.65	7.87
Variance	6.41	2.16	1.81

Note: Available time series for all seven countries were pooled for the complete period 1951–95, with the exception of France where the data from the IMF went from 1951–89 and the UK where it was readily available only from 1951–80.

Sources: International Monetary Fund, *International Financial Statistics*, Washington: IMF; Organization for Economic Cooperation and Development, *Labour Force Statistics*, Paris: OECD.

countries. As was the case for Canada, the phenomenon of real-interest rate pegging for the post-1979 period was repeated with dreary monotony in all the major industrialized countries, as central banks joined the monetarist bandwagon during the 1980s. The outcome of such measures are too well known to necessitate much elaboration – rates of inflation did come down but only at the cost of permanently higher rates of unemployment.

Contrary to the defenders of central bank austerity policy, these unemployment costs of disinflation will persist well into the future not only because of problems of hysteresis emphasized by some (compare, among others, Fortin 1993), but also because of the negative redistributive effects of such policies in favour of rentier income. The macroeconomic impact of what Smithin (1996a, p. 82) has described as the 'revenge of the rentiers' will continue to haunt Western economies because of the direct negative effects of this redistribution on aggregate effective demand, as well as because of the indirect effect that the overhanging public and private debt engendered by these high real interest policies are having on overall spending. Indeed, even after central banks have ditched NAIRU, as Galbraith (1997) has advocated, mass unemployment will inevitably persist. For instance, since the end of 1995, both nominal and real interest rates in Canada have come down significantly, yet unemployment remains stubbornly high at close to the 10 per cent rate, largely because of the negative effects of other elements in the *A* term in equation (12.7), above. Of particular importance is restrictive fiscal policy, which has been a major obstacle to economic recovery as governments saddled with huge debts caused by past high real-interest rates have remained firm in their deficit fighting. Hence, because of the adoption of hybrid Wicksellian anti-inflation policy over the last two decades, most Western economies remain stuck in a state that can appropriately be described as one of Keynesian underemployment equilibrium.

Notes

1. To substantiate this point let us quote from one of the many writers who was perhaps least identified with this Wicksellian framework but still accepted the basic Wicksellian precept in support of a discretionary bank rate policy that would impact on the growth of credit money and prices. R.G. Hawtrey writes that 'If [the central bank] leaves the market to itself, casual deviations of the short-term rate from the natural rate will be constantly occurring, and any such deviation may be exaggerated through the instability of credit' (Hawtrey 1932, p. 287). For further review of these neo-Wicksellian authors of the period, see Seccareccia (1990, 1992, 1994).
2. For recent reviews of the literature on the natural rate and/or NAIRU, see *Journal of Economic Perspectives*, **11** (1) March 1997, as well as *Journal of Economic Studies*, **20** (1/2) 1993.
3. In addition to the oil price shock, in Canada economists have referred, for instance, to exogenous supply-side factors pertaining to the labour market, such as the increased generosity of the unemployment insurance programme, high minimum wages, and so on, for the period of the early and mid-1970s. See, among many such studies, those of Rose (1988), Burns (1991), and Poloz (1994).
4. For instance, in the 1972 *Annual Report* of the Governor of the Bank of Canada it was recognized that there was 'some reason to believe that unemployment rates may no longer reflect the same degree of ease in labour markets as they formerly did. ... In particular, changing income maintenance arrangements may be tending to increase the number of those who are reported as remaining in the labour force but who want jobs only from time to time and may be lessening the urgency with which others seek re-employment' (quoted in Courchene 1976, pp. 182–3).
5. As former Governor John Crow was to affirm: 'In Canada, the preamble to the Bank of Canada Act does suggest a lot of different economic goals. But, as in Switzerland, the practical focus is unambiguously on price stability' (Crow 1993, p. 25). Any other objective, such as low unemployment, would merely set in motion cumulative inflationary pressures that would ultimately have to be paid for in terms of still higher rates of unemployment, such as supposedly had been the case during the 1981–82 recession (Crow 1987, pp. 24–5). This 1980s commitment to 'zero inflation' was heralded by some as one of the first price stability experiments since the *Sveriges Riksbank* in the 1930s, which was accompanied by New Zealand (1990), the United Kingdom (1992), Sweden (1993), and even the European Union under the Maastricht Treaty (compare Gavin 1990; and Laidler and Robson 1993).

Bibliography

Akerlof, G.A., W.T. Dickens and G.L. Perry (1996), 'The macroeconomics of low inflation', *Brookings Papers on Economic Activity*, **1**, 1–76.

Bank of Canada (1995–96), 'A proposed framework for the implementation of monetary policy in large value transfer system environment', *Bank of Canada Review*, Winter, 73–84.

Burns, A. (1991), 'The natural rate of unemployment: Canada and the Provinces', in S. Gera (ed.), *Canadian Unemployment*, Ottawa: Canada Communication Group Publishing, pp. 39–51.

Cassel, G. (1928), 'The rate of interest, the bank rate, and the stabilization of prices', *Quarterly Journal of Economics*, **42** (4), August, 511–29.

Clinton, K. and D. Howard (1994), *From Monetary Policy Instruments to Administered Interest Rates: The Transmission Mechanism in Canada*, Technical Report No. 69, Bank of Canada, June.

Cottrell, A. (1997), 'The Fisher effect: phenomenology, theory and policy', in A.J. Cohen, H. Hagemann and J. Smithin (eds), *Money, Financial Institutions and Macroeconomics*, Boston: Kluwer Academic Publishers, pp. 55–65.

Courchene, T.J. (1976), *Money, Inflation, and the Bank of Canada: An Analysis of Canadian Monetary Policy from 1970 to Early 1975*, Montreal: C.D. Howe Research Institute.

Creighton, J.H. (1933), *Central Banking in Canada*, Vancouver: Clarke & Stuart Co. Ltd.

Crow, J.W. (1987), 'The Bank of Canada and its objectives', *Bank of Canada Review*, April, 21–7.

Crow, J.W. (1993), 'Monetary policy, and the responsibilities and accountability of central Banks', *Bank of Canada Review*, Spring, 21–30.

Duguay, P. (1994), 'Empirical evidence on the strength of the monetary transmission mechanism in Canada', *Journal of Monetary Economics*, **33** (1), February, 39–61.

Eagly, R.V. (1974), *The Structure of Classical Economic Theory*, New York: Oxford University Press.

Eisner, R. (1996), 'The retreat from full employment', in P. Arestis (ed.), *Employment, Economic Growth and the Tyranny of the Market, Essays in Honour of Paul Davidson*, Vol. 2, Aldershot: Edward Elgar, pp. 106–30.

Fortin, P. (1993), 'The unbearable lightness of zero-inflation optimism', *Canadian Business Economics*, **1** (3), Spring, 3–18.

Friedman, B.M. and K.N. Kuttner (1996), 'A price target for U.S. monetary policy? Lessons from the experience with money growth targets', *Brookings Papers on Economic Activity*, **1**, 77–146.

Friedman, M. (1968), 'The role of monetary policy', *American Economic Review*, **58** (1), March, 1–17.

Galbraith, J.K. (1997), 'Time to ditch the NAIRU', *Journal of Economic Perspectives*, **11** (1), Winter, 93–108.

Gavin, W.T. (1990), 'In defense of zero inflation', in R.C. York (ed.), *Taking Aim: The Debate on Zero Inflation*, Toronto: C.D. Howe Institute, pp. 43–62.

Goodhart, C.A.E. (1988), *The Evolution of Central Banks*, Cambridge, MA: MIT Press.

Hargreaves-Heap, S.P. (1980), 'Choosing the wrong "natural" rate: accelerating inflation or decelerating employment and growth?', *Economic Journal*, **90** (359), September, 611–20.

Hawtrey, R.G. (1932), *The Art of Central Banking*, London: Longmans, Green & Co.

Hayek, F.A. (1941), *The Pure Theory of Capital*, London: Macmillan.

Homer, S. and R. Sylla (1991), *A History of Interest Rates*, 3rd edn, New Brunswick, NJ: Rutgers University Press.

Humphrey, T.M. (1990a), 'Cumulative process models from Thornton to Wicksell', in D. Moggridge (ed.), *Perspectives on the History of Economic Thought*, Vol. IV, Aldershot: Edward Elgar, pp. 40–52.

Humphrey, T.M. (1990b), 'Fisherian and Wicksellian price-stabilization models in the history of monetary thought', *Federal Reserve Bank of Richmond Economic Review*, **76** (3), May/June, 3–12.

Isaac, A. (1993), 'Is there a natural rate?', *Journal of Post Keynesian Economics*, **15** (4), Summer, 453–70.

Jonung, L. (1979), 'Knut Wicksell's norm of price stabilization and Swedish monetary policy in the 1930s', *Journal of Monetary Economics*, **5** (4), October, 459–96.

Keynes, J.M. (1930), *A Treatise on Money, Vol I: The Collected Writings of John Maynard Keynes*, Vol. V, London: Macmillan, 1971.

Laidler, D.E.W. (1991), *The Golden Age of the Quantity Theory: The Development of Neoclassical Monetary Economics, 1870–1914*, Princeton, NJ: Princeton University Press.

Laidler, D.E.W. and W.B.P. Robson (1993), *The Great Canadian Disinflation: The Economics and Politics of Monetary Policy in Canada, 1988–93*, Toronto: C.D. Howe Institute.

Lipsey, R.G. (ed.) (1990), *Zero Inflation: The Goal of Price Stability*, Toronto: C.D. Howe Institute.

Macklem, T. (1997), 'Capacity constraints, price adjustment, and monetary policy', *Bank of Canada Review*, Spring, 39–56.
McCallum, B.T. (1986), 'Some issues concerning interest rate pegging, price level determinacy and the real bills doctrine', *Journal of Monetary Economics*, **17** (1), January, 135–60.
Myrdal, G. (1939), *Monetary Equilibrium*, London: W. Hodge & Co. Ltd.
Nell, E.J. (1967), 'Wicksell's theory of circulation', *Journal of Political Economy*, **75** (4), Part I, August, 386–94.
Poloz, S.S. (1994), *The Causes of Unemployment in Canada: A Review of the Evidence*, Working Paper 94–11, Bank of Canada, November.
Rogers, C. (1989), *Money, Interest and Capital, A Study in the Foundations of Monetary Theory*, Cambridge: Cambridge University Press.
Rose, D.E. (1988), *The NAIRU in Canada: Concepts, Determinants and Estimates*, Technical Report No. 50, Bank of Canada, December.
Rowley, R. (1995), 'History, structure and the wandering natural rate of unemployment', *Économie appliquée*, **48** (1), 133–55.
Seccareccia, M. (1988), 'Systemic viability and credit crunches: an examination of recent Canadian cyclical fluctuations', *Journal of Economic Issues*, **22** (1), March, 49–77.
Seccareccia, M. (1990), 'The two faces of Neo-Wicksellianism during the 1930s: the Austrians and the Swedes', in D. Moggridge (ed.), *Perspectives in the History of Economic Thought*, Vol. 4, Aldershot: Edward Elgar, pp. 137–54.
Seccareccia, M. (1992), 'Wicksellianism, Myrdal and the monetary explanation of cyclical crises', in G. Dostaler, D. Ethier and L. Lepage, *Gunnar Myrdal and His Works*, Montreal: Harvest House, pp. 144–62.
Seccareccia, M. (1994), 'Credit money and cyclical crises: the views of Hayek and Fisher compared', in M. Colonna and H. Hagemann (eds), *Money and Business Cycles, The Economics of F.A. Hayek*, Vol. I, Aldershot: Edward Elgar, pp. 53–73.
Seccareccia, M. (1995), 'Keynesianism and public investment', *Studies in Political Economy*, No. 46, Spring, 43–78.
Setterfield, M., D.V. Gordon and L. Osberg (1992), 'Searching for a will o' the wisp: an empirical study of the NAIRU in Canada', *European Economic Review*, **36** (1), January, 119–36.
Smithin, J. (1994), 'Cause and effect in the relationship between budget deficits and the rate of interest', *Économies et sociétés*, **28** (1–2), January–February, 151–69.
Smithin, J. (1996a), *Macroeconomic Policy and the Future of Capitalism: The Revenge of the Rentiers and the Threat to Prosperity*, Aldershot: Edward Elgar.
Smithin, J. (1996b), 'Real interest rates, inflation, and unemployment', in B. MacLean and L. Osberg (eds), *The Unemployment Crisis: All for Nought?*, Montreal & Kingston: McGill-Queen's University Press, pp. 39–55.
Sparks, G.R. (1986), 'The theory and practice of monetary policy in Canada: 1945–83', in J. Sargent (ed.), *Fiscal and Monetary Policy*, Toronto: University of Toronto Press, pp. 119–49.
Spotten, B. and R. Rowley (1996), 'Monetary dialogue and dogma in Canada: the inside view', *Canadian Business Economics*, **5** (1), Fall, 20–32.
Sraffa, P. (1932), 'Dr. Hayek on money and capital', *Economic Journal*, **42** (165), March, 42–53.
Stokes, M.L. (1939), *The Bank of Canada: The Development and Present Position of Central Banking in Canada*, Toronto: Macmillan Co. of Canada.
Sylla, R. (1988), 'The autonomy of monetary authorities: the case of the U.S. Federal Reserve System', in G. Toniolo (ed.), *Central Banks' Independence in Historical Perspective*, Berlin: Walter de Gruyter & Co., pp. 17–38.
Thiessen, G.G. (1995), 'Uncertainty and the transmission of monetary policy in Canada', *Bank of Canada Review*, Summer, 41–58.
Watts, G.S. (1993), *The Bank of Canada: Origins and Early History* (ed. by T.K. Rymes), Ottawa: Carleton University Press.
Wicksell, K. (1898), *Interest and Prices: A Study of the Causes Regulating the Value of Money*, London: Macmillan & Co., 1936.

Wicksell, K. (1906), *Lectures on Political Economy* (Vol. II: Money), London: Routledge & Sons, 1935.
Wicksell, K. (1907), 'The influence of the rate of interest on prices', *Economic Journal*, **17** (66), June, 213–20.
Wicksell, K. (1958), *Selected Papers on Economic Theory*, London: George Allen & Unwin Ltd.
Wood, E. (1939), *English Theories of Central Banking Control, 1819–1858*, Cambridge, MA: Harvard University Press.
Wray, L.R. (1996), 'Government deficits and appropriate monetary policy', *Économies et sociétés*, **30** (2–3), February–March, 269–300.
York, R.C. (ed.) (1990), *Taking Aim: The Debate on Zero Inflation*, Toronto: C.D. Howe Institute.

13 New Zealand's experience with an independent central bank since 1989

Paul Dalziel   ES8 ES2

1 Introduction*

The reform by the New Zealand Parliament of the Reserve Bank of New Zealand Act in November 1989 continues to attract international attention as an example of how a central bank might be given autonomy to pursue an independent monetary policy, and yet still remain accountable to the country's elected representatives (Kirchner 1995; Evans et al., 1996; Robertson 1996; Dalziel 1997). In New Zealand, this has been attempted by: (i) reducing the statutory objectives of monetary policy to the single goal of 'achieving and maintaining stability in the general level of prices';[1] (ii) giving the Reserve Bank the freedom and responsibility to implement monetary policy directed towards its statutory objective; (iii) requiring the Minister of Finance and the Governor of the Reserve Bank to negotiate and sign a Policy Targets Agreement (PTA) that specifies a precise measure of inflation that will be accepted as consistent with price stability; and (iv) requiring the Governor of the Reserve Bank to publish a *Monetary Policy Statement* every six months to give account of the Bank's performance in achieving the agreed PTA target and how its current policies are expected to achieve that target in the future. It has also become standard practice for the Minister of Finance to write to the non-executive directors of the Reserve Bank to evaluate the Governor's performance every time there is a breach of the target, even if the breach is very small, and failure to achieve the target is one of the grounds contained in the Act for dismissal of the Governor.

One of the reasons why this arrangement attracted international interest is that New Zealand policy makers initially adopted a particularly tight definition of price stability. The first PTA under the reformed Act was signed on 2 March 1990, and defined a range of 0–2 per cent in the underlying inflation rate of the consumer price index (CPI) as the Reserve Bank's target (*Reserve Bank Bulletin*, March 1990, p. 26; for explanations of how the underlying inflation rate is calculated from the headline inflation rate, see *Reserve Bank*

* I am grateful to the conference organizers, Philip Arestis and Malcolm Sawyer, and to the Department of Economics and Marketing of Lincoln University, for financial assistance towards the expenses of attending the conference at the University of East London on 16 May 1997, and to David Mayes for written comments on an earlier draft.

Monetary Policy Statement, June 1995, p. 5, or Dalziel 1997). This range was then confirmed in the PTAs signed on 19 December 1990 and 16 December 1992. The midpoint of 1.0 per cent was chosen to allow for measurement bias in the CPI thought to be about that amount (Dawe 1990, p. 32; Brash 1996a, p. 312), while the range of 2 percentage points emphasized that the Reserve Bank was to have very little discretion in implementing its policies.

Experience under this arrangement has been mixed. By September 1991, the underlying inflation rate had been reduced to 2.1 per cent in the same quarter that unemployment peaked at 10.9 per cent. Inflation then remained between 0 and 2 per cent until June 1995, as unemployment improved to 6.3 per cent. After June 1995, however, the Reserve Bank found it very difficult to meet its inflation target, and between June 1995 and December 1996, the underlying annual inflation rate lay between 2 and 2.4 per cent every quarter. Actions taken by the Reserve Bank to move inflation back into the target band caused interest rates to rise and the trade-weighted exchange rate to appreciate, while unemployment continued to hover around 6 per cent. This high value of the New Zealand dollar led to arguments during the 1996 general election that monetary policy was harming farmers and other exporters. Consequently, the first action of the Coalition Government formed on 10 December 1996 was to change the PTA target band from 0–2 per cent to 0–3 per cent.

This experience provides the background to this chapter, which proceeds in four parts. Section 2 presents a summary of the principles that were used by the designers of the Reserve Bank of New Zealand Act 1989 reform. Section 3 explains how the Reserve Bank's monetary policies in 1995 and 1996 led to a strong political backlash from certain sectors of the economy, that undermined the Bank's tight 0–2 per cent inflation target. Section 4 discusses the implications of New Zealand's experience for ongoing international debates about the role of monetary policy in a modern market economy, before a brief conclusion in Section 5.

2   The Reserve Bank of New Zealand Act 1989

The Reserve Bank of New Zealand was originally founded by statute as a private central bank, incorporated on 1 April 1934 (Hawke 1973, Chapter 4). It was nationalized by the first Labour government on 1 April 1936, and since that date has been a Crown institution governed by its own legislation. From the beginning, however, when Sir Otto Niemeyer of the Bank of England was invited to advise the New Zealand government on setting up a central bank, there has been considerable controversy over the proper objective of monetary policy (Dalziel 1993a). Niemeyer's (1931, p. 7) recommendation was that 'the primary duty of the Bank shall be to ensure that the value of its notes remains stable', but the initial legislation watered this down to the following (*Statutes*, 1933, No. 11, Section 12):

It shall be the primary duty of the Reserve Bank to exercise control, within the limits of the powers conferred on it by this Act, over monetary circulation and credit in New Zealand, to the end that the economic welfare of the Dominion may be promoted and maintained.

Successive amendments to this statute in 1936, 1950, 1960, 1964 and 1973 eventually produced the following primary objective of monetary policy (*Statutes*, 1973, No. 16, Section 8, Clause 2):

For the purposes of this Act, the Minister may from time to time communicate to the Bank the monetary policy of the Government, which shall be directed to the maintenance and promotion of economic and social welfare in New Zealand, having regard to the desirability of promoting the highest level of production and trade and full employment, and of maintaining a stable internal price level.

By the late 1980s, there were two aspects of this statute that were judged by policy makers to be undesirable (Dalziel and Lattimore 1996, pp. 42–4). First, the Minister of Finance was able to insist that the Reserve Bank follow a particular monetary policy, without any safeguard that this should be subject to scrutiny by Parliament or even made public at the time.[2] Second, the inclusion of up to four goals (which might be contradictory in the short term) made it impossible to evaluate in a clear-cut manner how effective monetary policy makers were in pursuing their statutory duties. These concerns led to a major reform of the Act in 1989, so that the previous Section 8 of the new Act was simplified to the following (*Statutes*, 1989, No. 157, Section 8): 'The primary function of the Bank is to formulate and implement monetary policy directed to the economic objective of achieving and maintaining stability in the general level of prices'. Notice that the responsibility for formulating and implementing policy is given to the Reserve Bank (which therefore has a considerable degree of autonomy in this regard), and that the multiple goals of previous legislation are replaced by a single statutory objective of price stability. Indeed, this new statute is very close to the intent of Sir Otto Niemeyer's recommendations of nearly sixty years earlier.

In its promotion of this reform, the Reserve Bank has relied on the following fundamental principle (Brash 1996c, p. 21):

While monetary policy does affect the inflation rate, it cannot be used to engineer a sustainably faster rate of economic growth or a sustainably higher level of employment. In these circumstances, the most sensible rate of inflation for monetary policy to target is price stability, since any other rate of inflation involves both social and economic cost. Hence Section 8 of the Act gives monetary policy the sole task of 'achieving and maintaining stability in the general level of prices'.

The Reserve Bank acknowledges that monetary policy has short-term effects on output and employment in the short run, but has been convinced by evidence such as the empirical work reported by Fischer (1996) that inflation in the long run has a negative impact on growth. Archer (1994, p. 328) therefore draws the following conclusion:

> In essence, the new monetary policy framework tells the policy implementers to ignore the short-run output and employment consequences, because the economy will be better off in the long-run as a result, and because if the implementers do not ignore these consequences, the desirable long-run position will never be reached.

This theory has not been uncontested in New Zealand.[3] In a series of papers, for example, I argued that the output costs of monetary disinflation could have persistent effects because of hysteresis in the labour market or in the tradables sector (Dalziel 1989, 1991a, 1992 and 1993b), but particular mention should be made of the late Jan Whitwell. Whitwell (1987, 1990, 1992) consistently argued within a Post Keynesian framework that the money supply is an endogenous variable caused by nominal output growth, so that the Reserve Bank is able to produce price stability only by maintaining a high rate of unemployment. In particular, Whitwell argued that 'it is the real productive sector in general, and the traded goods sector in particular, which is fully exposed to the first-order effects of the monetary signals' (1990, p. 108). Her conclusion was based on a model in which the Reserve Bank produces a lower measured inflation rate by increasing the trade-weighted exchange rate (thus reducing the price of imported commodities) until rising unemployment caused by the overvalued real exchange rate impacts on wages. This insight assumed even greater relevance in the second half of the 1990s, as the next section of this chapter will describe.

More recently, Chapple (1996, pp. 46–7) has argued from the work of Akerlof et al. (1996) that 'the existence of downward wage rigidity along the lines found [in Chapple's empirical study of New Zealand data] can create a significant trade-off between inflation and unemployment even in the long-run'. The argument is based on the hypothesis that workers resist downward nominal wage movements (Cassino (1995) also finds evidence of downward nominal wage rigidity in New Zealand), so that any adjustment to real wages after an adverse shock can take place only at the rate of inflation. The implication that policy makers should be willing to tolerate a small amount of positive inflation to increase real wage flexibility has been bolstered by the empirical work of Sarel (1996) who finds in a cross-country study that 'when inflation is low [that is, less than 8 per cent], it has no significant effect on economic growth; the effect may even be slightly positive' (p. 200). More controversially, Bryant (1996a and 1996b) has proposed that monetary policy should be permitted to engage in some modest degree of output stabilization, but this has not found wide support (see the discussion in Dalziel 1997).

These criticisms will be discussed further in Sections 3 and 4 below, but first it is important to explain the role played by the Policy Targets Agreement. The Act does not define 'stability in the general level of prices', but Section 9 requires the Minister of Finance to 'fix, in agreement with [the Governor of the Reserve Bank], policy targets for the carrying out by the Bank of its primary function'. The resulting Policy Targets Agreement (PTA), which is renegotiated at certain prescribed times (for example, when the Governor's five-year contract expires) or by mutual agreement, sets 'the range within which inflation can vary without monetary policy being deemed unsuccessful' (Dennis 1997, p. 22). For the first seven years of the reformed Act, this range was very narrow (0–2 per cent in the underlying inflation rate), and some explanation must be given for why such a narrow target band was chosen.

The literature suggests two reasons why a narrow band might be preferred (see Ebert 1994, and Dennis 1997, for surveys). The first is that there is some empirical evidence that the rising costs of inflation are at least in part due to a higher variance of inflation at higher levels (Friedman 1977; Ball and Cecchetti 1990). The explanation is that a wider variance is likely to lead to more frequent inflationary expectations errors, and also requires economic agents to devote more resources to inflation forecasting. This suggests that inflation should be kept to a narrower range to reduce these costs.

The second reason is based on inflationary expectations, and the impact that a narrow target band might have on those expectations. There are several variants to this argument, but they all hinge on the idea first discussed in Kydland and Prescott (1977) and Barro and Gordon (1983a and 1983b) that policy makers face a temptation to create a surprise inflation if an announced commitment to price stability is believed and if policy makers receive some political reward for the inflation (perhaps as a result of a short-term reduction in unemployment, or perhaps by lowering the real value of non-indexed public debt issued in domestic currency; Dalziel and Wright 1993). Under these circumstances, the original announcement is not 'time consistent', leading agents to revise their expectations upwards, and the commitment to price stability can be honoured only by accepting ongoing recession (Dalziel 1991b, p. 341). To counter this effect, which may be particularly important if the central bank has inherited a weak reputation for monetary discipline as a result of high inflation in the past, a narrower target band may increase the credibility of the band's midpoint by giving the central bank very little room to manoeuvre between the midpoint and the ceiling of the band. This is because, given the unavoidable uncertainties associated with monetary policy and inflation targeting, the central bank reduces the chances of breaching the target limits if it constantly aims for the middle of its target band (Turner 1996; OECD 1996, pp. 43–5). Thus, the narrower is the band, the greater is the incentive for the bank to focus on its midpoint and to offset every small shock that threatens to move the expected inflation rate away from that value within the planning horizon of monetary policy.

This section has deliberately concentrated on the theories that were proposed in support of the single statutory objective and the tight PTA target band, partly because these were the arguments that led policy makers to accept this framework and partly because the weaknesses in those arguments became apparent as New Zealand built up experience under the new framework. It is to that experience that this chapter now turns.

3   New Zealand's monetary policy experience, 1989 to 1996

The easiest way to describe New Zealand's monetary policy experience under the new Act is to make reference to the Phillips curve diagram traced out in Figure 13.1. The Reserve Bank of New Zealand (1987, p. 104) adopted the view that 'the overriding objective of monetary policy is to lower the rate of inflation in the economy' at least from the middle of 1987, but progress on that objective was interrupted for 12 months after the introduction of a 10 per cent value-added tax (Goods and Services Tax (GST)) on 1 October 1986, and so the data in Figure 13.1 begin in December 1987. The horizontal axis measures the Household Labour Force Survey unemployment rate (seasonally adjusted), while the vertical axis measures the annual inflation rate in the CPI, unadjusted for interest rate changes, GST adjustments, or other supply-

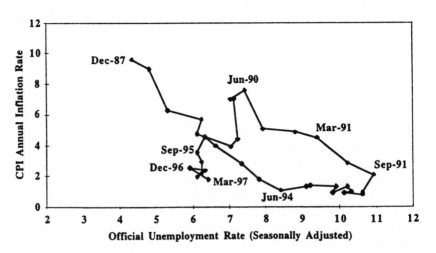

Source: Statistics New Zealand.

Figure 13.1   Phillips curve for New Zealand, December 1987 to March 1997

side shocks (that is, the vertical axis measures 'headline' inflation, not the Reserve Bank's 'underlying' inflation rate).

By the middle of 1989, the annual inflation rate had more than halved from 9.6 per cent in December 1987 to 4.4 per cent in June 1989. At the same time, however, unemployment had jumped from just over 4 per cent of the labour force to just over 7 per cent, igniting debate about whether policy makers could be content with the degree of disinflation achieved, or whether further reductions should be pursued. This was a very unsettled time for the government. The architect of its economic reforms, Roger Douglas, had resigned as Minister of Finance on 14 December 1988 after a protracted and bitter dispute with the Prime Minister, David Lange, over the former's proposals for a flat tax package. The Labour Caucus reelected Douglas to Cabinet seven months later, prompting Lange to resign on 7 August 1989. Meanwhile, the new Minister of Finance, David Caygill, had decided to increase GST from 10 per cent to 12.5 per cent (from 1 July 1989), while still pursuing a target of 0–2 per cent inflation by the early 1990s (Caygill 1989, p. 4). The Reserve Bank of New Zealand Act 1989 was passed in Parliament on 15 December without any dissenting vote and came into force on 1 February 1990.

The impact of the increase in GST in the data for September 1989 to June 1990 is clearly visible in Figure 13.1. The graph also suggests that policy makers suffered a loss of credibility during this period, since inflation did not return to 4.5 per cent until March 1991, even though unemployment passed above 9 per cent and continued to rise.

In October 1990, the Labour government was defeated in a landslide victory by the National Party. The new government announced substantial reductions in social welfare income support from 1 April 1991 (intended to reduce vote: social welfare by 10 per cent in a full fiscal year; Stephens 1991, p. 110) and the replacement of New Zealand's corporatist system of industrial relations with a decentralized system set out in the Employment Contracts Act 1991 (Walsh, 1991). The annual inflation rate immediately fell by 3.6 percentage points in three quarters, to 0.9 per cent in December 1991, even though the government had given the Reserve Bank until December 1993 to achieve the target of 0–2 per cent in the underlying inflation rate. Unemployment peaked at 10.9 per cent in September 1991, and remained at about 10 per cent for the next two years. The unemployment rate then fell quickly, to 8.3 per cent in June 1994 and to 6.3 per cent in June 1995. This was accompanied by rising inflation pressures, which pushed the CPI rate up to 4.6 per cent (with a large contribution coming from a rise in the rate of interest as the Reserve Bank tightened monetary conditions, which was excluded from the Reserve Bank's underlying inflation rate), but as inflation fell back towards 2 per cent, unemployment remained at about 6 per cent. This is well below its peak in September 1991, and is less than current unemployment rates in Australia and most of

Europe, but 6 per cent is still above the rate that prevailed prior to the beginning of New Zealand's economic reforms.

Thus, New Zealand's disinflation and subsequent experience under the Reserve Bank of New Zealand Act 1989 can be broken down into four periods: (i) the initial disinflation between December 1987 and June 1989, interrupted by the increase in GST on 1 July 1989; (ii) the passing of the Act and the implementation of its commitment to producing an underlying inflation rate between 0 and 2 per cent, achieved by late 1991 at the expense of unemployment above 10 per cent; (iii) the gradual and then sharp improvement in unemployment back towards 6 per cent by June 1995; and (iv) the struggle by the Reserve Bank to contain inflationary pressures in 1995 and 1996, culminating in a decision in December 1996 to relax the inflation target to between 0 and 3 per cent.

There is a paradox in this account that warrants further examination. In 1989, when inflation had been reduced towards 4 per cent and unemployment was at the historically high rate of 7 per cent, the government (supported by the major opposition party) determined to press on with reducing inflation to below 2 per cent. In 1996, when inflation was below 3 per cent and unemployment was about 6 per cent, the government (supported by the major opposition party) relaxed the target band's range and midpoint. In part, this might be explained by the new nature of party politics after New Zealand's first election of a Mixed Member Proportional Representation Parliament (the minority party in the Coalition government had campaigned against the high interest rates and exchange rate produced by the Reserve Bank's anti-inflation monetary policies), but there were deeper issues involved, which can be explained used the time series drawn in Figure 13.2.

The middle line in Figure 13.2 shows the behaviour of the Reserve Bank's underlying CPI annual inflation rate between March 1990 and December 1996. It shows that this measure moved to just above the 0–2 per cent target band in September 1991, and then remained within the band until March 1995. Notice, however, that at no time during those 18 quarters did the Reserve Bank actually achieve the midpoint of its target band, and in fact the average value of the underlying CPI annual inflation rate over this period was 1.7 per cent. This undermined the credibility of the Reserve Bank's commitment to a 1 per cent midpoint, with some observers 'publicly asserting that [the monetary authorities] really do not have a 0 to 2 per cent target at all, and seem happy to have underlying inflation constantly nearer the top of the range than the bottom' (Brash 1996b, p. 2). This credibility was further diminished as the underlying inflation rate remained at about 2 per cent (or higher) throughout all of 1995 and 1996 (Dalziel 1997).

Figure 13.2 also presents a breakdown of the underlying inflation rate into a tradables component and a non-tradables component. These data are calcu-

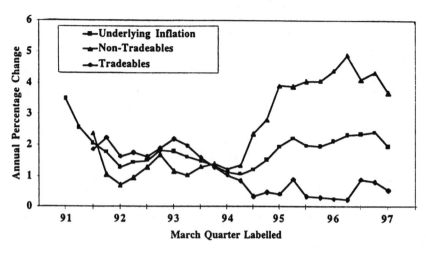

Source: *Reserve Bank of New Zealand Monetary Policy Statement*, June 1997, Figure 8, p. 19.

Figure 13.2 Underlying inflation in New Zealand, March 1991 to March 1997

lated by the Reserve Bank based on a classification of the 333 individual price series of the CPI into a tradables group and a non-tradables group, 'according to how sensitive they are to exchange rate changes ... checked for common sense' (Rae 1993, p. 61). The graph shows that the tradables group's inflation rate was below 1 per cent for every quarter between June 1994 and March 1997, but that inflation in the non-tradables group remained at 4 or 5 per cent, falling to 3.7 per cent in March 1997.

Such a wide divergence between the inflation performance of the two groups had the expected impact on New Zealand's trade-weighted exchange rate, depicted in Figure 13.3. The data in Figure 13.3 have been calibrated to equal 100 in the June quarter in 1984. This sets a useful standard for comparison, because on 18 July 1984, the New Zealand dollar was devalued by 20 per cent as the first act of the new Labour government that initiated New Zealand's programme of economic reforms (Dalziel and Lattimore 1996, Chapter 3). The New Zealand dollar was floated on 4 March 1985, but, despite some variance in the interval, it was still at its post-devaluation level at the beginning of 1990. The currency then depreciated steadily to a trough at the end of 1992.

Concerned about the impact this might have on its inflation target, the Reserve Bank tightened monetary conditions on 6 January 1993 (see *Monetary Policy Statement*, June 1993, pp. 33–4). It increased the penalty discount margin from 90 basis points to 150 basis points, it declined to sell back

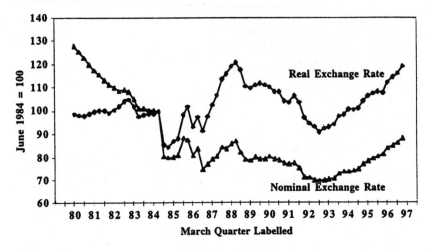

Sources: Reserve Bank Bulletins and IMF, *International Financial Statistics.*

Figure 13.3   New Zealand exchange rate, March 1980 to December 1996

to the market previously discounted Reserve Bank bills (the main non-cash liquidity instrument in the financial system), and it reduced the cash target from NZ$20 million to zero (draining the system of all cash reserves held at the Reserve Bank). This had the desired effect of signalling the Bank's commitment to price stability, the exchange rate stabilized accordingly, and the original liquidity settings were able to be restored within a month (3 February). There was a small appreciation in the second half of the year, but by the middle of 1994, it was becoming apparent that inflationary pressures were again increasing. This led to a substantial firming of monetary conditions as the market anticipated the Reserve Bank's response, and indeed the Bank described this as 'warranted and timely' in its December 1994 *Monetary Policy Statement* (p. 1). As underlying inflation (both current and projected) continued to hover around the ceiling of the 0–2 per cent target band, the Reserve Bank maintained monetary restraint. Figure 13.3 shows that in the two years between December 1994 and December 1996, the trade-weighted exchange rate index appreciated by 14.4 per cent.

Also shown in Figure 13.3 is the IMF's real effective exchange rate for New Zealand, which is, of course, an inverse measure of the international competitiveness of domestic production in the tradables sector. After the July 1984 devaluation, the process of monetary disinflation drove the real exchange rate back up to a peak of 20 per cent above its *pre-devaluation* value. It remained about 10 per cent higher throughout 1989 and the first half of 1990, but then depreciated to almost 10 per cent below the pre-devaluation value in September 1992. Subsequently, the real exchange rate rose by 27.5 per cent over the next four years, and was very close to its 1988 peak value in December 1996.

Bringing these observations together, the following is a summary of New Zealand's recent experience. From about the beginning of March 1994, domestic inflationary pressures threatened the top end of the Reserve Bank's target band of 0–2 per cent in the underlying annual CPI inflation rate. The tightening of monetary conditions induced by these inflationary pressures led to rapidly rising nominal and real exchange rates.[4] As a result, inflation rates in the tradables and non-tradables sectors diverged, causing differential impacts on firms depending on which sector their inputs and outputs were concentrated. Importers, for example, experienced windfall profits, while farmers and other exporters began to campaign for increased competition in the non-tradables sector and/or a relaxation of monetary policy to ease the profit squeeze they were experiencing.[5] This political pressure, together with the Reserve Bank's failure to achieve the lower half of its inflation target (discussed earlier in this section), provided the environment within which New Zealand's Coalition government could negotiate with the Governor of the Reserve Bank to raise the top end of the inflation target from two to three per cent.

4 Lessons from New Zealand's experience

The purpose of this section is to focus on three important lessons from New Zealand's experience with an independent central bank since 1989. The first concerns the ongoing debate about whether strict price stability is desirable in a modern market economy. The second contains a warning about the consequences of using a CPI as the measure of accountability for an autonomous central bank in a small open economy. The third points the way for further research into causes and controls of inflation, especially in the domestic non-tradables sector.

The introduction to this chapter commented that New Zealand's monetary policy framework initially adopted a particularly tight definition of price stability. The midpoint of its target (1 per cent, chosen to acknowledge measurement bias in the CPI) was less than the midpoints adopted by the Bank of England (2.5 per cent or less), the Bank of Canada (2 per cent) and the Reserve Bank of Australia (2.5 per cent), and below that which appears to be acceptable to the Federal Reserve in the United States. This feature of New Zealand's framework was based on a commitment to achieving strict price stability (allowing for measurement bias), and a rejection of arguments that a small amount of anticipated inflation does no harm (and may do some good) in a modern market economy. It is noteworthy, therefore, that New Zealand's initial stance has proved not to be sustainable (and indeed the 1 per cent midpoint was not achieved at any time during the first seven years of the reformed Act), and I have argued elsewhere (Dalziel 1997) that the increase in the target midpoint from 1 to 1.5 per cent represents an important shift in the attitude of New Zealand policy makers towards a cautious allowance that the previously rejected arguments may have some validity.

The second lesson is the one that Whitwell (1987, 1990, 1992) highlighted in her critique of the monetary disinflation policies of the late 1980s, concerning the transmission mechanism of monetary policy to its inflation target when the latter is based on the CPI. The CPI, of course, is a weighted average of tradable and non-tradable items. Let P_w be the international price level (measured in world currencies) of the tradables group and P_d be the domestic currency price level of the non-tradables group. Let E be the world price of one unit of the domestic currency, and assume that the domestic price of the tradables group is forced by competition to equal its international price divided by the prevailing exchange rate.[6] Finally, let z be a parameter measuring the proportion of tradable items in the domestic CPI, denoted by P. Then the CPI may be defined as follows:

$$P = (P_w/E)^z (P_d)^{(1-z)}. \tag{13.1}$$

Differentiating equation (13.1) and dividing the result by (13.1) produces the inflation rate in the domestic CPI. This is recorded in equation (13.2), where the lower case letter for each variable represents the variable's rate of change:

$$p = zp_w - ze + (1-z)p_d. \tag{13.2}$$

Suppose now that the central bank's inflation target for p is set at π. The inflation rate in the world price of tradables goods and services can be assumed to be outside the control of the domestic central bank; so denote the world inflation rate as the parameter $\prod$, and assume that $\prod > \pi$ (which is certainly true for New Zealand during the period under review). To complete the model, an assumption is required about the behaviour of P_d, the inflation rate in the domestic non-tradables sector. Two polar cases can be considered.

In the first case, suppose that either the inflation target has been chosen to reflect the core inflation rate in the domestic economy or firms in the non-tradables sector will produce inflation equal to the central bank's announced target, so that $\prod > \pi = p_d$. Equation (13.2) then implies that:

$$\pi = z\prod - ze + (1-z)\pi \Rightarrow e = \prod - \pi. \tag{13.3}$$

In this example, the exchange rate appreciates only at the rate necessary to offset the difference between world and domestic inflation, and there is no appreciation in the real exchange rate of the economy. In the second polar case, suppose that the connection between the inflation target and the core domestic inflation rate is weak, and that $\pi < p_d$ (which is again true for New Zealand after September 1994 and is what makes monetary policy so difficult). Equation (13.2) implies that:

$$\pi = z\textstyle\prod - ze + (1 - z)p_d \Rightarrow e = (\textstyle\prod - p_d) + (p_d - \pi)/z. \qquad (13.4)$$

In this example, the exchange rate appreciates at a rate that depends on two components: the difference between world and domestic production inflation rates, and the extent to which the CPI inflation target is below the domestic production inflation rate, scaled up by the inverse of the weight of tradable goods in the CPI measure. This second component, of course, produces an appreciation in the economy's real exchange rate, and domestic producers of tradables goods and services suffer a loss of international competitiveness. The lesson from this simple arithmetic is that policy makers in a small open economy can always achieve a 'low' CPI inflation target by engineering a suitable appreciation in the exchange rate, but that the initial brunt of this mechanism will be felt in the tradables sector if the inflationary pressures are in fact in the non-tradables sector.

This leads to the third lesson highlighted in this section, since the discussion just concluded reveals the critical role played by domestic inflation in the non-tradables sector in the achievement of any pre-determined CPI price target. Thus, it is vitally important that monetary economists understand the links that exist between monetary policy and domestic inflation, particularly in the non-tradables sector. This poses, however, some difficulties. In most models of monetary policy, it is assumed that the money supply is set exogenously by the monetary authorities, and that the growth in the money supply then determines inflation. The following extract from Barro and Gordon (1983b, p. 594) is typical: 'We assume that the policymaker controls an instrument – say, monetary growth, μ_t – which has a direct connection to inflation, π_t, in each period. ... In effect, we pretend that the policymaker chooses π_t directly in each period'.

This approach is hopelessly inadequate to capture the transmission mechanism that is actually being applied by policy makers around the world, and in my view progress is more likely to come from further development of Post Keynesian models of endogenous money and bank credit (see, for example, Arestis 1988 and 1993; Arestis and Howells 1992 and 1996; Chick 1992 and 1993; Cottrell 1994; Dow 1993, 1996a and 1996b; Earl 1990; Graziani 1990; Lavoie 1992; Moore 1988; and Wray 1990). This is because the Post Keynesian model takes seriously the ability of the banking system to create credit money for financing both productive and speculative expenditure, and so recognizes that a central bank is more akin to the conductor of an orchestra (Keynes 1930, p. 26) than the pilot of a money-dropping helicopter (Friedman 1969, p. 4).

5   Conclusion

This chapter has described the way in which the Reserve Bank of New Zealand Act 1989 made the achievement and maintenance of stability in the general level of prices the sole objective of monetary policy, and gave the Reserve Bank autonomy to formulate and implement monetary policy subject to stringent accountability requirements based around a Policy Targets Agreement negotiated and signed by the Minister of Finance and the Governor of the Bank. Section 3 explained how the failure by the Bank to achieve inflation in the lower half of its target range, and the costs imposed on the tradables sector by a tightening of monetary conditions in 1995 and 1996, undermined political support for the original PTA target band of 0–2 per cent, which created an environment in which the new Coalition government at the end of 1996 relaxed the inflation target to 0–3 per cent. In Section 4, it was suggested that this step represents a cautious acceptance by New Zealand policy makers that a small amount of anticipated inflation may not cause as much harm to the economy as the costs of achieving strict price stability. Section 4 also analysed the role played by exchange rate appreciations in achieving a pre-determined CPI inflation target in a small open economy, which drew attention to the need to better understand the relationship between monetary policy and domestic non-tradables inflation, along the lines being developed in the Post Keynesian research programme in monetary economics.

To conclude, I offer two quotations from Alfred Marshall that I think capture a fundamental principle in monetary economics that is often overlooked, but which is very pertinent to the political economy of central banking. In the first quotation, Marshall is responding to questions about whether an increase in currency (that is, gold or silver coins) increases the wealth of the country. His answer is as follows (1899, p. 323):

> It is, of course, real capital alone that can provide the substantial force needed to make business prosperous. A supply of currency is but the flux that makes real capital fluid, and enables it to get at its work. And a mere permanent increase of currency does not make capital more fluid; it simply depreciates the currency. What is wanted is a currency which expands when business expands, and thus enables real capital to become fluid when it is wanted to be fluid; and which shrinks when business shrinks, and thus preserves itself from becoming superfluous and falling in value.

As Keynes (1937, pp. 222–3) observed in his famous *obiter dictum*, the system that was developed to achieve this required flexibility is the bank overdraft system, where firms are able to obtain and repay credit according to their need for finance. This is a remarkable feature of modern money economies that should not be undervalued. At the same time, however, it is a system that is vulnerable to financial instability, particularly if the leading banks in the system do not operate with an element of public-spiritedness (Dow 1996a, pp. 704–5). The full implications of this remain to be worked out in analytical models (Dalziel (1996a and 1996b), presents a model, for example, in which firms are able to create inflation by increasing their average debt–equity ratio), but the consequences are well captured in this second quotation, from Marshall (1923, pp. 303–4):

> [People] saw that whoever could put his own notes into circulation got command over capital, which he could use in his own business or lend to others; and they did not see that he was in effect turning to his own use part of the expensive machinery of trade, which had been provided at the public expense by the national metallic currency, by political security and social credit. They did not observe that while making that machinery more efficient, he made it also more likely to break down; and that, while he reaped for himself the chief benefit of this increase in its efficiency, the chief evils from its increased instability fell upon others.

In this tradition, the central bank may be regarded as the guardian of a public good. This public good is not money *per se*, however, but is the ability of money to finance production and trade efficiently. Consequently, safeguarding the value of the currency (or at least protecting holders of money assets and liabilities from unanticipated changes in the average price level) is an important aspect of the central bank's role, but equally important is the way in which the value of the currency is protected. If it turns out that the mechanisms implemented to maintain price stability interfere in other ways with the ability of money to finance economic development (and the argument of this chapter has been that this is the case in New Zealand), then there remains further work to be done by monetary economists and policy makers.

Notes

1. There is a provision that allows Parliament to change the objective of monetary policy for up to 12 months at a time. This is designed to provide a transparent mechanism for Parliament to exercise its ultimate sovereignty over monetary policy without doing harm to the fundamental principles enshrined in the Act. This provision has not been used so far, and is not expected to be used except in response to a major economic crisis.
2. In fact there is clear evidence of a political business cycle in New Zealand's monetary data. The growth rate of the broad money supply (M3) rose in every election year from 1963/64 to 1984/85, and fell again the following year in all but 1985/86 (see Dalziel and Lattimore 1996, Graph 5.1, p. 40).
3. During the hearings of the Parliamentary Select Committee considering the Reserve Bank of New Zealand Bill, the Reserve Bank acknowledged that 'the general approach being adopted in New Zealand does not enjoy wide support in the New Zealand academic economics community', but went on to say that 'this lack of local academic support says

more about the state of New Zealand's academic economics than about the correctness of the Reserve Bank's and the Government's approach to monetary policy' (cited in Kelsey 1995, pp. 161–2).

4. In saying this, there is no suggestion that the Reserve Bank of New Zealand controls the exchange rate, or has a formal exchange rate target. Rather, the mechanism is that anticipation of a Reserve Bank response leads to an increase in domestic interest rates, which increases the net capital inflow into the country. This in turn increases the demand for New Zealand dollars in the foreign exchange market which causes the currency to appreciate.

5. The extent of this pressure is indicated by the Reserve Bank deciding to publish in August 1996 and December 1996 two pamphlets, *The Impact of Monetary Policy on Farming* and *The Impact of Monetary Policy on Exporters*, seeking to allay the concerns being raised in the tradables sector.

6. In fact, this last assumption may not be applicable, especially if a rise in the exchange rate is seen as a short-term phenomenon (imposed to offset a temporary rise in domestic inflation pressures) so that there are insufficient long-run profits to attract potential competitors into the domestic market. One of the difficulties New Zealand policy makers found in 1995 and 1996 was that tradables prices did not respond to the policy-induced appreciation of the exchange rate as they had in the past.

Bibliography

Akerlof, G., W. Dickens and G. Perry (1996), 'The macroeconomics of low inflation', *Brookings Papers on Economic Activity*, **1**, 1–76.

Archer, D. (1994), 'Monetary policy, output and employment', *Reserve Bank Bulletin*, **57** (4), 322–9.

Arestis, P. (ed.) (1988), *Post-Keynesian Monetary Economics: New Approaches to Financial Modelling*, Aldershot: Edward Elgar.

Arestis, P. (ed.) (1993), *Money and Banking: Issues for the Twenty-First Century*, London: Macmillan.

Arestis, P. and P. Howells (1992), 'Institutional developments and the effectiveness of monetary policy', *Journal of Economic Issues*, **26** (1), 135–57.

Arestis, P. and P. Howells (1996), 'Theoretical reflections on endogenous money: the problem with "Convenience Lending"', *Cambridge Journal of Economics*, **20** (5), 539–51.

Ball, L. and S. Cecchetti (1990), 'Inflation and uncertainty as short and long horizons', *Brookings Papers on Economic Activity*, **1**, 215–45.

Barro, R.J. and D.B. Gordon (1983a), 'Rules, discretion and reputation in a model of monetary policy', *Journal of Monetary Economics*, **12** (1), 101–21.

Barro, R.J. and D.B. Gordon (1983b), 'A positive theory of monetary policy in a natural rate model', *Journal of Political Economy*, **91** (4), 589–610.

Brash, D. (1996a), 'Modern central banking: discussion', in F. Capie, C. Goodhart, S. Fischer and N. Schnadt, *The Future of Central Banking*, Cambridge: Cambridge University Press, pp. 309–15.

Brash, D. (1996b), 'An address to the Canterbury Employers' Chamber of Commerce', Christchurch, 26 January.

Brash, D. (1996c), 'New Zealand's remarkable reforms', Fifth Annual Hayek Memorial Lecture to the Institute of Economic Affairs, 4 June.

Bryant, R. (1996a), 'Central bank independence, fiscal responsibility, and the goals of macroeconomic policy: an American perspective on the New Zealand experience', Wellington: Victoria University of Wellington Foundation.

Bryant, R. (1996b), *Alternative Rules for Monetary Policy and Fiscal Policy in New Zealand: A Preliminary Assessment of Stabilization Properties*, Reserve Bank of New Zealand Discussion Paper Series, No. G96/3.

Cassino, V. (1995), *The Distributions of Price and Wage Changes in New Zealand*, Reserve Bank of New Zealand Discussion Paper Series, No. G95/6.

Caygill, D. (1989), *Economic Statement to the House of Representatives, 21 March 1989*, Wellington: Government Printer.

Chapple, S. (1996), 'Money wage rigidity in New Zealand', *Labour Market Bulletin*, **2**, 23–50.
Chick, V. (1992), *On Money, Method and Keynes: Selected Essays of Victoria Chick*, edited by P. Arestis and S. Dow, London: Macmillan.
Chick, V. (1993), 'Sources of finance, recent changes in bank behaviour and the theory of investment and interest', Chapter 5 in P. Arestis (ed.), *Money and Banking: Issues for the Twenty-First Century*, London: Macmillan.
Cottrell, A. (1994), 'Post Keynesian monetary economics: a critical survey', *Cambridge Journal of Economics*, **18** (4), 587–605.
Dalziel, P. (1989), 'An independent Reserve Bank: the case against', Paper presented to the Summer Conference of the New Zealand Association of Economists, Victoria University of Wellington.
Dalziel, P. (1991a), 'The rhetoric of Treasury: a review of the 1990 briefing papers', *New Zealand Economic Papers*, **25** (2), 259–74.
Dalziel, P. (1991b), 'Theoretical approaches to monetary disinflation', *Journal of Economic Surveys*, **5** (4), 329–57.
Dalziel, P. (1992), 'National's economic strategy', Chapter 2 in J. Boston and P. Dalziel (eds) *The Decent Society? Essays in Response to National's Economic and Social Policies*, Auckland: Oxford University Press.
Dalziel, P. (1993a), 'The Reserve Bank Act: reflecting changing relationships between state and economy in the twentieth century', Chapter 4 in B. Roper and C. Rudd (eds), *State and Economy in New Zealand*, Auckland: Oxford University Press.
Dalziel, P. (1993b), 'The rhetoric of Treasury: reply', *New Zealand Economic Papers*, **27** (1), 89–97.
Dalziel, P. (1996a), 'A Keynesian theory of monetary inflation without government', Paper presented at the Royal Economic Society Residential Conference, Swansea, 1–4 April.
Dalziel, P. (1996b), 'Central banks and monetary control when credit-money finances investment', *Économies et Société's: Monnaie et Production*, **X** (2–3), 119–37.
Dalziel, P. (1997), 'Setting the Reserve Bank's inflation target: the New Zealand debate', *Agenda*, **4** (3), 285–96.
Dalziel, P. and R. Lattimore (1996), *The New Zealand Macroeconomy: A Briefing on the Reforms*, Auckland: Oxford University Press.
Dalziel, P. and J. Wright (1993), 'Policy credibility and debt management in a small open economy', *New Zealand Economic Papers*, **27** (1), 79–87.
Dawe, S. (1990), 'Reserve Bank of New Zealand Act 1989', *Reserve Bank Bulletin*, **53** (1), 29–36.
Dennis, R. (1997), 'Bandwidth, bandlength, and inflation targeting: some observations', *Reserve Bank Bulletin*, **60** (1), 22–6.
Dow, S.C. (1993), *Money and the Economic Process*, Aldershot: Edward Elgar.
Dow, S.C. (1996a), 'Why the banking system should be regulated', *Economic Journal*, **106**, 698–707.
Dow, S.C. (1996b), 'Horizontalism: a critique', *Cambridge Journal of Economics*, **20** (4), 497–508.
Earl, Peter (1990) *Monetary Scenarios: A Modern Approach to Financial Systems*, Aldershot: Elgar.
Ebert, C. (1994), 'Defining price stability: what should we aim for?', *Reserve Bank Bulletin*, **57** (1), 23–34.
Evans, L., A. Grimes and B. Wilkinson with D. Teece (1996), 'Economic reform in New Zealand 1984–95: the pursuit of efficiency', *Journal of Economic Literature*, **34** (4), 1856–902.
Fischer, S. (1996), 'Modern central banking', in F. Capie, C. Goodhart, S. Fischer and N. Schnadt, *The Future of Central Banking*, Cambridge: Cambridge University Press, pp. 262–308.
Friedman, M. (1969), *The Optimum Quantity of Money*, London: Macmillan.
Friedman, M. (1977), 'Inflation and unemployment: the Nobel Prize lecture', *Journal of Political Economy*, **85** (3), 451–72.
Graziani, A. (1990), 'The theory of the monetary circuit', *Économies et Sociétés*, **24** (6), 7–36.

Hawke, G. (1973), *Between Governments and Banks: A History of the Reserve Bank of New Zealand*, Wellington: Government Printer.

Kelsey, J. (1995), *The New Zealand Experiment: A World Model of Structural Adjustment?*, Auckland: Auckland University Press and Bridget Williams Books.

Keynes, J.M. (1930), *A Treatise on Money: Volume 1, The Applied Theory of Money*, London: Macmillan. Reprinted in *The Collected Writings of John Maynard Keynes*, Volume V, London: Macmillan, 1971.

Keynes, J.M. (1937), 'The "ex ante" theory of the rate of interest', *Economic Journal*, **47**. Reprinted in *The Collected Writings of John Maynard Keynes*, Volume XIV, London: Macmillan, 1971.

Kirchner, S. (1995), 'Central bank independence and accountability: the New Zealand case', *Agenda*, **2** (2), 169–80.

Kydland, F. and E.C. Prescott (1977), 'Rules rather than discretion: the inconsistency of optimal plans', *Journal of Political Economy*, **85** (2), 473–92.

Lavoie, M. (1992), *Foundations of Post-Keynesian Economic Analysis*, Aldershot: Edward Elgar.

Marshall, A. (1899), 'Minutes of evidence offered by Professor Alfred Marshall to the Committee Appointed to Inquire into the Indian Currency (1898), 16 February, 1899', in *Alfred Marshall's Official Papers*, London: Macmillan, 1926.

Marshall, A. (1923), *Money, Credit and Commerce*, London: Macmillan.

Moore, B.J. (1988), *Horizontalists and Verticalists: The Macroeconomics of Credit Money*, Cambridge: Cambridge University Press.

Niemeyer, O. (1931), 'Banking and currency in New Zealand', *Appendices to the Journals of the House of Representatives*, B3.

Organization for Economic Cooperation and Development (OECD) (1996), *OECD Economic Surveys, New Zealand*, Paris: Organization for Economic Cooperation and Development.

Rae, D. (1993), 'Measuring inflation', *Reserve Bank Bulletin*, **56** (1), 53–66.

Reserve Bank of New Zealand (1987), 'A layman's guide to monetary policy in the New Zealand context', *Reserve Bank Bulletin*, **50** (2), 104–10.

Robertson, B. (1996), 'The currency and the constitution: lessons from "a rather small place"', *Oxford Journal of Legal Studies*, **16** (1), 1–29.

Sarel, M. (1996), 'Non-linear effects of inflation on economic growth', *IMF Staff Papers*, **43** (1), 199–215.

Stephens, R. (1991), 'Budgeting with the benefit cuts', Chapter 6 in J. Boston and P. Dalziel (eds), *The Decent Society? Essays in Response to National's Economic and Social Policies*, Auckland: Oxford University Press.

Turner, D. (1996), 'Inflation targeting in New Zealand: what is the appropriate bandwidth?', Reserve Bank of New Zealand Monetary Policy Workshop, 20–21 May.

Walsh, P. (1991), 'The Employment Contracts Act', Chapter 4 in J. Boston and P. Dalziel (eds), *The Decent Society? Essays in Response to National's Economic and Social Policies*, Auckland: Oxford University Press.

Whitwell, J. (1987), 'Monetary policy with a deregulated financial sector', in A. Bollard and R. Buckle (eds), *Economic Liberalisation in New Zealand*, Wellington: Allen & Unwin with Port Nicholson Press.

Whitwell, J. (1990), 'The Rogernomics monetarist experiment', in M. Holland and J. Boston (eds), *The Fourth Labour Government: Politics and Policy in New Zealand*, 2nd edn, Auckland: Oxford University Press.

Whitwell, J. (1992), Money and inflation: theories and evidence', in. S. Birks and S. Chatterjee (eds), *The New Zealand Economy: Issues and Policies*, 2nd edn, Palmerston North: Dunmore Press.

Wray, L.R. (1990), *Money and Credit in Capitalist Economies: The Endogenous Money Approach*, Aldershot: Edward Elgar.

Index

Fortin, P. 64, 194
Foster, J.F. 97
France 138, 147–52
  capitalism 139–41
  monetary policy 139–40
  variance decomposition of interest
    rates 164
Franz, W. 110
Fratianni, M. 22
Friedman, B.M. 191
Friedman, M. 57, 65, 188, 203, 212
Frydman, R. 90, 91, 92
Fukuyama, F. 102

G7 countries 158
  mean and variance of the real
    discount and unemployment
    rates 194
  monetary authorities 166–7
Galbraith, J.K. 194
Gali, J. 166
Garber, P.M. 109
Gatti, R. 64
Gavin, W.T. 181, 195
General Agreement on Tariffs and Trade
  (GATT) 141
Germany 40, 114–17, 123, 126, 127–8
  and the European Monetary System
    (EMS) 74–7
  monetary policy 157–8
  price stability 81, 171
  variance decomposition of interest
    rates 164
Gertler, M. 157
Giavazzi, F. 112
Giusso, L. 171
globalization 137
gold standard 78–81
  different policy preferences in 73
  a model 67–70
  supply and demand shocks 77–8
Goldstein, M. 142, 154
Goodhart, C.A.E. 115, 118, 127, 168,
  180
Gordon, D. 21, 44, 203, 211
governments 22, 39
  and central banks 169–70
Gowan, P. 85, 92, 93, 99
Grabel, I. 84, 85, 98
Graziani, A. 211

Green, D. 131
Grilli, V. 51, 54, 171, 172

Hagemann, H. 113, 118, 171
Hall, P.A. 54
Hanke, S. 88, 89, 98
Hargreaves-Heap, S.P. 188
Harris, L. 24
Harrod–Domar model 64
Hasan, H. 64
Hawke, G. 200
Hawtrey, R.G. 182, 195
Hayek, F.A. 185
Henning, C.R. 86
Hicks, J.R. 20
Hirschman, A.O. 175
Holmes, A. 27
Homer, S. 188
Hood, N. 141
Horizontalists and Verticalists 26
Houthakker, H.S. 105
Howard, D. 192
Howells, P. 8, 18, 27, 211
Hume, D. 13
Humphrey, T.M. 181, 186
Huntington, S.P. 102

inflation
  and central bank independence 51–2,
    54–6
  and central banks 170
  history of (United Kingdom) 80
inflation rate targets, and central banks
  192
inflation rates
  Canada 61
  United Kingdom 61
  United States 61
Interest and Prices 182, 186
interest rates 5–6, 9–10, 170, 182–6, 192
  ARIMA weights and correlations 161
  and Bank of England 39
  causality relations 33–4
  and demand for credit 6
  and Federal Reserve 188
  and unemployment, Canada 193
  variance decomposition 164–5
International Financial Statistics 28
International Monetary Fund (IMF) 93,
  107, 127, 129, 194, 208

Vector Auto-Regressive framework
   (VAR) 158–9, 162–6
Viner, J. 20
voting behaviour 45
Vuchelen, J. 139, 143, 146, 154

wages 58–9
Waigel, T. 101
Waller, C.J. 22
Wallerstein, M. 143, 144
Wallich, H.C. 1
Walsh, C.E. 22, 42
Walsh, P. 205
Walter, A. 126
Weale, M. 133
Weintraub, S. 27
Wetter, W. 113
Wheale, M. 81

White, G. 87, 94, 98
Whitwell, J. 202, 210
wholesale markets 26
Wicksell, K. 80, 182, 183, 184, 186
Wicksellian loanable funds theory 182–3
Wicksellian norm 180–95
Wills, H.R. 18
Wood, E. 181
World Bank 93
Wray, L.R. 8, 12, 189, 211
Wright, J. 203
Wyplosz, C. 112

York, R.C. 192
Young, S. 141

Zeeman, E.C. 109
zero elasticity 8